In Full Flight

B

In Full Flight

TONY SPOONER
DSO, DFC

Tony Spooner

WINGHAM PRESS

WINGHAM PRESS — CANTERBURY

To my wife, Anne, and to all others of her
sex who have learned to share their men
with the Fair Goddess from the skies.

First published in Great Britain in 1965 by
Macdonald & Co. (Publishers), Ltd.

ISBN 1 873454 05 8

This revised edition published 1991 by
Wingham Press, Seymour Place, 28 High Street, Wingham, Kent CT3 1AB.
Typeset by Rowan Typesetters, Birchington, Kent.
Printed by Short Run Press Limited,
Bittern Road, Sowton Industrial Estate, Exeter EX2 7LW.

Acknowledgements

My memory of events that happened up to twenty-five years ago has been kindly jogged by the following persons who have helped me either by word or photograph. I take this opportunity to express my gratitude for their assistance.

C A Nepean-Bishop
Geoffrey Clapham
Captain and Mrs Duncan Davies
Desmond Haynes
Captain Vernon A M Hunt
Air Chief Marshal Sir H P Lloyd
Captain Eric Starling
E C "Chiefy" Wavell
Jeffrey Wilkinson

Also my wife Anne, who typed and edited the original text.

I would also like to thank Brenda Brooks and Norman Franks for their great help in producing this edition.

Unless otherwise stated, all names are as I now remember them; and the story is true, subject only to a fading memory and, possibly, to an imagination inherited from two Irish grandmothers.

Foreword

BY AIR CHIEF MARSHAL SIR HUGH PUGHE LLOYD

ON April 15 1942 King George VI wrote to the Governor of Malta in these words: "To honour her brave people I award the George Cross to the Island Fortress of Malta to bear witness to a heroism and devotion that will long be famous in history." In this book the author's last words are: "I was there."

Malta's other cross was the war in North Africa where our armies scurried up and down that coast. Malta's task was to sink Axis shipping as it sailed from Europe to Africa. No supplies—no campaign in North Africa. Victory depended on sinking ships. Tony Spooner was one of the pilots dedicated to that task and he tells a most vivid story.

Many books have been written about the operations on the ground in North Africa, but Malta's contribution has received scant recognition so that this book is timely and most welcome.

Had not the Axis convoys been destroyed, for example, as they sailed from Europe to Africa it is highly probable that the Axis armies would have been on the Suez Canal in 1941.

On the basis that the customer is always right, the author on page 176 quotes the shipping losses given by no less a personage than the German Admiral Weichold. The diary of Count Ciano the Italian Foreign Secretary is also interesting. On November 9, 1941 he writes: "Since September 19 the Axis have given-up trying to sail convoys through to Africa as every attempt has been very costly and the losses suffered by the merchant fleet so high as to discourage further experiments."

And on October 6: "The supplies for Africa are becoming more and more difficult. Only twenty per cent of the material set aside for September has been shipped and delivered."

It was obvious that unless Malta was captured the Axis had no future in Africa. So, late in 1941, a reinforcement of 400 German and Italian bombers arrived in Sicily under the command of Kesselring, with a similar number of fighters and parachute troops, etc, to follow. Then began that long and desperate battle over Malta which happily was crowned with the award of the George Cross. By attracting to herself such a mighty assembly of arms Malta provided perhaps just enough time to turn the tide of war at Stalingrad—or limited Rommel's drive from Benghazi in January 1942 with captured British petrol, transport and guns, to a few miles west of Alexandria instead of the streets of Cairo.

Success in sinking ships depended on good information and by the middle of 1941 much was known about the life and habits of the ships engaged on the North African traffic. The principal medium of information was the air photographs of such ports as Naples, Taranto and Tripoli, and the main architect of this work was Adrian Warburton, of whom the author writes with deep affection and admiration. When comparing the absurd simplicity whereby Warburton obtained his photographs with the difficulty of the Axis in obtaining theirs of Malta, one comes to the conclusion that Warburton's was surely the master hand.

Sinking ships was not a task for aeroplanes alone—not by any means. The submarines based in the Grand Harbour did great execution too. On a few occasions, also, surface ships of the Royal Navy took part, and a most graphic account of these most successful operations is given in this book.

This was Malta's other cross. That small, not to say diminutive, island, a mere eleven miles by nine, had as her nearest friend the British soldier in the North African desert (1,000 miles away, perhaps a little less).

There would have been no battle over Malta and no George Cross either had it not been for such gallant gentlemen as Wanklyn, VC, of the submarines, Warburton and his pictures, Agnew of *Aurora* and Spooner, the captain of a Wellington and author of this most splendid and inspiring book.

Contents

List of Plates

Introduction to First Edition

THE idea of writing a book about the daily happenings in the life of a British commercial pilot first came to me in Cape Town whilst enjoying a holiday there early in 1962. I had just finished reading Ernest K Gann's *Fate is the Hunter*, which expressed, in his attractive style, the simple adventures of an American airline pilot both in peace and war. This book impressed me and made me recognise that, to some sections of the public, our profession held a certain interest.

Later in the year I happened to be in Hong Kong on my twenty-fifth anniversary as a pilot. This landmark in my life seemed an excellent excuse for throwing a party and I duly pinned a notice in Operations Room at the airport inviting all visiting pilots and aircrew to my hotel room that night for drinks. I had friends in Hong Kong too, and it was quite a gathering. When the party was in full swing I stood aside and listened to the chit-chat, the like of which I had heard so often before at similar gatherings:

"I prefer Beirut to Hong Kong both for watches and worsteds."

"You can get Kodachrome processed in eight hours at Honolulu. . . ."

"There's a good barber's shop next door to Peter's Bar in that Tokyo Arcade."

"Montego Bay is still the best place for a haircut—the barber comes up to your room."

"Didn't we go to Lima together last year?"

"I used to like the Knickerbocker Hotel in Chicago."

"Good golf course at Delhi." "Ever play in Bermuda?"

"Tennis in Colombo and Tel Aviv."

"Tried to get into the Bibliotheque at Rome but the place was packed."

"Best place for Shish Kebab is Abdullah's at Istanbul."

"Got an excellent briefcase at Bangkok. . . ."

"Met a real beauty in Singapore last trip."

"Johannesburg . . . Mexico . . . Zurich . . . Cairo . . . Kano . . . Nairobi in the rain . . . Keflavik . . . Kuwait . . . Idlewild. . . ." The words and places came floating through the cigarette smoke whilst the lights of Kowloon, still brightly burning, filled the whole horizon outside . . . "The world is my oyster," as the poet said.

When the last guest had departed and whilst the Chinese boys swiftly made order of the room, I fell to thinking, "Maybe it *is* an exciting, strange life?"

A few days later in Delhi, where we were grounded till a horde of yellow locusts had passed, it struck me forcibly how very different it now was from that first day in October 1937 when I presented myself to the Brooklands Flying Club at Weybridge and said, "I've come to learn to fly."

In those days you could command attention by simply remarking, "Yesterday I went up in an aeroplane."

Nowadays people stop and stare only when you say, "I've never once been inside an aircraft."

In those days any Atlantic crossing was a nine-day wonder with headlines inches high; now I am one of the hundreds who stopped counting after 500 such transatlantic crossings.

All in twenty-five years.

Introduction to Second Edition

WHEN *In Full Flight* was first published in 1965, the World War II thirty-year rule had not yet come into force. In essence, this rule made public virtually all the official records of the War, enabling an official account to be available in the Public Records Office.

The original publication of *In Full Flight* was based upon the personal recollections of those involved, backed by my Civil and RAF Flying Log Books. However, with the new information now available, it is clear that the original edition of the book may be slightly at variance in some minor details.

With one exception, the text has been left unchanged because the discrepancies are small and the conveying of the overall atmosphere of the times is still there.

This one exception concerns Malta's most distinguished pilot. The pages covering the exploits of Wing Commander Adrian Warburton have been largely rewritten, because I have since written the biography of Warby* and feel that this unique, charismatic character should be portrayed as accurately as possible; though the general impression conveyed by the 1965 edition is correct.

I have now unearthed the log of the captain of the U-boat which I attacked at night, which I considered might well have been damaged or even sunk. It is now clear that, although the depth-charges dropped from my Liberator probably fell close enough to inflict some damage, unaccaountably none of them exploded. We shall never know why, but the result was that the U-boat escaped damage.

Further, I have now learned from an Italian who has examined the Italian Naval records that the ship which I and my crew bombed at

**Warburton's War* by Tony Spooner DSO DFC, published by William Kimber Ltd, London, 1987. ISBN 07183 0661 9.

night off the coast of Sicily in October 1941 was the 9,000-ton merchant vessel *Amsterdam*. It managed to reach Naples, to spend many months under repair.

Tony Spooner
1991

1: Decision to Fly

I WAS twenty and I was sitting in the bar of the Beach Hotel, Littlehampton, the seaside town wherein I had lived for all but the first year or so of my life. I was the Junior Inspector of the Worthing sub-office of the General Accident, Fire and Life Assurance Corporation. I was earning about £10 per month. From £39 per annum to nearly £120 in a little over three years was, I had been told, "a most promising start".

I had been fed up for weeks, and was morosely drinking away a pointless evening. In this mood I struck up a conversation with a young man more or less my own age.

"What do you *want* to do?" he asked, after I had told him that my heart certainly wasn't in the insurance business.

"I like driving motor-cars and adding up figures," I answered after some thought, and added, "playing squash too."

"Old boy," he said, "you should fly."

I didn't understand why, so he went on to explain why love of machinery, mathematics and a quick eye were of importance. It transpired that he was a young Royal Air Force officer but had failed to win promotion because his maths had been found wanting. In fact, he was equally morose.

As the evening wore on (we were both getting somewhat tanked up) this new idea kept recurring. I had never thought about flying. I had never, in fact, been to an aerodrome, never been in an aircraft, never seen an aircraft other than up in the sky. I had never made model aircraft or read books about flying. I didn't know the name of a single aircraft type.

Nevertheless the idea of flying attracted me; of soaring above the earth's surface; of controlling a machine which defied the laws of nature.

I was sufficiently interested to ask my new friend back to my house after the bar had closed. We had the family living-room to ourselves at that late hour and there, sustained by some more liquor which I "borrowed" from the home supply, I had my first "flying lesson". With a walking-stick serving as a control column and with books acting for rudder pedals, I turned this way and that. "Bank to the left." "Take your rudder off." "Ease the nose up." Luckily no one else was about, as we were obviously pretty "high", and my mother's chintz and Chinese cabinet must have seemed a strange background for the two young men on the settee who, in between sips, were bent upon "taking her off on another circuit".

I never saw my friend again, but the idea he had planted that night had taken some kind of root. Moreover, I remembered that he had advised me to join an organisation called the RAFVR, the week-end Air Force Reserve which taught people to fly for nothing. By joining this I could see for myself whether or not flying and I were to be good bed-fellows. I also remembered that he had said that there was a unit at Shoreham Airport, less than twenty miles away.

Next Saturday, therefore, I drove my car (actually it was half mine and half the family's car, but since I was the only one at home who could drive, I had become virtually its owner) to Shoreham Airport, and there tried to find the RAFVR. It took some doing, as the local flying club and the RAFVR seemed to be one inside the other, and at the bar I was nearly signed up as a member of the former. Later I wrote to somebody in London and had at least one interview. All was going swimmingly. I was the right age. I had the necessary scholastic qualifications and I told them I had my parents' consent. I passed their preliminary tests and was just about through my final interview when one of the examining board noticed that I had left blank the answer to the question: "Do you think you will remain in UK for the next few years?"

I explained that I couldn't answer this right now, as it so happened that I had applied for an overseas assignment with my insurance company and my application was then being considered. This was not at all what they wanted to hear, and with abrupt finality I found my application indefinitely shelved until such time as I could guarantee my continued presence in Britain.

Until then the idea of incurring any obligation in return for being taught to fly for absolutely nothing during my weekends had not occurred to me. Somewhat deflated, I returned home to have to face the fact that I couldn't at that moment be accepted.

I felt a little cheated as I reflected that I need never have told my interviewers about the possibility of my going abroad (about my application I could gain no further information from my employers). Just for being honest I now found myself rejected—or so it seemed to me then.

It was only then that I realised how much of my future hopes I had put into this attempt to join the RAFVR. I had seized upon it as a heaven-sent outlet, a chance to sparkle, a contrast to the rather dull tasks I was daily expected to perform for my insurance company. Life now seemed more pointless than ever. High summer was approaching and I couldn't even think how to spend my two-week annual holiday. The year before I had driven up to Lancashire to stay with the parents of a girl friend. But this venture had "fizzled". Now, more than ever, I felt I was stagnating, and in 1937 with "war-clouds gathering", time showed every indication of running out. I certainly didn't want to join the RAF proper as a pilot, not only because I didn't wish to risk an irrevocable plunge into a life about which I knew absolutely nothing, but also because I was being half influenced by some pacifist, politically-inclined intellectuals with whom I was on beer drinking terms. The RAF trained for war and war seemed no solution to anything. I held some sort of belief that if all the people of the world thought the same as I did (and it was reasonable to suppose that we held a ninety-nine per cent majority), then eventually all the armed services would shrink to mere police size and Hitler and Mussolini, Stalin and Franco and their followers would either have to become political gentlemen or lapse into obscurity.

So the RAF was definitely out! I also began to see that the "obligation" which I would owe to the RAFVR could prove embarrassing if by any chance war actually came.

I now definitely wanted to fly, and as the urge grew within me, so did the confidence that I could accomplish the task. Again I started to visit the Shoreham airport bar during my week-end respite. It was a welcome contrast to my daily routine of collecting premiums, sticking my foot in doors, buying lunchtime beers for agents, propping up the office counter and casting suspicious eyes over claim forms.

Shoreham Flying Club was, I now learned, a branch of a larger organisation whose headquarters were at Brooklands, then a celebrated motor-race circuit with a grass airfield within the steeply banked oval track. Anyone could learn to fly at Shoreham simply by joining the club over the bar (everything in pre-war flying clubs in Britain was conducted over bar counters!) and paying the sum of thirty or thirty-five shillings per hour for flying lessons. Since I was at most saving perhaps £2 per month, this obviously wasn't going to satisfy my new urge at any rapid pace. Also it didn't seem to be leading anywhere as I felt it should at that price. These were the days when best cigarettes were twenty for 11½d, beer 6d per pint, whisky 12s 6d per bottle, new cars £100 upwards and petrol about 2s per gallon. Bed and breakfast at a good hotel was 12s 6d, and for 30s or 35s one could just about manage a week-end in Brighton, for two if needs be!

Then I remembered hearing something about the son of a friend of my father's being some sort of non-military pilot. He too lived in Littlehampton. I was so ignorant of aviation matters that I wasn't sure of the difference between Imperial Airways and the other private aircraft companies operating in opposition to this Government-inspired giant. So I hunted out one Bob Derrington-Turner, and became aware for the first time of the very fine salaries which, at that time, were paid to Imperial Airways pilots (Bob turned out to be one of them). This man, perhaps about seven years older than I, was earning over £1,000 per annum, whereas my immediate manager at Worthing, a man way past fifty, was then earning less than £400 per annum. I knew because I had once seen his pay check and felt sorry for him.

The urge to fly now had an added attraction. Not only did it offer a challenge. The pay was right!

So back I went to the Shoreham Flying Club, where I now had a young friend, already an amateur flier, who was toying with the idea of becoming a commercial pilot. As rapidly as I could, I lapped up all the information which he could supply. I now also started reading the advertisements in the back of the weekly flying magazines, and posted off letters asking for terms from the various flying clubs which offered training for the Commercial A and B flying licences. Oddly enough I can't recall reading a single other word of these magazines. I still didn't know the name of a single type of aircraft other than that of the Gypsy and Tiger Moths which belonged to the Shoreham Flying Club. But I had, nonetheless, acquired a knowledge of the commercial pilots' licensing structure. The A was for private pilots: the much more advanced B was the commercial pilot's licence, and valid only for each type of plane on which the holder had passed certain tests.

I also learned that an instructors' endorsement issued by a mysterious body called "the Guild" gave B licence-holders the right to teach flying, and that by far the easiest and cheapest way of getting fully qualified and of earning a living as a commercial pilot was to get a B licence (only 100 hours' solo flying required), and then to add the "Guild Instructors" certificate. One could then instruct for money, whilst still flying the same type on which one had learned to fly. By assuming ten hours' dual instruction before acquiring the hundred hours solo requirement and adding another thirty to forty for further dual instruction and instructors' training, the job seemed to require approximately £2 x 150 hours—£300 outlay—the kind of starting money which a new instructor was paid per annum. My £10-per-month job began to look ridiculous. But at the back of my mind was Bob Derrington-Turner earning three or four times £300. I was really getting ambitious. So I delved a little deeper and learned that the flying licence which really opened the doors to the airlines was a navigational one, commonly called the 2nd N. The 1st N was something so high that it seemed that only the Almighty could hope to possess it. Its name was spoken with bated breath.

To get a 2nd N (An Air Navigator's Licence—2nd class), quite a lot of rapid maths were required; the need for speed and accuracy was stressed. Also the minimum flying time was 300 hours. The mathematic hurdle didn't unduly alarm me as the gift for this kind of rapid arithmetic was something which I had inherited from my father. I actually loved adding up, and used to do quite complicated sums in my head just for the hell of it (and as a show-off party trick). But the 300 hours' flying qualification meant that my outlay would now be nearer £1,000 than the £300 which I had first calculated when considering a B licence alone. If I was to hope to get 300 hours, obviously I couldn't do it in my spare time or at week-ends. With winter weather coming on I learned that the most flying a trainee pilot could hope to get was ten hours per week, and often far less than this.

Often none at all, in fact, at a place like Shoreham, which was exposed to south-west gales from the Channel. Anyhow, Shoreham didn't teach navigation. So. . . .

I think I had made up my mind to go for the higher objective, B licence plus 2nd N, almost as soon as I heard of the requirements and of the rewards it could bring. Maths was my one genuine asset, and I felt the advisability of being able to employ this to the full.

Again I cast around for training costs and schedules. Some would-be commercial pilots had advocated an alternative programme, to get the B licence and the instructor's ticket, and with the latter get a job at once in order to acquire the full 300 hours. This would enable the 300 hours to be obtained cheaply; also the money earned instructing would pay for the navigational instruction (nearly another £100). However, my particular friend Peter Dutt or Duth (I wish I now could be sure of his name as I learnt later to be truly grateful for all his good advice) doubted whether it would be feasible to break studies, get an instructor's job, study in spare time and pass the stiff 2nd N written exams. I doubted it too as I had just passed my ACII (Insurance) exams, and had found correspondence courses and self-study a particularly irksome way of learning. It wasn't suited to my temperament at all. I liked classrooms with lecturers I could talk to.

In terms of time one all-out effort at the B and 2nd N licences simultaneously was definitely preferable, and time meant money. By tackling the two together at the same aerodrome I would not have to kick my heels whenever the weather was against flying. If I couldn't fly, then I would study.

There appeared to be only two places in the country where I could combine flying training and navigational studies more or less simultaneously. There was AST at Hamble, and there was the Shoreham Club's parent organisation at Brooklands. AST was, however, more or less a complete air-training university, and their brochures spoke in terms of three years' training at prices up to £3,000 and beyond. Their courses included engineering and radio licences, and unquestionably offered the most comprehensive programme; in fact, their successful students went straight into the major airlines. By contrast, Brooklands was a do-it-yourself school. They had good flying instructors and a good reputation; they had workshops (and an engineering school at Chelsea) where one could get all the engineering knowledge one wished, and they had a qualified navigational instructor who had gained the reputation of getting pilots through exams. The drawbacks were that they were fifty miles from where I lived, so I would probably have to include "digs" in any costing, and that their flying charges were the highest in the country, 45s per hour whether dual or solo. Every other club charged lower rates for solo than dual, and I don't think any other charged beyond £2 per hour even for dual. Flying at Brooklands was about 40 per cent more expensive than it was at Shoreham.

All my spare hours were being given to this subject, which had by now become a frankly commercial undertaking. I seldom thought about "flying" as such and still took no more than passing interest in general aviation news. I had my sights on flying as a career.

The B licence medical was a stumbling block which I rather feared, since (according to a fond mother) in my early years I had only just survived every possible illness from meningitis to double pneumonia. Notwithstanding this I was obviously fit, as my performances on the squash courts implied. I was practically inexhaustible and used to play game after game without rest. At one time I belonged to about seven different squash clubs (the game was booming along the Sussex coast), and my car enabled me to travel with ease to the various inter-club matches, for which I sometimes played on both sides!

Arguing that my mother was probably exaggerating, and that anyhow her stories were only hearsay (so far as I was concerned), I duly wrote down "nil" against "serious illnesses" and sent up my application to take the B licence medical. This was an obvious precaution, as it would have been an appalling waste of money and effort to obtain all the necessary flight and ground qualifications and then fail to pass the medical tests. Still, just to make sure, and because around the Shoreham Club bar there were many tales about how severe this medical test was, I went into strict training.

To maintain fitness I now ran several miles before breakfast, and after work made sure that I played squash every night. I cut down on smoking, and drank nothing more than an occasional beer, and must have seemed as trained as a whippet when I presented myself before an examining doctor. I know I held my breath for so long that I was asked to stop, and that I blew up the mercury (a much dreaded test for some) for over two minutes before again being asked to "let go".

Incidentally this nearly failed me my *next* medical, when, after a year of free and easy club life around the Brooklands Club bar I could just about manage a bare sixty seconds of the mercury test and the pronounced "deterioration" worried the examining doctor more than somewhat!

Now all I needed was the money. By cutting costs, assuming that I could accomplish my whole training in one year (an optimistic figure in the opinions of Peter and others), and given certain fiddles which I was learning about (such as flying as an unpaid "safety pilot" with private owners who didn't wish to assume "full responsibility", they liked to drink *and* fly) I reckoned I could accomplish the full B licence, 2nd N 300 hours flight time, and instructors' endorsement on a budget of £900, including living costs away from home for the twelve months.

During these months of preparation my father had become desperately ill. He had, I believe, acute peritonitis. Mother never gave a coherent explanation as to his condition; nor the same one twice.She was a kindly, generous soul but not gifted with medical or specialist knowledge of any kind. Before approaching him as my only possible source of raising £900, I again went into the pay structure of Imperial Airways and that of their biggest competitor, British Airways. The pay was indeed attractive, as with their new four-engined Empire flying-boats, Imperial were on top of the civil aviation world. Flying pay boosted pilots' salaries to well over £1,000 per annum, provided they flew more than a certain mileage or number of hours per month. I had in effect drawn up a kind of balance sheet with "Life Expectation Earnings" prominently displayed; I hoped that this would make the £900 I wanted look relatively insignificant.

Father was in a private nursing home in one of the pleasant houses overlooking Littlehampton's esplanade. He was propped up and still the subject of fairly frequent wincing pains that made him shrivel and gasp. I had never seen my father, whom I both adored and respected, in such straits and I was staggered and dismayed by his distress. Nevertheless, I had my papers, costs, budget sheets, flying club brochures, medical certificate, etc, and I was determined to present my case, come what may. By now all the family knew that I had been chasing off to Shoreham Airport and latterly to Brooklands, too, and that I was taking an interest in flying but I had purposely played down this interest, and no one had any idea of the extent or intent of my enquiries. I think the general feeling was that "Tony was thinking about joining the RAF", since my initial enthusiasm had been towards the RAFVR and these familiar initials had stuck.

In my father's private ward I launched into my plans with costs, etc, but soon I was stopped. I had been blessed with an understanding father.

"Of course you can have the money. I have known for a long time that you have been dissatisfied with your present job. You could have gone to Cambridge as you know." (I had passed the exams but decided to go out and get a job instead as (*a*) I was in love for the first time, and (*b*) the family fortunes had taken a turn for the worse.) "Your brother went to Guy's for his long dental training. I have been waiting for you to find out what you really want to do. I know absolutely nothing about flying, but I dare say it will suit you."

To the general public, flying was then labelled dangerous, crazy and hare-brained. Nevertheless, in between spells of pain, my father accepted without the smallest demur an aviation career for his younger son before I had even started to enumerate the great commercial advantages of an airline pilot.

Weeks before I even had my first flying lesson, I had already determined to become a fully-fledged highly-paid airline captain—nothing less.

2: *Brooklands*

DURING September 1937 I had paid two visits to the celebrated flying club situated within the motor circuit at Brooklands—once to see whether and when they would take me as a pupil, and the other time to meet Bob Ashton, the navigation instructor. On the first of these occasions I was lucky to run into Duncan Davies, the part-owner and mainspring of the Brookland organisation which controlled some half-dozen flying clubs, maintenance hangars, etc, in various parts of England. As we chatted he looked up and remarked, "Oh, there is that Hart" indicating vaguely some aircraft on the airfield outside. "What," I asked, "is a Hart?" The Hawker Hart was then about as well known as the Hawker Hunter of today, and the question was an absurd admission of ignorance from one who, a few moments before, had blandly been telling Duncan of his plans to become an airline pilot within twelve months!

Duncan left abruptly. Later, when he and I had become good friends, I asked him what on earth he must have thought, and he told me that he was so certain I was an idiot that, against his usual generous habits, he had made a point of telling the barman, the timekeeper, his secretary and others at the club that "on no account was I to be given any credit". Cash or nothing it was to be!

Bob Ashton, the navigation instructor, was a quiet Scotsman with a delightful sense of fun. He had a wooden leg from an RAF crash, and he now ran, within the Brooklands empire, a civil navigation school which was probably the only independent one of its kind in the country. He had a good brain, much patience and proved to be a good friend.

Aviation in those days was so full of "characters" of every kind that the rare *ordinary* participant seemed utterly out of place. I don't recall the bar ever being seriously shut, and club life revolved around this room, from which an admirable view of the landing area could be enjoyed. A lounge and dining-room completed the premises. There were offices upstairs and Bob had his classrooms alongside one of the hangars near by. The engineering college was in Chelsea; otherwise everything was compact.

Flying took place from a timekeeper's hut where everything was logged, recorded and (in my case) paid for. This hut was run by a character called Jimmy the Boy (name slightly changed), a young red-faced beefy man with a thirst which was large even by flying club standards. He never had any money, so borrowed everyone else's. He had a fund of stories; could fly very nicely, but seldom did so for reasons I never understood—financial probably, and was always hale and hearty. He was extraordinarily generous and liked nothing better than to order up "drinks all round, chaps!" which was slightly ironical, as he invariably owed money to everyone in the bar!

Anyhow, it was to Jimmy that I first went—but I am leaping ahead a bit.

Looking back, I realise now that I must have met my unknown RAF officer in the bar of the Beach Hotel about late June or early July 1937, and that all the preparation first to join the RAFVR at Shoreham, and then for civil flying and finally for airline flying training, had been accomplished within about two months. Certainly it was the first week in September when I offered my resignation to the insurance company which had employed me for almost four years. I told them why I was leaving and what I was planning to do, and I asked whether the normal one-month notice could in my case be reduced to three weeks, so as to enable me to commence my flying training by October 1st. They readily agreed to dispense with my services, as these had been performed with absolutely no enthusiasm for far too long a time. The area manager from Brighton, in releasing me by September 30th, wrote a well-intentioned note in which he hoped I would find the excitement I needed in the Air Force and wished me luck. I couldn't resist replying that firstly I wasn't joining the Air Force but, as previously stated, I was preparing myself for a career in civil aviation and secondly, I wasn't doing it for excitement, but as a means of earning a proper living in a reasonable period of time. I really must have hated the Insurance business!

So, for the rest of September, I went around keyed up with anticipation and with an added jauntiness of manner. But why I didn't bother to read up aviation matters via the excellent *Flight* or *Aeroplane* weekly magazines remains a mystery. In this mood of *joie de vivre* I happened to drop in at the Littlehampton tennis club. Probably I was looking to see who I could have a beer with. I saw something far more attractive than a drinking partner, and I stayed on in order to get introduced.

Later that night I went round to her father's house to try and sell him my car (which I really didn't want to sell at all). I didn't make a sale. However, it wasn't a wasted evening, as he lived to be the grandfather of my three children! Henceforth I had a girl friend as well as aviation to pursue.

All in all, September 1937 was quite a month for me, since everything that has happened since inevitably stems from the two decisions I then made: to learn to fly for a living; and to learn to live with the girl I had noticed on the tennis courts.

On October 1st I duly presented myself at Brooklands, having driven up from Littlehampton to keep the 11 a.m. first-lesson appointment. My baggage was still in the back of my little Fiat 500. I had crossed my Rubicon. This was it. I still hadn't seen an aeroplane at really close range and I had no idea whether I would like flying or whether I had any aptitude for it. But youth is ever optimistic.

I was introduced to my instructor (who, I gathered, was the Chief Instructor). Ken Waller was a name known to everyone even remotely connected with aviation, but I hadn't heard of him. At that time, I believe, he held the London–New Zealand and return record, flying the De Havilland twin-engined racing craft—the first to be named the Comet.

Ken Waller was very tall, healthy and lean, and he possessed a drawling voice I was to come to know well. He was friendliness itself, but always slightly aloof, as British as any Wodehouse character.

"First," he said, "we'll have a brief look at the old Tiger Moth and its bits and pieces," and he lazily ambled up to the nearest of the neatly lined-up, smartly painted machines, which constituted the productive side of the Brooklands Flying School. I couldn't take in much of what he was saying, as I was trying to assimilate the shock of discovering that these aircraft were built out of mere wood and fabric.

I had been expecting strong-looking metal bodies like those of the various cars I had driven. The fabric was doped over and nicely silvered, and some of the more substantial surfaces were made of plywood, but all in all the Tiger Moth looked a most flimsily constructed piece of mechanism.

Next I had to borrow a helmet with Gosport tubes and earpieces, since I also discovered that he would sit in front of me. We would be several feet apart and only able to communicate via an old-fashioned speaking-tube system, such as we once had had installed at home for the purpose of calling instructions down to the kitchen. We couldn't possibly have sat in any other manner, as the whole fuselage was only about thirty inches across. The borrowed helmet didn't fit too well, but I nodded assent when Ken shouted "Can you hear me!" down the other end of the speaking-tube. I remember a careful lesson on how to get into my seat without damaging fuselage or wings. Then, after what seemed to be a laboriously antiquated method of starting the noisy engine by hand-swinging the propeller several times, we bumped away across the grass. The wheels appeared to have square tyres, judging by the jolts they imparted through the seat of my pants. I thought with nostalgia of my smooth silent motor-cars, with their steel bodies, self-starters, shock absorbers, leaf springs, comfortable seats and side-by-side seating arrangements. This aircraft didn't even have brakes!

Like all pupils I can't remember much about that first flight. Never having left the earth before, the wonder of the new perspective proved too much for other considerations. Until told otherwise, I kept my hands and feet as far removed as possible from the obvious controls—a vertical metal lever, like a crow-bar between my knees, and two pedals almost lost in the dark area around my feet. I must at some time have carried out the first simple movements to Ken's commands, which came drawling through my head with deceiving casualness. "That's good, old boy." "Not too heavy with the left foot, old chap." "Just relax, and we'll do it again." "Easy back, old chap." "Nice and gentle—that's the style." "EASY does it." "Good show."

I had found an instructor in a million. One who was never tense, who never wearied or gave up. A pilot with a smooth sure touch and a magnificent "pair of hands"; imperturbable and charming, on or off the ground. He had dark, close-cropped hair and a surprisingly small head on top of his long angular body. A smile which started in his eyes was never far away. At parties he didn't chat over-much, but was always there at the back of the room, leaning against a wall or mantelpiece with a glass of beer in his hand and a smile on his lips. One didn't easily establish a close relationship with this basically reserved man, but I never knew anyone who disliked him or who failed to respect him. He smoked cigarettes because all pilots seemed to do so then.

I returned to earth flushed by the wind which had seemed to howl around the noisy open cockpit and inside my ill-fitting helmet (which looked as if it had once belonged to a World War I veteran—and probably had). The lesson over, I enquired where I could find cheap "digs". I knew my money had not been advanced without some sacrifice on Father's part and with much misgivings on Mother's.

I found some about a mile away, run by a certain "Ma" Patterson, if my memory serves me correctly. They were typical "lodgings" of that time. Vaguely genteel, basically comfortable, run down, short of washing space, homely and simple fare reasonably cooked by someone who was perpetually worried about getting paid. Too many of her lodgers took advantage of her obvious lack of professional management. We were probably her only real interest in life, but this life at times, one felt, was rather too much for her overworked, somewhat exhausted frame. A widow, one assumes, left unprepared financially and otherwise.

My room was obviously the worst in the place (as is usual for last-to-come lodgers). It overlooked the main railway lines to London and the noise of the trains was amplified by a road bridge only a few yards away. Thus, it came in bursts, rose in echoes and disappeared abruptly as it had come. When two trains passed in opposite directions, the pressure waves shook my windows. There was a shilling-in-the-slot gas-fire and the inevitable china washbasin and jug of hideous rose patterns. Adequate bedclothes were supplied if one used the bedspread; nothing was new, and every fabric was faded, but there was a big, old-fashioned easy-chair which allowed escape from the so-called lounge if one desired it. I paid two weeks in advance, to her obvious delight and astonishment.

Those trains were a problem, and if I hadn't already burned my boats it is possible that they might have induced me to give up flying altogether.

Although I wasn't frightened at the prospect of flying, I was well aware of the dangers associated with it. Even more so than today, most aviation news in the daily press was dire and sensational. Every incident was given a banner headline. My dear fond mother had urged me to make sure that I always flew "low and slow", and I was too ignorant at the time to correct her. At best, a beginner received one flying lesson of up to forty minutes per day, often less than forty minutes. Ken's policy (normal club policy, too) was to let each lesson sink in, and, in spite of fair weather, I got only one lesson each day of that first week. They didn't alarm me and I have reason to think that I took to flying, if not as a duck takes to water, then as any normal healthy young man takes to flying.

But clearly, the unsilenced noise of the engine was leaving some powerful subconscious impression of power in my mind, as every time I went to bed all that first week I was awakened sooner or later by the damned trains outside, and on almost every occasion this noise had permeated into a dream in which I was diving out of control earthwards with my Tiger Moth's engine racing, the noise getting louder and louder. . . . At least once a night or early morning, I thus woke up in a sweating panic with my heart thumping. I could, perhaps, have changed rooms or digs, but I saw this as a challenge. I wasn't really worried, as I was aware, only too clearly, of the obvious explanation for these nightmares.

But after a week or so I resumed my normal habit of being able to sleep through almost any noise—a habit which is almost a first essential to any airline pilot!

I spent week-ends at home largely chasing my girl, and until she returned with her parents to their house in southern France, I stretched these a bit, due to the relatively easy schedule set for me at Brooklands.

Looking back now, I can't think what I did with myself for the rest of the days at Brooklands, as my lessons obviously didn't occupy too much of any day. I threw myself into the task of assimilating the language and "feel" of the flying fraternity. I devoured all the weekly and monthly publications, including all the back numbers I could find (very considerable at flying clubs). I went round the hangars and learned a few basic details of the aircraft. The skilled, experienced engineers there were always willing to gossip with any enthusiastic youngster. In the club I played chess, table tennis and draughts with fellow students, instructors and members. In the bar I budgeted for about two beers a day and made these last as long as possible, as I listened to the endless chatter. Nothing on earth can stop two or more pilots from talking about flying whenever they meet in a bar. Brooklands was more than a flying club. It was a social club and at weekends the place was often crowded out, and, though only a few of the members actually flew, they all displayed almost the same enthusiasm about flying as did we student pilots.

There were no fixed courses at Brooklands, but there were always three or four students, who were there for no other purpose than to train themselves for professional flying licences. Invariably we were at different stages of training and we tackled the common problems before us at varying paces and stages. When I started in October, 1937, Bill Orton and Vernon Hunt were nearly fully-fledged airline pilots. They had been at it for some two or three years, since they had first started in Chelsea in the Brooklands School of Engineering, where they obtained their B and D engineering licences. Now they both had their B flying licences and were putting the finishing touches to 2nd N training and flight hours. There had been a third member training with them who had crashed one of the club's aircraft, and though he luckily survived the accident, he never caught up with Bill or Vernon (nor regained his enthusiasm). This crash was much discussed, as it was about the only occasion on which the club had lost a training aircraft in all its long history. The pilot had flown about fifty or so solo hours at the time, when he had lost control and "spun in".

Bill Bailey and Eric Starling, both airline pilots flying in the north (Railway Airlines and Gander Dowers outfit respectively), had just been through the navigation school, as had some of the active British Airways Captains—in one rare case seeking the hallowed 1st N. I didn't see much of these experts at first as they were free to fly whatever, wherever and whenever they wished. Bill Orton and Vernon Hunt were, in fact, gaining their final hours and experience on a two-seater monoplane Puss Moth, which they had bought *n*th hand. G-AAXY was its registration, and some said that it was the machine in which the celebrated long-distance flyer, Jim Mollison, had first crossed the Atlantic. More about "Gaaxy", as she was called, later. She had personality as well as a history.

There was a cheerful rotund fellow called Harry Pepper, who had got as far as some fifty to a hundred hours solo, but who now progressed only in fits and starts. His friend, of about equal experience, was Tom Brooke-Smith, then well under twenty, but already displaying the talent which later made him one of the more famous of British test-pilots. At that time he was rather superior to us new boys, and he combined flying with a somewhat precarious personal life, which was not an unnatural or unusual occurrence at that time and age! He was "in-and-out" of navigation school, but his heart was obviously elsewhere.

Then there were a few young men of substance, who were learning to fly as an experience, or because they owned their own planes or hoped to do so. I can remember Ken Firth, who owned an Avro Avian (and a Lagonda), and Scotty, who drove a 100 mph open Alvis, and Cliff Mollison, then at the height of his fame on the London stage. Later came Alistair Cormack and his BA Swallow. Quite a few girls, also with obvious private means, used to dabble at flying. These were largely the pupils of another instructor who, needless to say, was both good-looking and unmarried! Eventually he departed to marry one of these elegant well-groomed pupils to the obvious satisfaction of them both.

There were, too, a few week-end flying enthusiasts, but none more so than the celebrated "Bish". C Nepean-Bishop was the doyen of the week-end pilots, quite the best of them, too, and the greatest enthusiast of all. Middle-aged, rather round, and wearing thick glasses, he had a Pickwickian look, and earned a living as a bank clerk. Nothing could ever keep "Bish" from Brooklands. Every week-end he was there, rain or shine. To me he was helpfulness and friendliness itself. His eyesight prevented him from ever becoming a professional pilot, but his experience, knowledge and handling of the planes were of professional standards.

My two great friends, as they were to become, were Jack Sewell and Rhona Stein (not her real name). This latter was a young tom-boy with a great urge to fly and with the desire to become a female commercial pilot. She had been training some six to nine months when I arrived, and had nearly completed the necessary flying hours and experience for her B licence; however, she was bent upon obtaining the much rarer 2nd N as well. Like so many other young enthusiastic aviators she drove an open sports car (she obviously had lots of money, and was the daughter of a banker). A good-looking girl, with an excellent figure, she was, nevertheless, so far as Brooklands was concerned, just another enthusiastic pupil.

She maintained her own car, smoked, swore and deliberately tried to minimise her own sex. Her other interest was ice-hockey, at which she was internationally well known. Only when one danced with her did one realise that her small frame was all whip-cord and muscle. I only once saw her dressed up in fine clothes: she looked really delightful. But normally, at Brooklands, she wore working slacks in winter, and shorts in summer, and what shorts they were! Later on, we used to spend long, hot days together, as we worked away for the 2nd N exam. It was then that she started her swear box as even she began to realise that her language was hardly ladylike. Plotting tracks over huge charts is a tricky business and one slip is apt to compound itself. Rhona would work away, biting one thumb until "F . . . .!" she would exclaim, somewhat to my embarrassment. So we devised a scale.

Each F . . . . cost her 1s. B . . . and S . . . . each went down for 6d, and lesser words tailed off to 1d for "Damns". I forget what we did with the money, but I collected £1 or more during those weeks before our exam. As for those short shorts, she took the hint when I started wearing dark glasses and complained that I couldn't study trigonometry under such trying circumstances!

Poor Rhona was Jewish, and her race was being bullied and mutilated all over Nazi dominated Europe. I suspect that her determined enthusiasm for flying was a form of escape from brutal realities. She had an excellent brain, and she and I were the only ones who persevered at Bob's school all that hot summer, by which time the senior pupils had all passed the exams and had left to rejoin the airlines.

Last but not least of my companions during the ten months which followed my initial introduction to Brooklands was Jack Sewell. He had started to train only a month or two ahead of me and we at once struck an easy friendship. For the rest of my time at Brooklands Jack and I trained side by side and, as will appear later, we even got our first jobs the same day. We became part of the club's formation-flying team; together we won the Doncaster Trophy for Brooklands. "Bish" had a hand in both these events too, and the three of us, two young twenty-year-old students and a middle-aged bank clerk, became an inseparable trio, bound together by a love of flying in general, and of flying for Brooklands in particular. All of which came much later.

These, then, were the companions with whom I cut my pilot's teeth. Poor and wealthy; old and young; male and female; enthusiasts all, whether performing or watching.

This was the strange society of devotees I had joined, and in a relatively short space of time I accepted as natural the perpetual "shop" talk and came to regard the club bar as my haven after a day's work. Our bar talk was richer than most in that the club was frequented by both the Vickers' and the Hawker's test pilots, for in those days both these manufacturing giants (who between them produced the war-winning Hurricane-Spitfire team of fighters) had their factories within the Brooklands circuit. They also used the same grass airfield as we pupils did.

One strange thing about learning to fly is that the pupil never quite knows how he is progressing. He has no yardstick by which to measure his progress against that of other pupils. Thus, the question "How many hours before you first go solo?" assumes a great importance—this being virtually the only guide to one's personal talent quotient. I was vaguely aware that I was "doing all right", and after about six hours began to wonder when I would be let loose on my own. Apart from anything else, this seemed to be the only question which my parents, brother and cousins at home, could think to ask me whenever I came back for a day or two. About twelve hours was regarded as normal, but youngsters usually did it in less. Rumour had it that Tom Brooke-Smith had flown solo in about seven. My friend, Jack Sewell, had to wait till about eleven.

I sensed that Ken Waller was beginning to consider the idea. He would casually mention such things as what to do if the engine should suddenly quit or how I should start keeping a watchful eye on the clouds and wind (how quickly I was to repent not paying full attention to this); and once, after about three or four circuits, which seemed absolutely OK to me, I thought he even started to get out. But he slumped back instead. This, I recall, set me back a bit and I started to make untidy landings again. I think I was resentful that he hadn't let me go solo at a time when I was about neck and neck with Brooke-Smith's recent "record". As in other sports where judgment is concerned, one's own confidence-level is so often the deciding factor between on-form or off-form performance. (Putting at golf is a good example.)

In fact, I was beginning to despair of ever going solo when, out of the blue, Ken casually drawled, "That's good enough, old boy. How about pushing off and doing a few on your own. Two or three at the most, I think." And before I could fully realise it he had climbed out, secured the dangling shoulder-harness in his front seat, removed the dual-control joystick and was leisurely sauntering towards the club-house. I can't now remember anything special about my first solo fiight, except that the second landing was slightly heavy, so I came in after two rather than three. My chief concern was that I wasn't sure that I had enough money to buy the traditional round of drinks which invariably followed a first solo! I have since sent pilots off on their own first solo, and I realise now that the right time is *not* when a pupil appears to have "got the secret", but when he had demonstrated his ability to make the right corrections to a poorly-executed landing. Until a pupil hits such a bad patch, he can't demonstrate how sensibly he will manage these vital corrections. In fact, I once had a pupil who simply *wouldn't* make any mistake at all, in spite of the slight upsettings which I, the instructor, was by then applying, and my chief and I were in two minds what to do about him. How would he react when inevitably he did start misjudging distances? We couldn't tell.

Anyhow, my time was nine hours twenty-five minutes, which was about right for my age and for the concentrated efforts which I had been making. I still had a week or two to run to my twenty-first birthday, so it had taken me just over a month to get this far—a fact which rather depressed me, as my budgeting was based upon the assumption that I would be fully qualified with 300 hours at the end of twelve months. Nor had I yet started any kind of navigational training, but at least I was over the first hurdle. I could now (just) fly by myself.

One product of teaching a person to fly (as I saw for myself so clearly afterwards), is that it does something beneficial to the personality of the pupil. The quieter types gain self-confidence, but even more noticeable is the way in which the extrovert types tend to steady down. I had been feeling very much of a devil ever since I had embarked upon this new venture, and the big moment I had been waiting for was when I would be telling my family about my first solo.

But by the time I got home (next day) I had begun to realise how insignificant was this first step. My flamboyance was fading fast. And for once they didn't ask me the usual question, but instead enquired "how it was going".

I didn't volunteer the information that I had gone solo and they didn't find out till a week or so later.

I was losing my amateur status. I was growing up.

3: "Worst Moment"

A PILOT is often asked: "Do you get some really bad moments?" or "What has been your worst moment?" Mine occurred before that year of 1937 was out.

Although Ken Waller was my instructor, I did from time to time occasionally fly with the other instructors. There was the handsome bachelor Roland, who was keener than anyone else to chalk up as many hours as possible, since an instructor's pay was increased by the amount of dual instruction which he gave. There was also the aloof Leslie Cliff, who had a near-ideal existence. He spent his summers instructing at Brooklands, and he was reported to spend the winters on some uninhabited Caribbean Island, where it was said he and his beautiful wife lived without the benefit of clothes. Somehow, he and his wife also found time to be internationally famous as an ice-skating team, but how they managed to fit in their practice I shall never know. Ice must have been at a premium on their private Virgin Isle. Leslie was an austere man, and getting to know him was a slow business.

Then there was "dear old Brem"; a vast hulk of beaming, booming goodwill; an ex-war-time flier, who went to South Africa in 1919 to grow oranges, only to be wiped out of business in one brief hailstorm of undue violence. So back he had come to UK. In the Brooklands organisation he officially filled the role of sales manager. However, very few aircraft changed hands in those days, so he became a part-time instructor too. During World War I he had been shot in the mouth, and this had added a whistling lisp to his natural hearty roar. He probably had other injuries too, as he lurched and swayed his huge frame around like an amiable grizzly bear. He had startling eyebrows, huge weather-beaten features, and was a bundle of energetic goodwill.

Everyone loved "Brem".

After a pupil first flies solo, he is still the subject of much further instruction especially at a school of Brooklands' high standing, and I suppose that I had now been flying about eight weeks and had acquired a total of about an hour and a half's solo, made up of about four separate flights—each preceded by a lesson just to make sure that I was keeping clear of bad habits, including over-confidence.

For some reason Ken wasn't available one day, so Brem (who had flown me about twice before) as usual stepped in to help. He and I went around the circuit once and he then got out of the front seat and told me to do "half a dozen like that" and come in at about half an hour's time. Then almost as an aside he said, "Don't climb her too fast; keep it as near 66 as you can."

I think this slightly piqued me, as in the first place Ken had always said "between 65–70, old boy", and encouraged me to keep nearer the upper limit rather than the lower. Also I figured I had flown a near perfect circuit and didn't deserve even this mildest of mild criticism.

"If Brem wants 66 mph on the climb I'll see that he gets it", I muttered and off I went. Finer points of accuracy were things of which I was now conscious—indeed proud.

To those not familiar with flying, the circuit requires a word or two of explanation.

An aircraft takes off and lands into wind for the same reason the birds do. It reduces the speed of contact and so reduces the distances involved whether taking-off or landing. Thus, after take-off the aircraft has to be flown round the circuit to a point from which it can glide back to land again. Modern aircraft technique is such that it no longer glides back with engine idling, but flies back under moderate engine power. But in those days pilots were taught to glide back, and if anyone was ever caught having to use engine power in order reach the landing end of the field it was a "drinks all round" Club offence.

The circuit naturally falls into five stages: (1) Climb out straight and level off. (2) Turn left and fly straight and level for a brief spell. (3) Turn left again so as to be flying past the field down wind. After passing the field, (4) Turn left again so as to put the aircraft 90 degrees to its final course; this is called the base leg. (5) Finally, the engine would be cut back to idle and the final 90 degrees turn made so as to glide gently down to the airfield. After landing, the aircraft would have to be taxied back to the take-off point and the process would be repeated.

The whole circuit was supposed to be carried out at 1,000 feet (plus or minus 200 feet) and the normal procedure I had been taught was to climb straight ahead to 800 feet before commencing my first turn. Naturally, the whole manoeuvre was carried out by visual reference to the ground, plus frequent checks upon air speed, which must never be allowed to get too slow (if it did get too slow, the aircraft would cease to fly and would fall to the ground out of control). The altimeter was also vital—to check that the plane wasn't being accidentally climbed or dived during any of the level flight phases of the circuit.

Good visibility was absolutely essential, as the pupil pilot had, at that stage, never been shown the much more complex business of flying and steering by instruments alone. If he lost visual reference with the ground he virtually had no means whatever of telling whether he was upside down, right way up or whether flying straight or banked in a turn. He would be no better off than a blindfolded man spinning in a cage suspended in a coal mine. Indeed he would be worse off.

Unknown to Brem the weather had unexpectedly deteriorated just at the moment when he was climbing out and telling me to carry on alone. The base of the clouds which had been above normal circuit height was now only about 600 feet and getting lower. Added to that I now had my 66 mph climb speed complex to think about.

The result was that soon after I had taken off, I decided to climb ahead with my eyes virtually glued to the airspeed indicator, and it was in this statuesque attitude that at 800 feet and at exactly 66 mph I glanced out in preparation for the first left-hand turn of the now familiar circuit. All I saw was cloud which was as unfamiliar as it was unexpected. I had never before flown in cloud. In fact, I had never before seen a cloud from the inside: grey, wet and swirling. But what was so nearly fatal to me was that I didn't even know that *I wasn't supposed to be able to fly in cloud.* So instead of pushing the nose of the aircraft down, and hastily getting back to familiar visual surroundings, I foolishly continued with the circuit as best I could, intending to keep to my usual circuit height of 800–1,000 feet. I remember muttering to myself the well-versed formula for a turn. "Apply back (aileron) and rudder together: take off bank, take off rudder and ease the nose up a little." But when to stop turning? When indeed?

By guess I decided that I should by now have turned sufficiently, so I went through the drill for coming out of a turn. But was I straightened out? Or was I still turning? Where in the hell was I? But by now more urgent considerations demanded my attention. The altimeter showed I was losing height—a dangerous mistake for obvious reasons with a bare 1,000 feet separating plane from the hard, unfriendly ground below. However, I knew how to correct this from my very first lesson. All I had to do was to ease gently back on the control column between my knees. This I knew would cause a gain in height accompanied by a slight falling off of the air speed. It did neither. So I pulled back some more—not so gently this time. All that happened was that the airspeed indicator, which should have been reading a normal 80–85 mph for level flight, increased beyond the 100 mph line (I had never seen it cross this mark before), and to my absolute horror the altimeter was showing 500 feet and still going steadily lower.

I was so bewildered that I don't think I did anything at all. The only corrective action I knew had been applied, and yet the two vital dials showing me my height and speed perversely continued to act in a directly opposite sense. I was like a man driving a car who takes his foot off the accelerator and applies the brakes only to find the engine speed increasing, and the car gaining further momentum. I had no other tricks up my sleeve, since I dared not shut off the engine at a time when I apparently needed every scrap of power to keep the aircraft from losing further height. I was utterly powerless to alter in any way the disaster which was obviously and rapidly approaching.

At about 300-400 feet the aircraft quite suddenly emerged out of the grey lowering clouds into the comparative brightness of the visible atmosphere. But never before had I seen the earth like his. It was all standing crazily on one side. As I looked forward down the nose of the aircraft I could see trees (mighty close to me) growing out of the ground sideways; houses, too. Quite a few seconds passed before it dawned on me that it was the aircraft and not the earth which had turned on its axis. I was in a near-vertical banked turn, and in a panic I jerked the aircraft out of this without the smallest consideration for smoothness or nice co-ordination of "bank-and-rudder" togetherness.

But now what? I was flying level at last and more or less under control, but cruising over strangely unfamiliar terrain at a height of little more than 300 feet perilously close to buildings, trees, high-tension cables and the like. And I soon learnt that from this low vantage point I could see precious little around me.

Where was I, and how was I going to find out?

My brain, partially numbed with terror, was being activated by automatic impulses. I determined to get up to 1,000 feet again and continue with the circuit. An utterly ridiculous decision as I didn't know where the airfield was. However, I managed to climb (at a steady 66 mph again, as I was now definitely living by past reflexes) up to 800 feet, levelled off and commenced my drill for a left turn before once again becoming a victim of the unbelievable, ie, the speed rose and the height decreased, yet when I applied the obvious correction and pulled back on the stick all that happened was that the speed rose crazily, and in a last desperate moment the Tiger Moth hurtled out of the cloud in a tight turn with the world not only turned once more on its side but even closer to me than before. I reckon I came out of that second spiral dive with only a few feet to spare, as by now the clouds had come down almost to tree-top level.

At about this point I mentally gave up. I was absolutely bathed in sweat but my mind was strangely calm. I could see only too clearly that it was imperative, therefore, to get up higher again. Also, I realised that it was only when I *turned* that the world started to go crazy. So, for the third time, I opened up the throttle and climbed back into the unfriendly grey clouds above. But this time, instead of levelling off at circuit height, I went on climbing in an effort to create the biggest possible gap between my plane and the obstacles of the ground. How long I would have been able to keep climbing straight without again getting into a tight spiral dive is conjecture, for at about 2,000 feet, I broke through the overcast to the clear, blinding brilliance of a winter's sky above the cloud. The relief was beyond words. I believe I sang aloud.

I was still utterly bewildered by the past behaviour of the plane, which was now reacting in a normal manner to joystick movements. The reasons for its previous wild gyrations were quite unknown to me. I had not then studied aerodynamics sufficiently even to have an inkling of what had occurred, although it was nothing in the slightest degree unusual, or even illogical. In a turn, an aircraft, by banking, begins to be affected by an exchange of control effectiveness. The rudder is no longer vertical nor is the elevator now truly horizontal to the *earth*. To take an extreme case, in a ninety-degree bank turn with the wing pointing straight up and down, the elevator, normally horizontal, is now vertical to the surface of the earth (although still horizontal to the body of the aircraft) so acts as a rudder. Similarly, the rudder is now horizontal and thus performing the function of the elevator. Since I had no visual reference and did not understand the very few instruments aboard, I had no way of telling whether I was banked or not and consequently my efforts to turn, or to come out of turns, had resulted in the aircraft becoming so steeply banked that when I pulled back on the control column in an attempt to raise the nose, all I was doing in effect was the equivalent of applying more and more rudder and thus tightening the already steeply banked turn. This further increased the bank angle, as the wing on the outside of the turn was now moving much faster, and so developing more lift than the inside wing. (The outside man has to move faster during a "wheel" in the drill parade—the principle here is the same.)

All this was quite beyond my knowledge then. All I knew was that I was up above the clouds with an excellent and clear horizon to look at, enabling me to control the plane according to the rules I had learnt. But my next problem was what to do with it. The Tiger Moth only had an hour and a half or so of fuel and, safe though my present situation was, it obviously wouldn't last for ever.

I began to look at the compass with new interest. It had always been there, in a round metal bowl between my knees, but no one had ever showed me how to use it. Still, all schoolboys know about compasses—so I thought. A plan was beginning to form in my head. It went like this: Brooklands was, as the crow flies, about 50 miles from the south coast of England and if I could fly due south for, say, 45 minutes at 80-85 mph. I reckoned to be over the English Channel for sure. Then I could glide down straight until sighting the sea. Then, once below cloud, I would turn back on to north. If all went well, I would soon reach the south coast of England in an area which I knew well. Once there I reckoned I could fly along the south coast till I came to a pier. I felt reasonably sure I would be able to recognise which it would be. With this knowledge I could then fly along the coast road to the airport at Shoreham. My plan, such as it was, avoided the two terrors which now dominated my every thought. It avoided, in theory at least, all turns in the clouds, and it avoided the possibility of having to confront *land*, with its hostile trees, chimneys, hills and other hazards. I knew how dangerously close I had been to striking these, and I was absolutely determined to do anything other than risk a third encounter with the uneven surface of mid-Surrey where, I knew only too well, the North Downlands rose up to nearly 900 feet in places.

One end of the compass had N for North affixed to it. All I had to do, I reasoned, was to go where the opposite end pointed. It (the South end) was to my left, almost due left, so left I went, whereupon the pesky South-end of the needle swung violently further left. As I gave chase by turning further to the left the needle commenced swinging in circles and I became aware that all I could possibly be doing was going round and round. Where, damn it, *was* South?

Now I felt tired; matters were beyond my comprehension. Firstly, the controls had acted as never before whenever I got into a turn in the cloud, and now the stupid compass refused to obey what I thought was the one basic rule of magnetism, namely, to stay in one place pointing North-South. I didn't then understand the gimbal-ring around the precariously balanced magnetic needle, nor did I understand that this instability was merely the well-known "South turning error" and that all I needed to do was to turn a little and—wait: check how near South I was, then turn a little more and wait again. I made two or three further efforts to get my aircraft on to a South heading, but it proved quite beyond my skill, so I abandoned the idea and with it all hopes of ending up at Shoreham Airport.

This time I was licked and I knew it. My petrol wasn't going to last for ever and when it ran out I knew I had no chance whatsoever.

The inescapable thing about an aeroplane is that it has to keep going. A ship or a car in a hopeless fog can stop, conserve its fuel and wait for better conditions. Even the cyclist can dismount. The aircraft, by contrast, has a minimum speed below which it ceases to be a flying machine and falls like a crumpled, inanimate body to the ground. Even the elementary Tiger Moth requires to be kept going at a minimum of 50 mph. I didn't know what to do or where to go, but nevertheless I did have to keep going. And I had to do this at a minimum rate of about one mile per minute—and thus keep on burning up the few gallons remaining which alone kept me aloft. I was like an exhausted man running hopelessly nowhere till all strength had gone.

All I can remember thinking about was that no one knew where I had left my car that morning and this was worrying me. I had had a puncture on my way to Brooklands and had left the car at a garage which happened to be *en route*. I had then walked the rest of the way. The garageman had no means of knowing that I was connected with flying, so he wouldn't think to connect the reported flying death with the Fiat which a stranger had left with him. I had no idea even of where I would ultimately crash. It could be miles from Brooklands; on Leith Hill for example, or possibly I had by now travelled to the other side of London or, even worse, I could be *over* London. I wanted my brother to have my car, and the way my luck seemed to me to be running that morning it seemed almost certain that I had chanced upon a dishonest garageman who would, after waiting a short time, sell the unclaimed car.

These were my ridiculous thoughts as I aimlessly flew hither and thither above the clouds, which still completely blanketed from sight every vestige of the world I knew below.

The petrol gauge began to assume great importance. There was absolutely nothing I could do to keep the aircraft up in the sky, and at the same time prevent this tell-tale gauge from getting remorselessly lower and lower.

If I had had a parachute and even the remotest idea of how to use it I wouldn't have hesitated a second. But parachutes are no part of civil aviation or its training. From the start, pupil pilots of the airliners of the future are taught to stay with their planes and rightly so.

One inescapable fact was gradually overtaking all others. This was that I had to leave my crystal clear world of sunshine above the pure white clouds and go down into the grey peril of the unknown yet again. There was no choice at all.

I half-closed the throttle and, keeping my hands and feet as still as humanly possible, I allowed the aircraft to sink gently into the swirling cotton wool beneath. On the way down when I again encountered the start of another unaccountable increase in speed I happened upon the idea of stirring my right hand in a slow, steady circular movement and began to "feel" the slight differences in pressure and note the effect upon the air speed that the joy-stick made at different phases of the "stir". The aircraft more or less stayed under control, but great as was my joy at this, I was now obsessed by the image of the North Downs and of the tower on top of Leith Hill (1,001 feet) in particular, so when the altimeter crept down to below 1,000 feet, my heart was in my mouth.

I had to keep going down or, as I visualised it, *the ground had to keep coming up.* At least, more by luck than judgment, I was coming down more or less on my own terms very gradually and economically and at about 60 mph. Varying degrees of darkness in the cloud tended to play me tricks and gave several false hopes and/or scares that I was emerging into the visible area betwixt clouds and earth. These false alarms tended to divert my attention from the various tasks I had in mind such as keeping the feet absolutely still, slowly stirring and "feeling" the joy-stick to detect the favourable segments, keeping the speed as low as safely possible, keeping the engine running at such an rpm that the altimeter gave up its precious height as gently as possible. If I had known that it was regarded as virtually impossible to fly blind in the clouds without understanding either the crude ball and bubble bank indicator or the directional compass, I suppose I would have been in an even worse state than I was. But in this case ignorance was bliss. After all, I felt I was an experienced pilot now with nearly two hours solo in my log-book, and I felt I ought to be able to manage with what I had got, airspeed indicator, altimeter, rpm counter and that awesome, bobbling, ever sinking fuel gauge.

At about 400 feet I broke out of the cloud apparently nowhere near any hills and more or less on an even keel. Words can't describe how I felt when I realised that Lady Luck had somehow come around to my side again. I hadn't spun hopelessly into the ground nor had I emerged into or on to the cruelly hard hills, factories, buildings, trees, pylons or any of the other obstacles which I had so dreaded.

However, it was raining remorselessly and although I took my goggles off, I still found that I couldn't see much. And of course I had no idea in what direction I was going, nor of where I was or how on earth to get the aircraft back to Mother Earth in one piece. I seemed to be passing over typical mid-Surrey landscape. Towns of no great size, country houses, agricultural land, railway lines, woodlands and roads. At times I was able to get up to 600 feet without getting ensnared by the clouds above. Petrol was low but should last another half-hour at least if the gauge meant anything. I simply didn't know where to land, but I was vaguely looking for a huge level field or a piece of flat common ground. Later I learnt to land the Tiger Moth on a patch as small as a football field. What I now wanted was a man-sized airfield or its reasonable equivalent. In the gloom and depression of a wet and filthy winter's day, I suddenly became aware that I was passing over an unusually long field and one which appeared to be man-made and absolutely flat. I peered forward, but at first could see little, then, with a stab of astonishment that I can still feel today and one that I will never again sense with the same degree of amazement for as long as I live, I passed right over Brooklands' own clubhouse!

By a miracle, I had happened to return to the very aerodrome from which I had taken off some 15–20 minutes before. (They tell me it was only 15–20 minutes but I know otherwise.) I wasn't quite out of trouble yet, as by the time I had taken stock of this heaven-sent haven, I had passed over the banking and, at 80 mph, was out over the countryside again. I turned back as smartly as I knew how in order to try to regain visual contact with the clubhouse or the banked racing circuit. I had some agonising seconds (Had I missed it? Was it all going to be snatched from me at the last moment?) and then familiar objects, starting with the long Hawker hangar, began to reappear. I was the wrong side of the airfield for landing and didn't know enough to land down-wind—I didn't chance it, anyhow, but elected to fly a low circuit to get into a landing position. I was utterly determined not to lose sight of the airfield so turned the plane steeply inside or over the racing oval until, from a low altitude and with a really bad skidding turn and with the speed too high, I bumped the aircraft clumsily but safely back to its home base.

I was down.

My heart was pounding crazily and I was visibly shaking.

I saw Jimmy, the club timekeeper, literally haring across the field, his fat, florid face as red as a beetroot. He was hatless and was being soaked by the merciless rain but he sprinted the whole distance between his hut and my plane. He obviously wanted to speak to me but I couldn't move a muscle. I was locked stiff by a nervous tension. He had to climb up on to the wing, fumble inside my cockpit and release the inside catch to drop the side flap so that he could get his face level with mine. I sat there staring and shaking, still quite beyond movement. Jimmy finally had to force the flying helmet off my ears and bellow against the noise of the idling engine, the wind and the rain.

"I've come to tell you," he roared and panted, "I've come to tell you—NOT to take off again. Brem says NOT . . ."

This was the trigger I had been waiting for. This, without question or doubt, was the funniest sentence I had ever heard. This big, fat, friendly chap had run as fast and as far as he ever was likely to do in his whole life, in order to tell me that I wasn't to take off again! Not for all the gold in Fort Knox, not under any threat, or for any value on or off this earth could I have been persuaded to open the throttle, still clenched in my left fist, for the purpose of taking off again.

Laugh! How I laughed! I rolled and shook with laughter: tears from my eyes got all mixed up with the rain till I couldn't see a thing. I groaned and gasped with laughter long, loud and weirdsome. It was a bout of uncontrollable hysteria, and all poor Jimmy could do was to stand there with the rain dripping all over him and observe with undisguised astonishment the ravings of a maniac. After quite a few minutes I was drained of energy, emotion and tension and when I recovered my breath I found I was back to normal.

"Can I give you a lift in?" I enquired almost casually.

With some natural misgivings, Jimmy agreed, and he stepped gingerly on to the wing. He didn't dare get into the cockpit's vacant front seat for fear of what I might do next. Crouched as he was on the lower wing he was able to benefit from the shelter of the upper wing, and at the same time he was in a good position to leap off should I decide to go flying, or go berserk again! He never took his eyes off me the whole way back to the apron.

This story is true. The real sufferer, of course, was poor old Brem, who had sent me off solo in the rapidly worsening weather and who had died a thousand deaths during the next twenty minutes. He, alas, is now dead. A pupil landed on top of his training aircraft during the early days of the war. Jeffrey Quill, the celebrated Vickers Supermarine test pilot, was in the Brooklands bar when first I sloughed my way, at 66 mph, into those treacherous clouds. It appears from his and from others' accounts that I was seldom far away from the airfield, and that on my first two spiral dives they actually *heard* the plane roaring earthwards to its expected end. The increase in speed during those dives raises the engine note to a scream, due to the working of the fixed-pitch propeller.

Jeffrey Quill and I both happened to come from Littlehampton and I had just started to play squash with him at the St George's Club, Weybridge. When next we met, he couldn't help but comment that he had been more than a little worried by my peculiar behaviour and gyrations with the Tiger Moth in the cloud, rain and poor forward visibility. I don't think he realised how little I knew about the instruments and compass and he was a little curious, to say the least, to know why I had lost control and why I had dived so close—yet stayed up so long.

"You were quite some time up there," he remarked. "What were you doing—aerobatics? We could all hear you."

"Just fooling around," I said.

"You did well to get it back in one piece, so I gather," he volunteered.

"Yes," I admitted. "I figured I had had enough at the time, so I decided not to go up again!"

He looked at my strangely not quite knowing whether I was just plain mad, crazy, lucky or bewitched. He, the most famous young test-pilot in the country. Me, the newest recruit to Brooklands. The incident didn't seem to upset me unduly and I began to realise that I should be grateful for the frantic hysterics which had purged my system so thoroughly.

But, nonetheless, I decided that I had better learn a lot more about compasses, aerodynamics, aircraft controls, instruments and blind-flying. Bob Ashton was obviously the best source of such knowledge and to Bob I went, as avid for learning as any student could be.

4: An Eventful Visit to France

AFTER this adventure, my life at Brooklands settled back into a pattern dictated by the English winter weather. Pupil pilots need relatively calm and steady winds, good visibility (no one now knew this better than I), with neither low cloud nor heavy rain. England in winter offers such conditions but occasionally. And when it did, I flew; when it didn't I would spend my time with Bob Ashton, or go tapping the brains of Ken Waller, Brem or of the more advanced pupils. I now not only did what I was told to do but I made a much more determined effort to find out why. Ken encouraged me to ask all the questions I wanted.

My hours slowly mounted, and by the time my twenty-first birthday arrived at the end of November I was allowed to take up an aircraft by myself, provided my instructor thought that the conditions were suitable. Naturally enough, after such a big scare, meteorology, along with the theory of flight and aerodynamics, became almost an obsession of mine. In all these subjects Bob Ashton was my mentor, whether actually in his class-room (for which fees had to be paid) or at the bar or poring over a chess board. I also became less of a pupil and more of a friend with Ken (never one to make friends easily) when we discovered that at squash racquets there was barely a point between us.

Cars occupied a lot of our spare time. They were nearly all open cars and it was rare indeed that the hoods were put up. Ken had the biggest—one of the six or so huge eight-litre Bentleys made early in the 1930's. Its engine was big enough to lay dinner upon, and it ticked over so slowly that I could almost count the engine revs. My Fiat, by contrast, was the smallest, with an easily raised hood and an engine which sounded more like a sewing machine. We were all fresh-air fiends and dear old Brem used to arrive each morning muffled to the eyebrows astride some fierce-sounding motor-cycle. The boss, Duncan Davies, had a saloon Rolls-Bentley but we didn't see him much as he and his skilful business partner, Bill Massey, had many more fish to fry than the flying club at Brooklands. Brooklands was almost unique amongst flying clubs in that it seemed to make money. Consequently our clubhouse and bar were always nicely decorated, the buildings were painted and the aircraft spic and span. Most of the other clubs, though not noticeably less comfortable, didn't look so smart, nor did their aircraft, although I am sure that the vital parts of these were as carefully maintained as were ours. Aeronautical engineers are a dedicated breed and I never heard of any single case of suspect maintenance.

Since our cockpits were open in every sense of the word, we used to dress up to combat the really frightful cold which existed aloft. Generally, up in the winter sky, it was freezing and even at our slow 80–85 mph the atmosphere could cut like a knife. When fully dressed up we wore a long padded suit, which extended from ankle to shoulder. It was quite a job to get this over our normal winter clothes. Thick seamen's stockings came over the leg part of this suit and we wore sheepskin lined leather boots as well. On our hands we donned firstly a pair of silk gloves both for warmth and (supposedly) for "feel" and over these we put leather gauntlets. Atop the padded suit (which was known as a Sidcot suit) we wore a woollen scarf which we pulled up to cover the mouth and nose. Over our heads we wore leather flying helmets with tube earpieces and big padded flying goggles.

As the year drew to a close an idea began to visit me insistently. The girl-friend had gone back to her home in the South of France and I began to wonder whether or not it was possible to fly there. The idea hardened when I learned that there was an airport at Nice. About 90 per cent of my flying had been limited to what was known as "circuits and bumps" around the familiar and easily recognised racing circuit, but I had made one or two cross-country flights of up to 15–20 miles distance in order, at my own request, to study how that pesky compass worked.

A word or two about that compass. It was a thoroughly temperamental (and inefficient) instrument, although at that time it was about the best on the market. If I wanted to turn the aircraft towards north, I would firstly make what I judged to be about the right amount of turn, and then I would have to wait. The compass needle would either do absolutely nothing whatever, or move slightly in the wrong direction. However, when it had thoroughly "digested" the aircraft's movement it would gradually condescend to take up the right position for the new heading. A turn towards South had the reverse effect. The needle would wildly gyrate way beyond South and then slowly realign itself to the correct heading. East and West were less frolicsome, provided the speed was steady, but any acceleration or deceleration had an adverse effect upon attempts to alter heading towards these points.

Without a precise knowledge of how the compass was going to react, all attempts to choose a new direction were bound to end in failure—as I had personally discovered.

In a Tiger Moth flying around England, navigation was very largely a matter of map reading in spite of the fact that it wasn't all that easy to balance the map on one's knee inside a draughty cockpit. (Folding and unfolding was even more difficult.)

I knew little about the effect that a strong wind has upon a slow aeroplane. But I began to realise that it was considerable. Wind to the aviator is like tide or current to the mariner. In extreme cases it can even make the aircraft go backwards!

Also, I refuse to this day to believe that any aircraft has ever been built from which it was possible to see less than from the rear seat of a Tiger Moth. The pilot peering forward through the narrow gap between the two wings is so placed that he can scarcely see either up or down.

At 80 mph a simple calculation showed that it would require about ten hours flying each way to get to the South of France and back, excluding refuelling stops. (We only carried 17 gallons and used about seven gallons each hour.) This gave me an incentive, as 20 hours at the Brooklands rate of £2 5s 0d per hour added up to £45. Hours were what I wanted, so I had £45 of my training budget to play with. Could I get to Nice within this budget in such a manner that the flying time counted towards my ultimate goal of 300 hours? If so I reckoned the trip would, in effect, cost me nothing.

It so happened that Bill Orton and Vernon Hunt had just about finished all their training and were in two minds whether to sell their

Puss Moth G-AAXY. For £30 or so they would be most happy to hire me "Gaaxy" for two weeks provided I could find someone to fly it. It was out of the question that I could fly it myself, never having made a real air journey nor having flown a Puss Moth. However, another student called Harry Read showed an interest. He didn't have a girlfriend in France but he, too, wanted cheap hours, and the prospect of a holiday over Christmas in the South of France was an added attraction.

"Gaaxy" was not registered for overseas flying, but Harry discovered that for a small fee we could take out a tryptique which was cheaper than, and the equivalent of, the international carnet (so we thought). This latter is normally carried by planes outside their homeland frontiers. The touring section of the AA supplied maps and we earnestly began to plan a route. "Gaaxy" would stay in the air longer than the Tiger and also went faster, as it was a monoplane cruiser—not a training biplane. This meant that less stops would be necessary. We hoped, in fact, to get there with stops at Croydon or Lympne (to clear Customs), Paris, and Dijon, with possible extra stops at Lyons or Marseilles just in case things didn't work as planned.

Harry, who had about 150 flying hours in all, spent a half-hour or so at the controls of "Gaaxy" and seemed satisfied with her. In many respects she was much nicer to fly than any training aircraft. For one thing, you could see where you were going! Also, it had a totally enclosed cabin, so the maps were less likely to blow away. It even had a heater and, a great luxury, brakes to help it stop after landing. By contrast, the Tiger merely bumped along till it came to rest.

Just prior to departure I spent a few days at home where my father was now recovering from his illness.

We took off on a cold, clear day with snow obscuring the ground, and right from the start I found I had a host of things to learn. Technically, I was navigating. The first thing I learned was that it was at least twice as difficult to recognise ground features after a snowfall. Railway lines (the map reader's greatest single aid) were almost indistinguishable from roads: also woods (another great help since these were always marked green on our maps) lost their shape and became merged with the surrounding fields. However, Harry was doing almost all the work and he appeared to know his way down to Dover (Lympne) without difficulty.

Prior to crossing the Channel we climbed up to about 8,000 feet (I had never been higher!) in order to give us a long glide should we happen to suffer engine failure during this "dangerous" part of the trip. We also carefully checked both magneto switches. It was hazy, so we couldn't see the other side, and a tense silence fell upon us as Harry carefully set a compass course and headed towards Cap Gris-Nez. Like Channel swimmers we had elected to cross the Channel at its narrowest part. I often think back to this "dangerous" crossing. After more than five hundred Atlantic crossings as an airline pilot I have never lost the flavour of this—my first "big" overwater venture!

Once on the other side we had to locate and circle the Cap Gris-Nez lighthouse just to show them that we had made the journey successfully. Failure to do this would have resulted in a sea search beginning.

We arrived at Le Bourget airport in Paris that afternoon just before it was dark (neither of us had ever flown abroad or at night) well satisfied with our first efforts at international aviation.

In Paris we had planned to spend a short night and press on at dawn for our next refuelling stop at either Dijon or Lyons, depending on whether we thought we could reach the latter. But first we had to find parking space for the machine, refuel it for the morning, clear Customs and go through the other irksome formalities which even in those days seemed to be unnecessarily annoying.

As it happened our tryptique was not, after all, such a good substitute for a carnet. It appeared that the French authorities were deeply suspicious of us. With the Spanish Civil War raging across the Pyrenees, they seemed to think we were agents of Franco, intent on smuggling our plane to the aid of his Nationalist forces—the side with which France's Communist government under Leon Blum was practically at war.

In the event, and after much haggling, we were placed under open arrest and our plane was impounded until such time as we could deposit the sum of 100,000 francs (then the equivalent of about £400).

This was a formidable, if not impossible, proposition for us. We phoned the British Consul, whose only advice, after emitting sounds of sympathy, was, "Better raise the money!"

It was now late on Friday evening and we had already wasted a precious day and a half. After much difficulty I got through by phone to my girl-friend's father in Cagnes-sur-mer. Not surprisingly this produced little positive result as far as finding the money was concerned. After sleeping on the problem, I sent a telegram to my home asking that a credit of 100,000 francs be wired to Paris. Once more my dear father, who had supported me so much already, rallied round and sent the money and by Monday lunch-time we were free to depart.

We decided that we could just reach Lyons before the early darkness of mid-winter set in, and, favoured by good weather, we just about did so. By now I had assimilated from Harry quite a few points about drift and ground-speed checks, and had become accustomed to recognising features in the snow below. In fact, I was no longer such a burden to Harry. He now gave me the maps and told me to get on with it. So with protractor, dividers and ruler I was able to offer him courses and ETAs to the nearest minute, which must have been a pleasant surprise to one who had little enthusiasm for navigation, nicely though he flew.

We tried to make a very early start out of Lyons the following morning, since Christmas Day was almost upon us and we naturally wanted to arrive at our destination prior to this. But "Gaaxy" had other ideas.

At best she was a bitch when it came to starting. Under normal winter weather conditions she could be made to start rather reluctantly but only when the secret of her peculiar innards had been learnt. She suffered from fuel starvation, and to get her to fire her cylinders on a cold day it was necessary to soak a rag with petrol and stuff this into her air intake— treatment unbecoming to a lady but, in her case, obligatory. At Lyons in the half-dark of 8 a.m., with the temperature a bare 20 degrees and with deep, frozen snow lying everywhere, "Gaaxy" decided that this was too much for a person of her age and dignity. She refused to fire a cylinder.

Starting drill for the light aircraft of that era was carried out with priest-like rites. There were fixed intonations and responses. One person had to sit inside with one hand on engine throttle (all cars have foot throttles, all aircraft hand throttles), leaving the other free to manipulate the dual ignition switches and to control the aircraft. The other person had to swing, swing and swing the propeller, and on a cold morning this called for considerable effort. I, the assistant, was doing the swinging and, cold as my feet were from much tramping about in the frozen snow, the rest of me was wet with sweat after nearly an hour of this exercise.

So we tried other tactics which, with luck, would sometimes help to start the Gypsy Major engine which powers the Puss and most of the DH Moth series. We persuaded a local Frenchman to pick her tail up and hold it over his head. It can be done but it takes strength. But to no good purpose. In desperation we removed a couple of plugs and poured petrol direct into the engine's cylinders. Even this produced no sign of life. Perhaps happily so, as it is a trick which is as likely as not to set fire to the engine. Finally, in desperation, we drained the sticky cold oil from the sump, took it into the hangar and cooked it over a stove before replacing it. Then, and then only, did she give up her obstinate struggle—but even after starting she managed to defy us for another ten minutes before we could record any oil pressure.

By now we were several hours behind our intended schedule. It was mid-morning, and with several hundred miles to go it seemed that our only hope of arriving at Nice before darkness (and we were unwilling to fly at night, having no experience, generator, battery, navigational or landing lights) was to draw a straight line to that seaside metropolis and fly direct to it. This we set out to do, although the height of the French Maritime Alps stood ominously in our way and the fuel reserves for such a flight were hardly conservative.

Until we reached the mountains all went well. I was able to keep a fairly close check upon our progress, as there was no cloud to obliterate ground objects. Harry kept "Gaaxy" on track. Speed checks showed that we were making good time and we would not have serious fuel problems. But as the ground started to rise before us, so did the cloud begin to form around us. The contour lines in the maps told us all too clearly that we needed to reach a certain height or else we would fly into the mountains. A figure of 13,000 feet became all important, especially as in the cloud we could no longer be sure of keeping to any pre-ordained track. Harry was an able instrument pilot, and the flying presented no great difficulties to him. In fact, apart from the fact that we didn't know for sure where we were, and I was wondering when we should be in a position to dare to let down on the Mediterranean side of the French Alps, we were not unduly worried until Harry reported that the controls were beginning to feel "queer". This he illustrated by moving them from side to side with little apparent result to our bank angle. Next, he said that he could hardly move them at all. Round about this time the engine started to backfire violently and we knew we were in real trouble.

Ice accretion was something I personally had never heard of and it was an experience that Harry hadn't encountered seriously.

Ice can be hell!

Under certain conditions of cloud and low temperature such as we were then encountering, ice builds up (rapidly at times) and endangers the aircraft in a number of different ways. It builds up on the leading or forward-facing edge of the wing to such an extent that it both creates high additional drag which slows up the aircraft, and upsets the smoothly designed contour of the wing surfaces, thus destroying their designed characteristic of providing "lift". Without "lift" an aircraft will not fly any more than a brick will. This build-up eventually results in complete loss of speed and a fall earthwards. Ice also builds up in the hinges of the control surfaces and on the mass balances of those surfaces, until after a time the control surfaces cannot be moved or, in the latter case, cannot be balanced. Either way the aircraft flounders out of control without the pilot being able to do anything about it. Ice also adheres to the blades of the propeller, partially destroying its ability to pull the aircraft through the sky. Ice additionally obscures the windscreen much as does a freezing fog in a motorcar. Lastly, ice collects in the throat of the carburettor, upsetting the fuel-to-air ratio and causing the engine to cough, splutter and stop.

I reckon we now had the lot.

The plane was nearly stalled; it could hardly be turned or made to descend. We couldn't see a thing through the frosted windows in front and the engine was coughing badly. Harry struggled to turn the aircraft back on to a reciprocal track and had to use all his skill to keep the engine firing at all. We dared not descend to warmer, cloudless levels as we were somewhere over the rising ground.

"Where are we?" he demanded.

"Can't tell, Harry. Haven't seen the ground for ten minutes."

"How low can we go?"

After some searching for high peaks I ventured the information that *if* we were still holding to our intended track we should be able to get down to 8,500 feet without hitting the ground.

I stressed the IF.

We had little option anyhow, as the Puss Moth even under full staccato throttle was now losing height.

Usually there is a gap between cloud and ground, and this proved our saviour. Luckily it was a considerable one and we found ourselves with several thousand feet of clear air in which to coax "Gaaxy "back to normal or near-normal operating habits. *She* had known it wasn't a good idea to start up that morning and we should have listened to her protests with greater appreciation and understanding.

We had no idea where we were, but the more we flew north the more the ground fell away from us and the more "Gaaxy" returned to normal as she slowly cleared her wings, her control surfaces, and her throat of her obnoxious ice covering.

Eventually it became safe to turn west and seek the Rhone valley, which, surely, would be an unmistakable and recognisable feature.

Once we had located this, and after checking that the petrol would, or should, be sufficient, we had no thought other than to attempt to reach Marseilles before nightfall.

This we did, and after sending a telegram to our hosts-to-be we repaired to a cheap hotel near the airport where, if memory serves me right, we got more than somewhat drunk. It was, after all, Christmas Eve, and an awful lot seemed to be happening to us one way or another. At one moment we had been very close to sheer panic in a "blind" aircraft with little control, a hesitant engine, Alps all around, and no accurate idea where we were.

Marseilles was as cold as Lyons, which had been as cold as any place I had ever visited, and an icy, howling Mistral wind chilled us to the bone. I thought with some qualms that Nice was on the same latitude, and began to wonder what was in store for us. I wasn't equipped for an Arctic holiday, amour or no amour.

However, next morning, when we finally landed at the narrow beach strip which then constituted Nice Airport, the sun was shining, the air was warm and She was there to greet us.

Happy Christmas, 1937.

The holiday turned out to be one of the most idyllic and important of my whole life, but this need not concern us here.

We went ski-ing up the Alps and I was lucky (as a novice) not to break more than I did, since I was tempted to have a go at a minor, very minor, ski-jump after only three days on skis. I escaped with broken ankle straps and a split across my upper lip. I believe I landed face first.

But we had a glorious time and about a dozen of us spent New Year's Eve in a small ski shack. It was no coincidence that the numbers were even!

Since Harry and I only had the "hire" of the plane for two weeks (and it had taken us nearly five days to get to Nice) the time for return came around all too soon.

Optimistically, we allowed ourselves only two days for the return flight, completely ignoring the European winter weather.

We didn't dare tackle the Massif of the Alps again but compromised by heading for the Frejus Gap, which cuts diagonally across from the Côte d'Azur to the open Rhône valley. On this leg, which was intended to take us at least to Dijon, we encountered reasonable weather—but the faithful Gypsy engine began to display bronchial symptoms which we felt sure were nothing whatever to do with ice. We struggled along for a while, but when we discovered an airfield at Montelimar it seemed prudent to land and investigate.

A French mechanic appeared to be satisfied with his diagnosis of the situation and conveyed to me that he could easily fix it, whereupon he promptly went to lunch for what seemed to be hours! Dirty fuel and filter trouble was the cause, and he alone had the tools to rectify the fault. So it was after two o'clock before we could depart.

We had no option but to night-stop at Dijon, whereas we had hoped to reach Paris.

However, a good start from Dijon and the cutting out of Paris in favour of Le Touquet (we had to clear Customs out of France at some designated Customs airport) enabled us to be over the Channel by 2.30 p.m.

The weather was not now bothering us (almost for the first time since we had departed from England two weeks before). For this homeward flight we had been blessed by relatively clear skies, as a stationary high-pressure system was controlling the weather of Europe, and incidentally keeping it gripped in cold. But this kind of weather is always liable to produce fog, and it was obviously now about to do so. Since we had had no weather information since departing from Dijon at near dawn, and since neither of us really understood the French weather chart that we had seen there, Harry sensibly decided to land at Lympne so as to be able to check the weather along the route and at Brooklands itself. I undertook to clear Customs for us whilst Harry obtained the operational data.

We were really anxious about returning the aircraft on the right day. We didn't figure that Bill and Vernon would be bothered, but we knew that the two weeks' insurance which we had been obliged to take in our own names would expire at midnight.

Harry came back from the weather office and said that it looked grim, but that since he knew the way so well he would continue. He had to make the decision quickly as the early darkness of winter was fast approaching. Some well-meaning official personally went out of his way to warn us that "even Imperial Airways had cancelled its flight into Croydon", but we were not to be put off by such an obvious omen as this. We put all faith in the navigational value of the railway line which ran straight from Dover almost up to Redhill Airport. "If the worst came to the worst," we consoled ourselves, "we will land at Redhill."

So in the gathering gloom of a foggy afternoon we took off from Lympne. The visibility was so bad that we had trouble in even finding the railway line. Yet it was only two to three miles away! When, eventually, we had truly located this guide-line we headed north-west, keeping the lines in sight whilst flying as high as we could. The most height we could maintain was at first a mere 400 feet and when we had gone a bare quarter of the distance we were forced down to 100 feet, and even then could barely see anything. Clearly we had to turn back before the evening fog completely obscured everything. But to turn was a risk in itself. To do so meant that temporarily we had to abandon the railway tracks which were our only indication of where we were. We were now so low that the smallest hill would have been sufficient to snare us, but we had to turn. Harry skilfully completed this nerve-racking manoeuvre, and we soon found ourselves back above the steel rails heading south-east, towards Dover and Lympne. A small tunnel almost had us in a panic, for here the ground rose and we were obliged to hold our course and pray that the lines would reappear. When they did so we both realised that we were in such a precarious situation, virtually hedge-hopping, that even if we could keep the lines within sight the whole way to Dover, our chances of then being able to find Lympne Airport were almost nil. It was at about this point that an unexpected turn in the line brought home to us the horrible fact that we were no longer tracking above the dead straight broad lines which ran between London and Dover. Somehow we had got on to a branch line, and the map told me that it could be one of several. So now we had no idea where we were, where the lines would take us, how high the ground was or how to get to any airport before the whole countryside became enveloped in thick, impenetrable fog.

Harry rose to the occasion. "I'm going to try and land in the first field of any size," he shouted to me over his shoulder, and the words were barely out of his mouth before he slammed the throttles closed, reared the Puss Moth on to one wing, swerved round a tree, and plonked the aircraft on to the rough ground of a grazing pasture. It was steeply up-hill, and this enabled us to land and stop in such a small distance that we avoided over-running into the hedges which loomed out of the mist.

Strangely enough no one came near us or seemed aware of what had happened. We had plenty of time to take stock of our position and decide what next to do. We picketed the aircraft down and trudged around the heavy soil trying to locate any sign of habitation or life.

Eventually a surprised farmer was confronted with two young aviators carrying suitcases. Once over his surprise, he proved to be kindness itself. The nearest village was called St Mary's or St Martin's in Kent (I forget which), and I later learnt that Ken Waller was well known in it, and this was an asset in establishing friendly relations. We had virtually no money whatsoever, so were only too pleased to accept the offer of accommodation. We phoned Brooklands as soon as we could, but were unable to say whether we would be able to depart next day, as the visibility was such that we could not even guess at the length of the field in which we had landed.

Next morning the fog slowly cleared and we went to see where Harry had landed the aircraft. It appeared to be quite undamaged in spite of the rough nature of the pastureland and the steepness of the hill. Harry had done an excellent job. He now offered to fly it back empty if I would look after the baggage and follow by train. He didn't know whether the aircraft could take off or not, but he thought it possible. In the end we loaded it up and I decided to accompany him. We had been together so far and I didn't feel like deserting him now. Anyhow we had no money for the train fare!

After playing her usual tricks "Gaaxy" decided to start, and as she warmed up we dragged her uphill to the very apex of the field. There was no question of taking off into wind, but simply one of charging down the lumpy field and heading for the most obvious gap in the trees at the bottom. We roared up the engine, let go the brakes and charged. A friendly bump jerked us into the air near the bottom, and Harry was able to keep her airborne till the hedge came up, by when we had sufficient speed to lift ourselves up and over.

The insurance had by now expired, but we managed to return home to Brooklands without further incident.

I had seen the Girl Friend and I most certainly had accumulated much experience. Luck had been with us. "Toujour l'amour" had triumphed, and the dual objectives of the exercise had been accomplished.

5: Progress—and Two Accidents

LOOKING back, I am at a loss to understand why, at this point, Brooklands didn't expel me from their club and wash their hands of an obvious bad risk to their good reputation. In just over three months I had made more determined efforts to get myself killed by my own foolhardiness than, surely, had any other pupil in the past. At the time the thought never entered my head. The way I looked at it, I was acquiring experience at a faster rate than most and was really beginning to enjoy it all! I had learned about blind flying instruments and low clouds in that early solo. From this I had made a study of control behaviour at unusual flight altitudes. I had learned about ice and snow on the ground. I had seen at first hand the problems of navigating by map-reading under unusual circumstances. I had been introduced to the dangers of ice in the clouds, both to the engine and propeller, and understood the adverse effect it had upon the airframe and controls. I had acquired foreign-touring experience. I could claim to be almost an expert on the subject of aircraft carnets and import regulations as applied by the French government of that time. I had learned the need to personally ensure that fuel was strained through chamois leather filters (as it always was at Brooklands). I was now a great respecter of fog; I had flown two types of aircraft and could casually mention my "various forced-landings" in bar conversations.

I had, in fact, sampled so many unexpected situations and been so lucky to survive on each occasion that I was fired with an even greater determination to know "everything that there was to know" about the life to which I had committed myself.

I now spent as much time with Bob Ashton as it was possible to do. Rhona was almost as keen as I, and with Jack, Tom and others occasionally joining in, we became quite an enthusiastic school. We were all great friends with Bob and with each other, and this made our task as pleasant as it was constructive. In flying I progressed, because I had come to realise that I had so very much to learn. I began to see now the great advantage in the Brooklands system of charging the same £2 5s 0d per hour for dual instruction as they did for solo flight, and even though I was soon to be allowed solo whenever I wanted to do so, and was issued with a passenger-carrying certificate, as often as not I went flying with Ken Waller or one of the other instructors. But principally it was with Ken, and together we practised hour after hour "forced landings", aerobatics, compass and course keeping, aerial navigation, blind-flying and everything that there was. When I finally left Brooklands I had a total of ninety-one hours' dual instruction, which was some kind of a record, as in the normal way once a pilot had learned to fly and been passed as fit to fly on his own with passengers, he ceased to go back for further instruction, in the same way as motorists cease to go back to their driving schools after passing their licence tests.

However, in winter the opportunities for light-aircraft flying are far too few. Low cloud, strong wind, fog, heavy rain, all more or less prohibit club flying. As a result of this and still being determined to obtain all my licences—flying, navigation and instructor's—within the year I had set for myself, I began to realise that I was far behind schedule, and that the budget costs were up. Inevitably my living expenses increased as I widened my circle of acquaintances. My car was an expense, as was the St. George Hill Club where I played squash. I had fallen almost without choice into the habit of spending part of the evenings around the club bar, for it was here that so much aviation learning was to be found. The various Hawker and Vickers test pilots were regular customers, as were the British Airways and other airline pilots who came and went to Bob's navigation school. Also there were private owners like the immensely capable Alistair Cormack, and other very experienced club pilots such as Bish, Ken Firth and the co-owners of "Gaaxy", Bill Orton and Vernon Hunt, both of whom were now virtually fully qualified and more than usually competent.

War-talk had temporarily died down. The *Daily Mail* and even *The Times* seemed to think that Hitler was "not such a bad chap" after all, and the Spanish war was revealing the limitations of Mussolini's much vaunted forces, so, adding it all up, I decided once again to try to join the RAFVR—not, let it be said, from any patriotic motives, but simply as a means of getting flying hours for nothing. An RAFVR pilot was allowed to fly up to 25 hours per year and one could put two years together and thus do 50 hours straight away. Fifty hours meant a saving of £112 10s 0d to me.

This time I had no bother in enrolling, as I could truthfully state that I now had no intentions of going overseas, and I was fortunate to find an RAFVR school only about eight miles from Brooklands at a place called Fair Oaks, Chobham. Here, too, they trained pupils in the Tiger Moth, which by then I could fly reasonably well.

This airfield was interesting. It was so small that it was necessary to cut a gap in the trees on each side of the rectangular landing ground. It was so narrow that landings had to be made up or down as in the fashion of today's runways. It was necessary to be really accurate, both as regards a precisely timed glide and as to direction, in order to get the aircraft through the "gaps" artificially created by the tree-fellers.

I was soon checked out solo at Fair Oaks, but for some time had to resort to tricks like side-slipping in order to place the aircraft at the exact height and speed through the narrow gaps. I remember a charming young instructor called Seth Smith, and soon he and I were going up together and were playing tricks with the aircraft in much the same manner as Ken and I were doing.

One asset about the Fair Oaks Tiger Moths was that they were all fully equipped for blind or instrument flying, whereas at Brooklands there were only one or two planes so equipped. Blind-flying aircraft additionally had a hood which was raised over the pilot's head, shutting out all vision of the outside world, forcing the pupil to solve all his problems entirely by reference to his instruments whilst the instructor up front kept a visual look-out for other aircraft. In this way I learned to steer by compass, turn, climb, dive, spiral and even spin the aircraft out of control (and later regain control) solely by the few instruments aboard. It was, in fact, exactly the same as being in cloud, and it taught reliance upon instruments rather than on instinct, for in cloud (as I knew only too well from my early near-fatal experience), when firmly strapped in by shoulder harness (always worn), it was impossible to tell *by feel* whether the aircraft was flying straight, in a steep banked turn or even flying upside-down, although the rush of blood to the head sooner or later gave warning of this last.

Blind flying became quite an obsession of mine, and it gave me two nasty moments. At every opportunity I used to get myself into a genuine cloud and practise real instrument flying. On one such occasion, whilst gliding down and practising turns on to various of the more awkward compass courses, I *heard* the familiar noise of a British Airways Lockheed 10 airliner climbing through the cloud presumably out of its base at Heston. With a helmet strapped tight over my ears and in an open cockpit with a far from quiet engine even when ticking over, it was hard to hear any outside noise at the best of times. So, to hear another aircraft was a certain indication that it must have passed only a few feet away in the cloud. There was then very little positive Air Traffic Control, the theory being that the sky was a mighty big place and that the chances of two aircraft colliding were remote, so little was done to safeguard against this contingency, although there were times when Brooklands, being close to both Heston (British Airways) and Croydon, London's "big" airport, were obliged to restrict flying to strictly visual flights only. Fair Oaks, however, was situated outside the London QBB area and was, as far as I knew, not similarly curtailed by such restrictions.

The other occasion when I was in trouble on instruments was too silly for words. I had been practising aerobatics, such as looping the loop and slow rolling, on instruments alone, and I wanted to check very carefully exactly what happened to the instruments whilst manoeuvring upside-down. The engine, I knew, soon cut out because the carburettor float-chamber wasn't modified for inverted flight, also the fuel system was gravity-fed from a tank placed on the upper wing. I knew, therefore, that I would be gliding rather than flying under power whenever upside-down, and since I wanted to make a detailed study of the instruments under varying flight conditions first climbed to about 9,000 feet in a clear-blue sky.

Half-rolling the aircraft on to its back I began a careful study of the dials under normal inverted behaviour. The elevator control, I knew, worked in reverse, but I wasn't sure what reaction the turn and bank needle would show in, say, steep inverted turns. Most of all I wanted to study this instrument during the various phases of a slow roll. I kept a fair speed throughout as the camber of the wings was now the opposite to their designed efficiency, and I knew that my stalling speed was considerably increased. Thus I weaved, turned, half-rolled, rolled back, all upside-down, quite happily until, carrying out a routine check, I noted with horror that the altimeter showed a bare 1,000 feet. The rate of sink in the inverted position had been far greater (due to the lift characteristic of the wing being negatived) than I had anticipated. One glance above my head (for I was still flying upside-down) confirmed my position as being dangerously low. I half-rolled the aircraft to its normal altitude as fast as possible, but try as I might, I wasn't able to get the engine to restart. I knew this would take time as the carburettor would have drained itself whilst inverted, and I had to wait for it to replenish itself from the tank above my head. Meanwhile all I could do was to glide down gently and pick the field most suitable for landing whilst at the same time looking out for smoke, wind ripples in long grass, landing birds, flags or any other clues to the wind direction.

In an aircraft like a Tiger Moth the landing run could be twice as long landing down wind as landing into wind. Much recent practice was a great help, and I had a fair-sized field within my sights and had manoeuvred the aircraft into wind when the first faint splutters came from the engine. This was by no means more than half alive so I decided to continue with the forced landing, and indeed settled comfortably into a field every bit as big as Fair Oaks's own restricted landing area. By now the engine was more or less functioning normally, and after giving it time to warm up I taxied back and took off again, returning to my RAFVR base and hoping against hope that no one would note and report the odd behaviour of one of His Majesty's training aircraft. I was anxious for some weeks but no report came in. Later I told my instructor friend, Seth-Smith, about it, and once he had got over my amazing stupidity in gliding upside-down almost into the ground without even realising the danger, he saw the funny side too.

The RAFVR commitment also meant that I had to attend classes in London alongside members of several other RAFVR schools, and in these we learned simple navigation and meteorology. Generally it was less complicated than the studies I was now undertaking with Bob Ashton and thus gave me little trouble. I learned that there were at least two different ways of doing or interpreting most things in aviation. The RAF didn't use quite the same navigational technique as did the civil pilots. We, in Bob's school, used an instrument called a CDC, Course and Distance Calculator, whereas the RAF computed the course, wind and speed from the more advanced CSC, Course Setting Computer. Likewise the meteorological data was processed somewhat differently.

Another great difference between the two modes of flying was that in the RAFVR, I was introduced to, and was obliged to carry with me, a parachute. On every flight we had the thing strapped to us. It was, in fact, the only seat we had to sit upon! I cursed the thing, as it was heavy, awkward and hindersome, and having absorbed the civil flying lesson of never deserting one's aircraft, I had no intention of using it. We used to waddle out like ducks, with this loaded seat banging behind our knees, and try to clamber with some semblance of adroitness into the cramped rear-box generally called the "pupil's seat". Once installed we had to strap ourselves in with our webbing lap-straps and shoulder harness. More than one pupil got the two sets of straps confused, and instead of unstrapping himself at the end of his lesson he released himself from his parachute.

All this while I was also reporting to Brooklands, though during that spring I probably did more flying at Fair Oaks until I reached their limit of 50 hours. Eventually I was detailed to transfer to one of the RAF light bombers, the Hawker Hart or Hawker Hind. These aircraft had no civil equivalent and seemed generally too war-like, so I decided not to proceed further with the RAFVR for the time being, but merely kept up minimum class attendance in London.

During that spring or possibly earlier there was a comic, near-tragic incident at Brooklands that impressed itself on my mind. Brooklands motor-race circuit was the home of a dozen engineering enterprises, often one-man bands. In the sheds behind the pits cars were hotted-up, racing cars built and tuned, special equipment supplied, etc. One man had the hobby of rebuilding pre-1914 aircraft. One of these reached the stage of being flyable, and on a calm day, with all of us watching and making caustic comments, this veteran-plane enthusiast got the little castor-oil engine to start, and at what appeared to be no more than about 10 mph began to taxi over the grass to become, to our surprise, airborne. The flimsy plane proceeded a few feet off the ground very slowly, only to tilt a wing and crash in a heap of splintered wood, tangled wire and fabric. It all looked so absurd that we only stood and laughed till Brem rushed by yelling, "For God's sake, lend a hand. It might well catch fire and the poor fellow is trapped." And so he was. He was hurt, too. Yet it had not occurred to me that tragedy was even a remote possibility. Flying accidents were something one read about and were not, in my mind, connected in any way with what we all did at Brooklands. I felt heartily ashamed of myself, and when I reached the scene the hot smell of castor oil and the fact that we all had to trample through the wreckage to get the pilot out of the debris rubbed home the force of Brem's admonition.

One day at Fair Oaks, whilst awaiting my turn to fly, I was looking at the other aircraft overhead. I was in full flying dress, flying suit, gloves and boots, with helmet loose about my neck. I was alerted by the noise of an accelerating engine overhead, and I gazed up in disbelief as one of the RAFVR Tiger Moths spun wildly down, obviously out of control and with engine roaring. A last-minute desperate effort to rectify its earthward spiral resulted in a shallow, sweeping turn which took it straight towards me. It crashed about fifty feet away from where I stood, landing right on top of two other aircraft which were neatly parked side by side, luckily without occupants. It had all happened in seconds and the crashed aircraft ended up nose deep into the wings and fuselage of the others with its tail pointing vertically upwards. The same strong smell of hot oil was at once noticeable. No one else was in sight and the pupil pilot dangling some ten feet above me obviously needed help. He had blood all over his face, which had smashed into the woodwork ahead of him, and he was now hanging forward unconscious, loosely supported by his shoulder harness.

Brem's words were still on my conscience and I ran forward with the sole thought of getting the pilot out before all three planes caught fire. But he was over my head beyond reach, and my efforts to climb up to him were frustrated by the flimsy nature of the wings I had to climb upon. Almost every step resulted in my going through stringers and fabric. I found I had to climb up cautiously and not be in such a hurry. When at last I got to the pilot I released the pin of his lap-strap and shoulder harness, with the result that he fell forward out of his seat and right on top of me, sending us both crashing through wings and light wooden frames. By then others had appeared, and they swiftly carried him indoors. I wasn't hurt but I was a bit shaken, and I wobbled as I extracted myself from the mess of broken wings around me. Unknown to me at that time I was covered with the other poor fellow's blood, and it was in this state that the ambulance men found me when they arrived on the scene. Seeing the horrible wreckage of three aircraft, and seeing a pilot in flying clothes gasping from effort, and almost dripping with blood, they naturally seized me and began to help me into the ambulance.

"I'm all right," I kept saying, but they were not to be denied and nothing I could do or say would make them go to the building where the real casualty had been taken. I almost got into a fight with one of them and was by now getting rather hysterical, which didn't help put right the obvious misunderstanding.

The pupil was badly smashed up, but lived. However, he never appeared at Fair Oaks again whilst I was there.

The incident made me cautious for a while, as I had never before (nor since) had another's blood pouring over me and I didn't relish the experience.

6: Golden Summer

BROOKLANDS was not just a flying club, it was a social club, too, and it had an atmosphere which attracted many different types. The sportsman, the engineer, the aviator; the rich and the comparatively poor, all gathered together at Brooklands on Sundays, because on Sundays Duncan Davies saw to it that something of interest took place.

By the summer I had learnt quite a bit. And in time I found myself on all the Brooklands short-lists. I was now allowed to carry passengers; I could hire the Puss, Leopard or Fox Moths; also I was qualified to go anywhere in the UK at any time, and I was even permitted to fly the strange aircraft which often visited us on Sundays for sales or demonstration purposes.

These were new types, or modified or unusual designs brought along for interest. I remember, for example, flying a Belgian-made Tipsy, and on another occasion a single-seater plane with a Ford 10 (Carden Ford) engine. I also flew an experimental type with the first nose-wheel tricycle undercarriage I had ever seen (at that time all aircraft were made with one rear wheel or tail skid, and had their main landing wheels in front— such as the old DC-3 still does). I also flew various Swallows, some earlier Moths and an Avian—in fact, anything that presented itself. It was all good experience for me and, of equal importance, it usually meant a free 15-20 minutes' flying as well.

I marvel now in the trust that Ken Waller and Duncan Davies placed in me, when only a few months before they would have had every justification for expelling me from their midst.

Duncan was one of those wonderful people who had never fully grown up. He loved aeroplanes and had his first start in aviation with the famous Colonel Cody in about 1910. He had been a pilot and instructor throughout most of World War I, and afterwards he had gone barnstorming and joyriding in patched-up planes. Now he rode around in a Rolls-Bentley and was the main-spring of an organisation controlling maintenance hangars and flying clubs up and down the country. Like most old-time airmen who had long looked life straight in the eye with an unblinking gaze, he was partial to his whisky. I remember two incidents which portray his schoolboy enthusiasm.

One of the daily papers produced a print of a glider which it encouraged its young readers to cut out and make, and later to fly after fitting it with elastic bands. Duncan Davies, a pioneer aviator, was the first amongst us to cut it out, glue it up and fly it. On another occasion a group of pilots were fooling about in Tiger Moths with flour bags trying to do "hand bombing" onto the circle which had been cut and whitewashed over the grass, and which now marked the centre of our airfield. Duncan, who hadn't flown an aircraft for the best part of three months, joined us in a flash and with some of the craziest stunt flying I had then seen, he was soon lobbing flour bags over the side of his Tiger Moth, and dead on target too. I suppose he was then aged about fifty. On another occasion, just before I joined the club, he had startled everyone by taking one of the club aircraft around the steeply banked motor circuit so low that he flew *under* the foot bridges spanning the track. He was not above breaking all club flying rules, which was probably the reason why he retained me in spite of my early rashness.

The flying club encouraged its members and their guests to have tea at the club, knowing well that tea-time soon ran into bar-time and as usual with clubs, bar-time meant putting money into the bank. Brooklands, in fact, instigated a shilling tea on an eat-as-much-as-you-like basis.

Jack Sewell (who later became an ace fighter pilot in the Fleet Air Arm) and I, who were perpetually counting our pennies, could hardly believe our ears when first we heard about this. In our respective digs we got bed and breakfast and a stodgy evening meal. Now by persuading the staff to start serving tea from about 3 pm onwards we cut out all attempts at lunch, and began our 3 pm tea with at least two or three boiled eggs each and followed these with piles of sandwiches, bread and jam, cakes, etc. We were, respectively, aged twenty and twenty-one and had the normal appetite of youth plus what was added by the open-air existence we led, either in cockpits or cars.

As the days lengthened and the weather improved new faces appeared. Private owners arrived, new pupils were enrolled Roland's lady pupils were inexhaustible in number, and we commenced the Club Raids and Dawn Patrols.

The Club Raids would take place for no known reason. All that happened was that in the late afternoon someone would say, "Let's go and visit Redhill" (or Shoreham or some other flying club), and then business at Jimmy's timekeeping hut would become brisk. In a matter of minutes every club aircraft (we had about seven) plus a few private owners' would be on their way, usually with passengers aboard too, to "beat up" the other flying club. Once there, we would be entertained in their frugal but friendly club huts with as much beer as we could drink. Brooklands, with its posh buildings and bars, was the Rolls-Royce of flying clubs. The others, though no less enthusiastic, seemed always on the verge of bankruptcy. Suddenly we would realise that it was getting dark and since we all knew that the club's aircraft were not insured for night flying we would all fly back, a cheerful crowd of instructors, pupils, passengers and private owners hurrying home like so many naughty schoolboys. More than once we all landed back in darkness with Duncan driving his Bentley on to the field and putting on his headlights to guide us. He would give us a frightful ticking-off and then, as often as not, ask us all back to his house for more drinks! Mary, his wife, was a charming hostess, and although her life can hardly have been an ordered one, she was always smiling and was held in high regard by all of us.

Dawn Patrols were organised in advance and each club in turn, from as far north as Liverpool and as far south as Lympne or Wiltshire, gave warning that on a certain day a free breakfast would be provided to all visiting aircraft which arrived before 9 a.m. in such a manner that its registration could not be spotted before touch down. On the day in question the club got all their aircraft aloft at first light and guarded their own airfield. They did their best to get close to each of the invaders and so read their registration letters. These letters were, by law, painted on all aircraft very prominently, and thus it was difficult to get down without having been spotted by one of the home-based defending aircraft.

These Dawn Patrols took us all over the countryside in most kinds of weather, and we were by now experienced coursekeepers and map-readers. We usually had passengers with us too, either girl friends or more usually wealthier club members who "flew a little" but who used to prefer to "hire" one of the club's advanced pupils by the simple process of paying for the time flown.

Once in the area of the host field, the paying member usually gave over the control of the aircraft to the likes of Jack and me, and we used a variety of tactics to get in unobserved. Sometimes we would fly the last twenty miles hedge-hopping, hugging the contours of the ground. Or else we would appear from the opposite direction. At Shoreham, for example, we would first fly well out to sea and appear as if from France. Or we would try crazy approach tactics, such as that of spinning down over the top of the airfield and delaying recovery till near the ground. It is surprising that no planes ever collided, but there were lots of near-misses and much crazy flying, just to earn a free breakfast.

Other owners or wealthy members would occasionally "hire" us to fly them to Le Touquet for gambling weekends. Since all flying which we didn't actually pay for was a gain at the rate of £2 5s 0d per hour, Jack and I jumped at every chance to go with anyone in any plane anywhere. Bish was equally keen during weekends, as financing flying out of his bank pay was an obvious strain.

Gradually Bish, Jack and I came to call ourselves or be called "the Three Musketeers". Bish was about twice our age but in all other respects we were well matched, and I never recall a cross word or disagreement occurring amongst us. We also conceived the idea of forming ourselves into an aerobatic formation team. But first we had to learn formation flying, and we had to do this in secret as we had a strong idea that it was neither taught nor encouraged at Brooklands!

At weekends (I had long since ceased to go home to Littlehampton for weekends since club activity was at its height then; however, I often went home on weekdays instead) the three of us would book a Tiger Moth at about the same time, and by pre-arrangement rendezvous at say 3,000 feet over Frensham Ponds or some other landmark well known to us. We knew the district from the air so well that we scarcely ever carried maps.

In this way we practised station keeping in formation. We learnt to fly really close to each other—for example, I used to read Jack's instruments, finding this the easiest way to anticipate his movements.

We soon got to the stage when we wanted to practise formation take-offs and landings but dare not do so at Brooklands. Instead we used to fly to other neighbouring clubs. Soon the news came back home and instead of being asked to stop our activities we were asked to show what we could do. Brooklands was truly a most trusting kind of school. We did our little act for Ken and Duncan and I don't recall that they made any effort to curtail our activities. The Tiger Moth lacked the power for spectacular formation exhibitions. We could dive, turn, climb, loop, change stations, take-off and land, and that was about the lot. We worked out a five-minute pattern with fixed heights so that we could show off all our few tricks in a minimum time and at the optimum level for spectator enjoyment. We used to end up with a bomb-burst or a Prince of Wales feather going vertically upwards in formation, then fanning out and dropping down in different directions to re-form as quickly as possible at the bottom, in order to land as adjacent to each other as we dared. Each aircraft had slightly different flight and stall characteristics, so the landing was not as neat or as well tucked in as we would have wished. I know I once landed at Hamble in a haze without realising that I was even near the airfield! In the gloom I was watching Jack's panel so intently that I didn't realise that he had decided to land in order to check the Brooklands weather before the return flight. I figured he was practising a slow fly-past, until my wheels touched the grass!

I used to try to bear in mind that if we ever did touch wings or otherwise collide, all would be well as long as I extricated my plane by the same route as it had gone in and as slowly and gently as possible. Luckily it never came to this.

Some well-known artist even painted a water-colour of us (we were the only civil aerobatic team in the country). I treasured this picture, but unfortunately it got lost during one of the forty-one moves which I had to make at the RAF's behest during the war years. It was signed by us all, and since Jack was killed in the Fleet Air Arm during the war it is irreplaceable. Anyone seen three red and black biplanes flying over the Brooklands oval in about a 12 by 9 inch frame?

Brooklands was always full of ideas for drumming up more flying business. For one such, they started a series of monthly competitions for pupils and members. Usually Brem, Bob or Ken had thought them out. They varied, and included spot landings, blind navigational exercises, forced-landing tests, map-reading exercises, manoeuvring tests or combinations of these. A trophy was offered for the person getting most points throughout the summer season. A small prize went with each competition.

I think there was fairly general surprise when I won the first (with Jack second). We both received handicaps after this, but I also won the next two. By then my handicap had become an impossible burden. The club's idea was *not* to give Jack or me monthly prizes but to encourage the half-hearted members to sharpen up their flying, and to encourage them to hire more aircraft hours in so doing.

I was now past the 100 hours solo required for my B licence tests, and Ken had been preparing me for my commercial licence flight test, to be given by an approved Ministry instructor.

At about this time the Girl Friend came across from the South of France, and as she was staying with relatives in South Wales, I arranged to fly down and meet her at an air display which was taking place at Filton, near Bristol. I hired one of the club's smart Leopard Moths for this flight, and from then on she was either staying at my home in Littlehampton or in a hotel near Brooklands. Ken, too, had acquired a steady girl friend, and often the four of us would attend the parties which were such a feature of the club life.

7: *"Pilota Piknik" in Hungary*

A BRILLIANTLY clever young man from the shipping world joined the club. Vernon, Bob and I quite fancied ourselves at chess, which game we used to play by the hour during bad weather periods. John Holder, however, was in quite a different class. He told us in which move he would beat us—and he usually did. He and Vernon (a gifted mathematician) worked out rules for three-dimensional chess and built a wire cage in which to play the game, but since no one else could understand their rules it got no further.

John learned to fly, but not too neatly as he was a bulky youth; he then delighted Brem by buying up an old Moth which he had had for sale for some time. In fact, the club found John to be nearly the ideal customer as he wanted to learn it all and was never short of money for any purpose. He decided to fly his newly acquired aircraft to Hungary to join in the annual "Pilota Piknik" organised by the son of Admiral Horthy, then Regent of Hungary and, like other Hungarians of the time, very pro-British. (The Hungarians had recently offered their vacant throne to Lord Rothermere.) Each summer anything from ten to twenty aircraft from the flying clubs of Britain made the journey to Budapest, where for about ten days they were lavishly entertained by the Hungarian government. (Admiral Horthy's son was Aviation Minister.) When John asked me to accompany him as safety pilot, I jumped at the chance. It meant about thirty free hours; free living, too, as he also agreed to pay for my expenses.

The Gypsy I which John had bought was really ancient, but it handled much like a Tiger Moth and went as fast (85 mph).

On the first day of our flight we reached Cologne, the very day after Joe Louis had knocked out Max Schmeling and thus deprived Hitler and Germany of their world heavyweight boxing champion. It was largely for this reason that we experienced our first taste of Nazi rule. We had our newspapers confiscated and our bags were thoroughly examined to make absolutely certain that we carried no other newspapers giving details of the German hero's defeat. During a beer-hall conversation that evening we learned that all local papers were proclaiming that Schmeling had been fouled rather than flattened.

Next day I chiefly remember a tricky descent into the airfield at Linz, situated in a steeply banked curve of the Danube. After Linz we flew to the Austrian capital.

Vienna had but recently been "liberated" by the Nazis, and the night we spent there should have taught us far more than it did. The town was dead after 9 pm, and a cloak of fear and depression hung over it. We were both young, enthusiastic and bent upon high adventure, and in this carefree mood we hardly took note of what was happening to the Europe we saw around us.

Hungary and Budapest in June, and under the auspices of a government trying desperately to alert Britain to its needs for help and friendship, were all that we could wish for. The Hungarian people proved to be charming. I loved their food, wine and music and was utterly captivated by the coffee we sipped through two inches of deep cream. I admired, too, their horses, their love of animals, their manners and friendliness. Lord Rothermere's picture was often seen prominently displayed in the shops. Wherever we went, after we had established the fact that we were British, every door opened in friendship.

The flying party next assembled on the shores of Lake Balaton at the airfield of a seaside resort called Siofok. It was about 100 degrees in the shade, but the lake waters were cool. There was music, wine and song but some inkling of the country's underlying problems was revealed to me when air force officers questioned me fairly closely about the performances of the Hurricane and the Spitfire, both of which I had frequently seen at Brooklands and which were often parked on the other side of our airfield. I knew a little about both, as I had heard their test pilots discuss them at our bar, and I gave them both a near-perfect report. Hungary, I began to realise, was frightened and genuinely expected another war. This was at the time when the *Daily Mail's* Ward Price was still persuading many Britons (including me) that Hitler was really quite a decent fellow if left alone. I didn't pay much heed to these Hungarian fears. I had, I suppose, shut my eyes to the strange scene at Cologne Airport and chose to ignore the ghastly feeling of utter defeat which had surrounded us in Vienna.

I met a pretty girl who appeared to be Jewish at the lake-shore and dated her for the dance which followed. Later, when she followed up our casual acquaintance by seeking me out in Budapest and indirectly asked me to marry her (whilst indicating that a good "settlement" would be mine if I did so), I again began to wonder what was going on in Europe to make people like the Jews so desperate.

Politics were not our concern, however. We were having fun. We next flew to Szeged for some religious parade and festival, and then back to Budapest, where we explored the celebrated night-clubs on the island in the Danube between the twin cities which made up the capital. We heard zithers and zimbolas galore and we consumed much good local beer as well as the famous Tokay wines. We were permanently thirsty in the heat-wave which followed wherever we went. We were taken on conducted bus tours; we attended parties, functions, dances and fiestas. Few of us had ever been fêted like this before.

The highlight of the Piknik was when we all flew to attend the rodeo show held on the famous Hungarian grass plains of the Hortobagy. Here, once a year, the horses which then played such an important part in Hungarian life, were rounded up and for a few days a tent town sprang up in the heart of the plain. An airfield was easily marked out and we were due to spend two days camping out under the stars, enjoying to the full, alongside the gaily-dressed cowboys, the good local wine and the wild strummings of the gypsy bands. It was a glorious experience.

On the second day after our arrival I was having a snack with an American friend I had happened to meet, when John came to me somewhat crestfallen and simply said that: "I had better have a look at the aeroplane." This surprised me as I hadn't given it a thought since checking that it had been securely tied down the day before.

As we walked out to the airfield he told me what had happened. He, too, had met an American and had offered to give him a "joy-ride". He had "come in a bit high" and had dropped the Moth on its wheels instead of gently landing it.

It was a very sad-looking little machine that he led me to. It was down on one side rather like a tired bird with a broken wing. And there was an ominous wrinkle and hump showing on top of the right lower wing. Various members of our party were already examining it. I suppose we had some twenty to thirty pilots-cum-engineers in the Pilota Piknik party, and one came up to me and told me that undoubtedly one of the main longerons had gone and he strongly suspected a wing-spar fracture too. The longerons were the principal fore and aft stress members and it was easy to examine these from inside the cockpits. This was all too clearly broken. The suspect spar lay inside the fabric covering the wing and was not actually visible, but this too showed obvious signs of having been broken.

Admiral Horthy's son was with us as usual and he immediately placed all necessary facilities at our disposal. We lacked neither interpreters nor goodwill and in less than an hour I was back finishing my lunch and awaiting the arrival of the Hungarian Army carpenters, who had been designated to carry out the repairs. I realised that officially all repairs had to be certified by an ARB licensed engineer familiar with the type, but I could not conceive that there should be one within 500 miles and decided to forget this. It was, perhaps, some indication of the progress that I had made in the past six months, that I was really furious with John. Since he was a very inexperienced pupil, it had been agreed that I would do all the flying except when I decided otherwise. He was there to learn from me the rudiments of navigation, meteorology, foreign rules and regulations and general airmanship. It was his personal aircraft, but in flying it without my permission he was breaking our verbal agreement.

Since we were in Central Europe and it was at least 100 degrees, I didn't expect much to happen rapidly, so I was somewhat startled when another friendly pilot came to me shortly afterward to advise me to "see what they are doing to your aircraft". He suggested that I had better "supervise the wings being removed". It was still early afternoon and barely three hours since the accident had happened. I hastened to the aeroplane, but arrived much too late. Already the upper and lower wings on both sides had been removed and a body of about twenty troops were packing the remains into the back of an open army truck. They appeared to be working with brutal efficiency. The plane had literally been torn to pieces and, whilst I watched, the remains were trussed up with rope and the wings were lashed to the sides of the truck. I had no clear idea to where they were taking her, as Debrecen (where the unit was stationed) was just a name to me.

The whole Piknik party was due to fly back to Budapest again next morning, and John and I were offered lifts in various other machines, but the industrious Aviation Minister had gone one better. We were informed that he had arranged to supply John and me with another aircraft, and shortly afterwards a biplane military trainer of German design appeared. It was a two-seater, one in front of the other in open cockpits, and in this respect somewhat like our damaged Moth. All the dials were in either metres, litres or kilometres. It had, however, a self-starter, which eliminated the danger of hand-swinging an unfamiliar propeller. Our interpreters had flown off with the main party, and I couldn't get anyone to tell me how much fuel it used per hour, but everyone assured me by signs and gestures there was enough to get us to Budapest. We obtained some kind of map of Hungary and it was obviously another cloudless day, so off we went.

It was a frightfully noisy machine and rather uncomfortable inside, as we had to improvise seats from cushions, lacking as we did the parachutes we were supposed to use as seats, but it flew easily, being a fully aerobatic trainer with ailerons on both sets of wings. It was, I think, the warmest day and/or the warmest plane I ever experienced. Even in our open cockpits we were absolutely roasted, and as I flew towards Budapest I managed to rid myself of all my clothes except for trousers, shoes, helmet and goggles.

To my horror, I found upon arrival at Budapest Airport that the Aviation Minister had arranged a formal reception. There were heel-clicking officers (anxious about their plane?) and, even worse, journalists with photo-flash bulbs. I realised this when only about fifty yards from the apron and I had to stop where I was and, in full view, go through the awkward motions of dressing myself within the cramped confines of an open cockpit. John was doing likewise. My hair was hopelessly out of place and I was glistening with heat and embarrassment but, at least, I was wearing a shirt and tie when photographed shaking hands with the reception committee.

We enjoyed ourselves for a few days in Budapest with the rest of the party, but after they all left to fly home—and after the final banquet—it all seemed to go very flat. Left to ourselves as we now were, we began to realise how much had been done for us by the organisers. It was like looking at the ashtrays the morning after the party. Hungary obviously was scared by the Nazi threat, which had so brutally subjugated neighbouring Austria. Also, she had long-standing squabbles with all her neighbours from whom she claimed enclaves of territory. Hungarians were especially bitter against the Czechs, but I never really understood the historical background to it all.

We were very anxious about the plane. I couldn't get the picture out of my mind of our Moth being dismantled, tied, trussed and driven off over the bumpy plain in an Army truck with a dozen or so roughly uniformed men sitting and smoking all around her. I was also aware that John was paying the bills, and that I was wasting both my time and his money. At home I had the Girl Friend and my aviation training schedule. Thoughts of these increased my impatience and boredom.

We decided to visit Debrecen to see what was going on, and we went there by train. It was a grim provincial town—a garrison town, I suspect—and our visit was only made tolerable by meeting an extraordinary American, who was studying medicine there for no better reason than that the Magyar (Hungarian) language was supposed to be the hardest to learn in Europe and that he liked to do things the hard way!

One night he and I got hopelessly drunk, and after spending some futile hours trying to play a game of European billiards, we emerged into the blazing sunshine of 6 a.m., summoned an ancient horse buggy and demanded to be taken to the nearest brothel. In due course we arrived at the most appalling place I have ever seen in my life. I conclude that it must have been the brothel for Hungarian Army prisoners! The "inmates" or "residents" all looked much the wrong side of fifty with straggly grey hair and coarse hanging breasts. They wandered about either naked or half-clad with an utterly "lost" look on their faces. I could not conceive of such human degradation. I was stunned. Even my strange American friend was shocked. These creatures pawed us like animals and began their disgusting tricks. We gave what money we could spare and got out as fast as we decently could. The place was built around an old barrack square and the women were obviously not allowed to leave their grim, sordid confines.

Soon after this the plane was declared ready and I went to the nearby airfield to inspect it. The broken longeron had been glued, screwed, spliced and then had been given a stoutly bolted overlapping plate. It wasn't a neat job, but the sight was heartening. This repair now looked by far the most substantial part of the whole aircraft! I wondered, in fact, if the plane would fly level with so much massive additional timber added to one side! I couldn't see the wing repair as this was underneath a freshly doped layer of new fabric. The wings all appeared to be securely replaced. I could only think of one way of finding out if the wings were O.K. Clearly I must fly it.

I left John behind and tested his aircraft as severely as I knew how by diving it to its maximum permitted speed and by straining it in the steepest of steep turns. It seemed as solid as a rock, so after many adieus and efforts to express our thanks (no payment was suggested) we flew her firstly back to Budapest, and thence home as quickly as we could.

After quitting our last port of call—again Germany—the engine half stopped near the Belgian frontier. We were determined not to return to Germany, if any reasonable alternative existed, and I was able, by carefully nursing the "popping" engine, to fly the wounded Moth into a Belgian military airfield, a bare mile or two across the frontier. Only after we had landed did I realise that John had opened the altitude valve in his cockpit. This valve, when opened, gave a reduced mixture to the engine and should not have been opened below 8,000 feet. The only control for it was in the rear seat where he, the pupil, was sitting, and he had caused our predicament by fiddling about with it, quite unaware of what it did.

I was not best pleased, as this emergency landing delayed us quite a while, and we had to await the arrival of officials and then complete further entry and departure forms.

We returned home in rather a strained atmosphere.

8: Disappointment—and Success

THE maintenance engineers at Brooklands were aghast at our makeshift repairs, but admitted that they met the strength requirements. However, they had to do both jobs all over again in order to get the official ARB approval without which the certificate of airworthiness, and consequently the insurance, was invalid. Air legislation was one of the subjects I had been studying with Bob, and I knew this was the case and had been slightly edgy on this account all during the flight home.

It was now high summer and I pressed on with my various plans. The Girl Friend was either at a hotel near Brooklands or was staying with my parents and it was obvious to all that we were "going steady". When she was at Littlehampton I drove the fifty miles to Brooklands daily and she often spent a day or two there with me. I remember that we taught her the Morse Code so that she could transmit practice messages for Rhona and I (and sometimes Jack) to read and copy.

I had in my Log Book more than the required number of hours to enable me to qualify for the coveted B licence and Ken had prepared me for the tests. As soon as I could gain my B licence I would be able to fly for "hire and reward". It was essential to have a Commercial Pilot's Ticket, as without it I couldn't legally earn money as a professional pilot.

Soon the day of the test came. Brooklands seldom allowed a pupil to take this test unless it was felt that he had a reasonable chance of success. My examiner was an RAF officer who had been officially approved by the Ministry of Civil Aviation. I was to meet him at Northolt Airport at 10 a.m.

I flew myself there in one of the Brooklands Tiger Moths. I had been well instructed what to expect during the test.

First, there were simple manoeuvres; turns, climbs, dives, climbing turns, steep turns, stalls, spins, spin recovery, power application, speed control and co-ordination tests. I rather prided myself upon my accuracy and smoothness and went through these familiar drills as expeditiously as possible. After lunch we set off together on the second phase of the test, which included map-reading, course-keeping, turning on to various compass headings, drift and wind exercises, including the pinpointing and finding of objects such as obscure church spires in the West Country. Instrument flying was included, as was the inevitable emergency landing drill, brought about by the usual method of the instructor switching off the fuel at unexpected moments.

He failed me.

I was thunderstruck. He had barely passed a comment throughout, and I honestly felt I had done a reasonable job.

I felt I had a right to know why and enquired accordingly. I was told that I had lost some height in the early simple turns. There was nothing for it but to fly home with my tail between my legs. I felt I had let Ken down, also that I had been harshly treated. I dreaded my arrival back at Brooklands, where I knew my friends were waiting for my return. "I'll put the champagne on ice," were the last words I had heard on departure.

I was so pre-occupied working out my excuses and deciding what to say that I made a careless approach to the airfield and obstinately refused to correct the glide during the early stages when the misjudgment first became evident. I nearly hit the Hawker hangars (where the Hurricanes were being assembled) and arrived short of the actual airfield, landing almost behind Jimmy's hut. This way I escaped being seen from the bar windows for, as ever, the gang had taken root there.

For this last foolishness I deserved to fail every test.

Everyone was awfully decent about my failure, which made things worse for me, but, inside, I felt absolutely shattered.

Jack went off to do his tests shortly afterwards and passed, as did Rhona. It is true that they had both started ahead of me, but I reckoned that I had at least caught them up. Luckily my enthusiasm was revived soon afterwards by a decision of the Brooklands organisation to hold a four-club trophy meeting.

They owned four flying schools in various parts of the South of

England, and some kind person had put up an enormous silver trophy to be competed for annually. Each club was to choose three pilots who would be examined and marked by a senior RAF instructor from the famous Central Flying School. I nearly missed the Brooklands qualifying competition as I had to pay a visit to Fair Oaks on the day selected and was barely back in time. The Brooklands team had, in fact, been chosen, but, thanks to Brem, they agreed to let me take my entry test late. Bish had scored most points in this with Jack second. I managed to edge Bish out of first place and this restored my jaded spirits. We three were to represent the club. What could be nicer!

There were some hard feelings when the other clubs nominated their teams, as one of them had included an instructor. The fact that he was not officially a professional pilot enabled them to do so. This pilot was a diabetic, and could never pass the medical examination which every professional pilot must take. He was, however, a sensible and much-respected man, who had been instructing for years—by some unofficial arrangement with his club.

Duncan, with his canny commercial sense, staged the competition one weekend and combined it with a large, general air-meeting and a "dawn patrol", held for once at tea time. He had arranged to have an aerobatic team from the RAF give one of their startling "tied-together" demonstrations, and had also arranged for the appearance of both the Hurricane and the Spitfire (an early public showing of this latter). The meeting was very well attended with about fifty planes scattered around the field, and the bar must have had a record day's takings. Our four-club competition took almost all day and was conducted out of sight of the public, but Duncan Davies presented various displays of crazy flying, an aerobatic display (both by Ken Waller), displays of new aircraft and other eye-catching events. The big crowd were getting their money's worth.

The Doncaster Trophy was won by the host club, Brooklands, and what was of greater importance to me than winning, was that a club member had put up a prize of £25 to be shared by the winners. I also collected another money prize for being the overall top scorer of the day. The diabetic instructor was second and Jack came third. The trophy was handed over by Duncan's wife, and we filled the monster pot with beer (it would have held several bottles of champagne and we hadn't been paid our winning bonus yet!) and all those present had their swig.

1. "Bish" dressed up as Father Christmas departs on an errand. Rhona is the pilot.

2. A Brooklands Flying Club Tiger Moth over the famous race track. The Hawker assembly shed is under the tail. The large Vickers factory is at top.

3. The Three Musketeers: Author—Jackie—"Bish".

4. Three Flying Instructors at Brooklands, Leslie Cliff, Ken Waller and Roland.

5. Jackie Sewell, "Bish", and Author with Doncaster Trophy.

6. *"Gaaxy", the Puss Moth with a personality and character unto herself.*

7. *Eric's Redwing in the streets of Calais after his night landing there.*

8. John Holder, Tony Spooner and John's ancient Moth.

9. John's Gipsy Moth G-ABLZ provided an interesting passage to Hungary—and back.

10. Geoffrey Clapham, whose honest face and twinkling eyes drew me to Liverpool. Later, when aged nearly 50, he became an operational pilot in the R.A.F. with the rank of Wing Commander.

1. H.M.S. THETIS. Later on one of the sailors perched on the tail and tapped messages to the 100 men trapped inside.

12. *The Avro Anson 1 or "Faithful Annie", used as a flying classroom. No safer plane was ever built. She was viceless.*

13. *Digging out one of the specially equipped Wellingtons after it had slithered into a bomb hole at Malta.*

14. *The "Goofington" or "Stickleback" Wellington. Every single aerial (for its ASV) was an ice-trap.*

15. *Eric Starling and his Navigator taken in Iceland after a successful U-boat attack there.*

16. H.M.S. AURORA. *This light cruiser (5270 tons) made the Italians pay heavily.*

17. Captain W. C. Agnew. *"Agnew of the Aurora"—the brilliant leader of Force K.*

18. Lieutenant-Commander Husse *Commander of the gallant H.M.S LIVELY.*

19. H.M.S. LIVELY. *No ship fought more actions in and around Malta than this destroyer commanded by Lt.-Commander Hussey.*

20. *Total damage to Force K after sinking over 20 enemy ships—one shell splinter.*

21. *Two pages from Author's log-book, showing messages of congratulation and relevant newspaper clippings.*

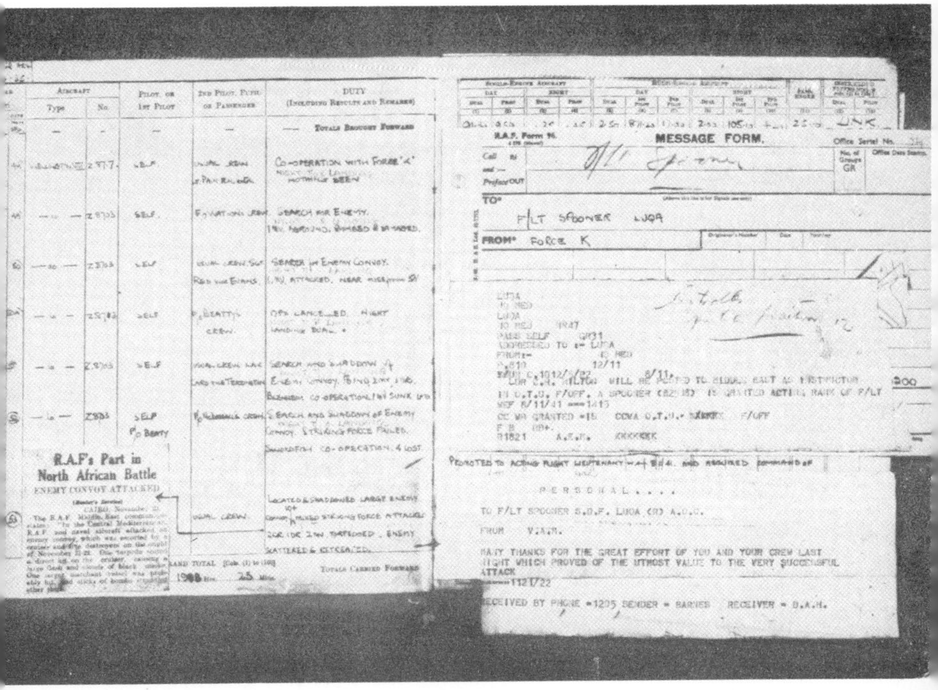

22–23. *"A bi-plane that would not have looked out of place in World War I." The Swordfish handled with incredible gallantry by the FAA. Top: The ASV equipped flight leader. Bottom: Strike aircraft with torpedo.*

Later, during a hiatus in the day-long programme, the three of us were asked to show off our formation exercise, and this we did. After our usual formation landing, I was tempted to take-off again as I had been working out a new aerobatic—a vertical figure "S" manoeuvre built around an inverted half-loop. This last was commonly called a "bunt" and was an illegal manoeuvre due to the negative "g" it imposed upon the wing roots of the plane. However, several of us had been trying it in secret—we had once seen Ken do it during an aerobatic display. I reduced my height to as low as I dared, the better to show off my own variation of this manoeuvre. It all worked out OK, and all I got by way of reproach was a kindly talk from Ken, emphasising the need to keep such unofficial over-stressing of the aircraft to those days (such as this one) when the sky was void of rough air turbulence. "Else," he said slowly, "the wings will come off and we wouldn't like that, old chap, would we?"

Later, in my presence, he loudly asked the visiting examiner from the CFS, who had spent all day judging the twelve of us, whether, on the results of his flight with me that day, he, the examiner, considered I was fit to take the B licence flying-test. When the examiner said that Spooner would walk through, the gentle Ken gave me a nod and I saw a savage gleam come into his eye. Not till then did I realise how much my failure had hurt him.

All in all this was a fantastic day for me. I had helped Brooklands to win the trophy for the club. I had been judged the individual winner. I had filled the cup, taken part in a formation flying display, publicly displayed my own little aerobatic innovation, and after the fifty-mile drive home to Littlehampton late that night alone with the Girl Friend (who had been at Brooklands all day, too), she and I sat in the garage at the end of our garden and there agreed to get married. With about £15 coming to me as prize money, I felt I could now buy her a decent engagement ring, and this is what I did with my winnings. Up till that moment, whilst we both more or less had accepted an "unofficial engagement" tag, we hadn't actually got down to discussing details, nor had there been any definite proposal and acceptance.

Quite some day, that long summer's day in June, 1938.

9: *Commercial Pilot*

SOON after my "day of days" I again flew away to take my B licence tests and this time I passed. As I had already passed the written tests in navigation, air-law, engineering, etc., and as I had the required 100 hours solo flying and had passed the medical standards, I was soon in possession of the coveted B licence (No. 13667), and this meant that I could now charge for my flying services. However, this made no immediate change in my circumstances, as I continued to train at Brooklands as planned in order to get the 2nd N (Navigators) ticket, for which the full 300 hours was required. I also decided to study and train for an instructor's ticket, since this seemed the easiest way to get a paid flying job.

I passed the navigational examination towards the end of summer at the first attempt. Rhona sat the examination alongside and passed all but one of the five subjects. Jack, like Tom Brooke-Smith before him, never really got to grips with these subjects. Pilots fall into two main categories. There are those with engineering sense and backgrounds, such as Jack, Tom and many others, and those with mathematical, or to be more accurate with arithmetical, sense, and it is rare that the two go together. I belonged to the latter school. Alistair Cormack and Vernon Hunt (who had left to join a small airline flying out of Heston) were rare examples of pilots with both abilities. Vernon's colleague, Bill Orton, was more of the engineering type. It was bad luck for Jack and Tom that the 2nd N licence was the licence which really opened the doors to the better-paid positions. Their superior engineering knowledge didn't greatly enhance their prospects as pilots.

My fiancée's parents had by then come to spend the late summer months in England as was their custom. They arrived to find their beautiful daughter, a débutante too, wearing an engagement ring. This could have hardly fitted in with their plans for her, as almost all they knew about me was that I still hadn't got a job and that I once had visited them in France, arriving three days late with a friend on Christmas morning, after having failed over the phone to borrow 100,000 francs a few days earlier. Still, they were very decent about it all, even though they did put in a word about the need for me, as a pilot, to get my life properly insured! Luckily her father and mine were occasional golfing friends and they had a quiet respect for each other.

Before passing from the Brooklands scene, before indeed being allowed to possess my B licence, I had to carry out the well-known B licence night-flight requirement. The flight invariably went from Croydon to Lympne, this being about the minimum distance for licensing purposes. None of our planes were equipped for night-flying, so one had first to be prepared. Electrical power was provided by fitting a small wind-driven generator underneath the fuselage. Airflow in flight turned a miniature propeller, which in turn rotated the dynamo, thus enabling the wing-tip lights to illuminate. Thus equipped, Brem and I flew off to Croydon.

There he first checked me out as a night pilot. He did this as soon as it was officially dusk. Actually, it was still light enough to see the airfield, and we barely benefited from the single Chance light which was designed to illuminate the landing area without blinding the pilot. Most operators had long ago abandoned this apparatus, and later aircraft were equipped with their own proper landing lights, but our Tiger Moth had no such luxury. After checking that the weather at Lympne would be OK and that someone would be there to turn on their airport beacon and Chance light at the time when I was expected, Brem went back to Brooklands just as it really got dark.

Having never before flown at night, except in rather beery condition over very familiar routes, such as Redhill to Brooklands, or Shoreham to Brooklands, I was rather thrilled by the whole procedure. The insurance company wanted an extra £25 *per flight* (about ten per cent of the value of the aircraft!) and this I would have to pay. Naturally, it was all instrument flying, and with no cockpit lighting it was quite a task in the open cockpit to shine a torch to read the map and fly the aircraft all at the same time. I had never flown the route Croydon to Lympne before, but had calculated that I would pass near certain towns at certain times. Later, I felt sure I could find the south-east coastline, thence locating Dover harbour and from there would see the Lympne airport flashing beacon. This beacon would by then (I hoped) be switched on. It all went reasonably well even if I landed rather clumsily. Duncan Davies's brother (who ran the Lympne, or Cinque Ports, Club) was there to meet me, and he kindly put me up for the night. It was all over in an hour. I returned home by air next day duly passed fit to fly anywhere in the world, for a living if needs be, by night!

One of the most remarkable of aviation stories is connected with this B licence night-flight. The person concerned was Eric Starling, an experienced airline pilot, known to me only by name, as he had departed from Brooklands just before I arrived there, after successfully studying at Bob's school for his 2nd N. Later, Eric and I spent much of the war years together in the same squadrons, and I was able to get the story from him in full.

On the particular night when Eric set forth from Croydon to Lympne he was a student pilot with a hundred or so hours and was flying, I believe, a small biplane called a Redwing. Eric had the bad luck to run into a sea fog which had drifted inshore completely blanketing Lympne and the SE corner of England. Thus he could neither find Dover nor the Lympne airfield with its friendly beacon. This set Eric a real problem, as there was no other nearby airfield where he could land at night, and his plane did not carry overmuch fuel. Meanwhile he had to keep flying somewhere. All he really knew was that according to his watch he should be over SE England, though there was absolutely nothing visible below except fog. Climbing higher, he saw some lights in the distance and flew to explore. They came from a town on the other side of the English Channel, and he circled it awhile whilst considering his next move. By circling he could at least avoid losing his direction in the darkness. Setting a northerly course back to where Dover should lie he again timed himself across the Channel, but again saw absolutely nothing where Lympne or Dover should have been: no sign of a cliff or coastline even, and these he knew *would* show up in the moonlight, with the white breakers contrasting with the dark sea and shore. He had a moment or two of utter confusion when on one of his Channel crossings he meant to turn back towards Dover and was overjoyed at finding lights ahead of him, only to realise that he had turned the whole way round and was, in fact, heading once more towards the lights which he rightly assumed were those of Calais. The setting of any kind of course on those early unstable compasses was tricky in daylight, as if the pilot accidentally lined up a black pointer against a red one (instead of another black one) he was at once set to fly in exactly the opposite direction to that intended. Most of us had made this error during our early attempts at course-keeping. At night, with black and red equally obscure, it was easier than ever to make this mistake.

Once more Eric found himself back over the French town. His first thought was to attempt a landing on the beach nearby or in shallow water, but he realised that he knew nothing whatever about the details of the French shoreline. Would there be rocks? How about cliffs? Was there a flat sandy area or would it all be shingle? Were there breakwaters? At night a pilot can see precious little of such details.

He then conceived the startlingly original idea of deliberately landing his aircraft in one of the streets of the town which he could still see below him. The thought that this, too, might soon disappear from view in the fog was at the back of his mind. He flew over the town and scientifically began to eliminate certain of the broader streets over which he could detect overhead tram wires. Keeping his head throughout, he finally selected the broadest and best lit street which appeared to have neither tram wires, statues, fountains or other obstacles along it. After a test run down to roof-top height he decided that his small biplane could be fitted into the width of this back street, and with luck could be stopped before coming into contact with anything too hard.

With petrol running low he again approached as slowly and carefully as he could, and by the exercise of great skill, judgment and, above all, calmness (remember he had never previously flown at night) he successfully pulled off the most discussed and controversial emergency landing in civil aviation for that year. His plane had no brakes and with a hard road surface, rather than grass, to act as a deceleration agent the Redwing took longer than usual to come to a standstill, with the result that it gently slewed itself into a statue when at little more than walking pace. Otherwise it was completely undamaged. It is almost a miracle that no cars or carts were abroad, even though, as Eric said, it was very late at night and the town seemed practically deserted except for the main boulevards.

The landing was executed as planned and, although I have never heard of it being attempted before or since, it undoubtedly extricated Eric from a most perilous position and one with which he had only been faced due to sheer bad luck. After all, "the proof of the pudding lies in the eating". If people ever doubted his decision Eric would ask them, "What would you have done in my place?" I, for one, have always found this unanswerable.

Eric always looked at things calmly and philosophically, and this incident certainly didn't dampen his enthusiasm for flying. Eric was one of those who simply was "born to fly".

The worst part, so he told me, was that although he was dead tired, he had to stay up all night telling the story—and waiting for it to be interpreted. Firstly he had to explain it all to the gendarmes who appeared. Then in a police station. Then in police headquarters. Then to the newspapers, to the aviation people, to the British consul and to Croydon by phone, and each time he related the story it tended to sound more ludicrous. The Frenchmen shook their heads and muttered with respect "c'est formidable". The incident so appealed to their Gallic sense of drama that Eric awoke to find himself the local hero, and found, too, a host of friends to help him get the plane back to its anxious owners at Croydon.

10: Nearly a Test Pilot

BACK at Brooklands I now began to see light at the end of the tunnel. I had my B licence, endorsed for Tiger Moths only, but nonetheless a valid certificate enabling me to earn money as a pilot. I also had the 2nd N technical examination behind me. The required hours for this would soon be accomplished and all I would then have to do would be to pass the simple signalling and semaphore tests. Furthermore I was officially fit. The instructor's ticket was not issued, as were the other licences, by the Ministry, but by a City Guild calling themselves GAPAN (The Guild of Air Pilots and Air Navigators).

There was a carefully laid down curriculum for instructing, and a standard "patter" by which all pupils were (or should be) taught. Ken had stuck very faithfully to the correct patter throughout all our flying together, so when he had to teach me how to teach others it came naturally. I soon applied to take the Instructor's Endorsement flight test. Some days before I was due to take it, I began to seek a job. I had studied all the "situations vacant" in the aviation magazines, and was lucky in that quite a few flying clubs were looking for qualified instructors. This was a by-product of the fact that the government had recently announced their Civil Air Guard scheme, which was to teach the youth of Britain to learn to fly at the subsidised cheap rate of 5s per hour. They wanted fit young men who, they hoped, would later join one of the Flying Reserves of the RAF.

But first I must tell you about "Lamps"—the uncrowned King of Civil Aviation in those happy-go-lucky days of 1938, when Henry Cotton could win the Open, and England, thanks to Hutton, could defeat Australia and Bradman. Lamps truly belonged to these times.

Captain A G Lamplugh, to give Lamps his full name, was officially the Chief Assessor of the British Aviation Insurance Co. But he wielded power far beyond this, as on his say the insurance rates of every civil aviation enterprise, *and that of each of their pilots,* were based. Yet for all this Lamps was welcomed everywhere. He was a unique man who did an immense amount of good to the growing profession. Any time any professional pilot even thought about doing anything rash, the mental picture of Lamps loomed up, for no pilot ever committed a flying error without Lamps learning about it in quick time. I shudder to think what my potential insurance rate must have been at one point in my career when after three months, I had committed almost every folly in the book. However, my consistent record of being top scorer in the Brooklands competitions throughout the summer was, I hoped, in process of cancelling out my earlier transgressions.

Brooklands was one of Lamps's favourite flying schools, and any pupil passed out there started his professional career with many advantages. It was certainly a great help to me. Bob Ashton doubtless contributed, too, and I think it likely that Ken had been impressed by the amount of dual hours I had voluntarily flown with him, although long since approved as fit to hire the club's aircraft without further instruction.

On Duncan's advice I wrote to three of the biggest flying clubs—these were at Birmingham, Liverpool and Newcastle—offering my services as an instructor. I still hadn't passed the instructors' flight test but Duncan, so I now think, wanted these clubs to check with Lamps about me in good time. To my surprise all three wrote back and offered me a job! The Liverpool Club at Speke Airport offered the best money, but Ken said, "Money wasn't everything", and anyhow I knew that the actual money usually worked out somewhat different from what was officially offered. It was suggested to me that I should go north to see which club I liked best.

I filled up a Tiger Moth and headed first to Elmdon, the airport for Birmingham, where I met their chief instructor, saw the club's aircraft and premises, liked all I saw and half agreed to start with them as soon as I had passed the necessary instructors' test. Looking back now this all seems very odd as I had never actually tried to teach a pupil and I might have been psychologically incapable of teaching anyone to fly. It was impossible to avoid the impression that they were more or less bidding for my services, whereas in reality I was anxiously seeking my first job as a commercial pilot.

My next stop was at Speke, where I met the chief flying instructor, the club chairman and the club accountant. Speke looked a most business-like flying club. It had well-decorated, soundly constructed club premises instead of the usual wooden huts. It had clean smart aircraft and bore the authentic stamp of permanence which I had thought was peculiar to Brooklands alone. The club accountant even went through the books to show how healthy the club's finances were. This was another rarity. They also told me about plans to extend their activities thanks to the Civil Air Guard contract they had been awarded by the government. I doubt whether these assets were really of importance to me in making up my mind. Speke was sold to me by their chief instructor, Geoffrey Clapham. I took an instinctive liking to this man who was somewhat older than most practising pilots. He was a square-cut, rugged, dependable-looking figure with the healthy complexion usually associated with open cockpits. I felt sure that Geoffrey Clapham and I would see eye to eye. I was so sure, in fact, that I decided then and there to accept the offer which his club made me. This was a well-paid appointment, being only £15 per year less than the salary of the 55-year-old Worthing insurance office manager under whom I had worked just twelve months before. It was over three times the pay I had been receiving at the end of three and a half years with that same company.

I now saw no point in flying to keep my appointment in Newcastle, so sent them a telegram stating that I was already suited. But I called in again at Elmdon on the way back to Brooklands, and there explained that Liverpool had offered a better contract. I asked whether they would be interested in employing Jack Sewell, who was at the same stage of progress as I as a pilot, though he had abandoned his navigation studies.

Thus it was that I flew home, and on being met by Jack and Rhona could announce that I had taken the job in Liverpool and arranged for Jack to have the one in Birmingham if he wanted it. But there was no offer of a job for poor Rhona. She wasn't welcomed in the profession as Jack and I had been, yet in some ways she was the best all-round aviator of the three of us. She had some of Jack's engineering skill plus some of my love for mathematics and navigation. She had good flying ability allied to the toughness and stamina of any man. But she was a woman.

In between taking time off, when my fiancée and I did the rounds of seeing her relatives and mine, I finished my "patter" training and duly went to be tested by a Guild examiner, an RAF officer and test pilot instructing as "chief", at a training school at Yatesbury in the West Country. This belonged to the Bristol Aircraft and Engine Company.

I went through the routine as best I could, and was happy to find that my examiner was a very pleasant character who seemed to accept the fact that I had been properly instructed by Ken on this subject. His name was Kerr, if my memory of an incident of long ago is reliable. Anyhow, we spent the last fifteen minutes of my test flight chatting together rather than being examiner and examinee.

Through the Gosport tubes of our headsets he asked me what kind of job I was aiming to find. He suggested that I took my 2nd N, and he was surprised when I told him that I had recently taken it. He later offered me a job as part-time flying instructor with his RAFVR training school at Yatesbury, plus part-time work as a Bristol test pilot, since they were looking for pilots to test out the latest versions of the Mercury engines fitted in their famous Bristol Blenheim. A set number of hours had to be logged for each new engine type, and after the experienced test pilots had given the new engine type their OK, a "boy" was wanted to just fly and fly these twin-engined bombers around the country, in order that the new Mercurys should qualify for their type certificates. To me this was a wonderful offer and a glamorous one, since the Blenheim was at that time Britain's newest, fastest and most publicised bomber, with a top speed of over 250 mph, then regarded as terrific. It was, as far as I knew, the fastest bomber in the world, and the thought of flying this for a big firm like Bristols quite took my breath away. Also, the money was a great advance on what I had been offered.

However, I had definitely agreed to go to Liverpool and I was disinclined to go back on my word. The offer was made whilst we were still in the air. . . .

I have since speculated what fate would have had in store for me if I had accepted this remarkable offer. With war soon to explode, I would obviously have become a very busy test pilot as, for example, did my friend Tom Brooke-Smith.

Test pilots had much glamour in those days, and the Brooklands Flying Club bar was where they often gathered. I actually saw poor

Johnny Hindmarsh killed. The Hurricane he was testing dived vertically almost into the Vickers works on the other side of the airfield. It plummeted in at full speed like a gannet after a deep-lying fish. A few minutes later a change of shift was due and the casualties might well have run into hundreds. As it was he just missed all vital buildings and workers. Did he black-out? Did a control cable fail? The usual speculation took place, but no one would or could ever be sure since nothing salvageable remained.

With Hawkers building their Hurricanes just behind Jimmy's hut, and Vickers across the airfield working day and night building Wellesleys and perfecting the Wellington; testing and rejecting their own fighter, the Venom; but gaining great acclaim with their subsidiary company's Spitfire (already in test-flight stage), Brooklands had become a centre of RAF production. Our club bar had become a meeting place for test pilots too.

The most spectacular of all test pilots in my opinion was Dick Reynell of Hawkers. He could make those early Hurricanes do anything he wished. We used to leave the bar to watch his displays and I knew that I would never have a "pair of hands" like his. I once remember seeing him glide a Hurricane the whole way round the Brooklands circuit upside-down until, when practically over the banking of the race-track, he half flick-rolled the aircraft, lowered the flaps and landed as neatly as possible. It was an incongruous sight to see him "lower" the Hurricane wheels "up" whilst still gliding inverted. He used to pull enormous "g" in this high-speed aircraft whilst making spectacular high-speed turns at low altitude. He was the tall, hard, lean Gary Cooper type, with long thin hands of enormous strength and delicacy. Phil Lucas was his chief, and the No. 1 Hawker test pilot after Major George Bulman was promoted to higher things. Johnny Hindmarsh, until killed, was a frequent visitor to our friendly club.

Over at Vickers the celebrated "Mutt" Summers ruled supreme. He was busy winkling the "bugs" out of the prototype Wellingtons. Although senior in age he could make this big, rather whale-like bomber practically sit up and beg. He used to barrel roll it, and then "swish-tail" it right down to the ground in a series of perfectly judged left and right sideslips. His landings were always perfect. After one such landing—it was a gem—I saw the Wellington keel slowly over on to one side, coming to rest on its crumpled wing. One main undercarriage leg had collapsed. Naturally this was a great tragedy as the machine was only in prototype form, and it was the future white hope of Bomber Command. The story at the time was that Mutt, who at all times was a practical rather than a slide-rule type of test pilot, had long before looked with doubt at this particular undercarriage link which in his opinion "looked too flimsy". The experts rechecked their calculations and told Mutt that since all the stresses were being routed so as to pass through this link in a horizontal line it did not need to be too robust. This was the link that did in fact fail, and Mutt, who was unhurt after the incident, was rightly triumphant. However, the experts re-calculated their stresses and strains and blandly announced that "their slide-rules showed that the accident could not possibly have happened"! What Mutt said next is not recorded!

Jeffrey Quill, his assistant at Supermarines, Vickers' subsidiary company, was a great test-pilot. He was almost the only one of the Vickers pool of pilots who would willingly fly the Venom, Vickers' own miniature fighter, which could exceed 300 mph, although it was powered by a Bristol Aquila radial engine of little more than 500 hp. I saw it come in and land once or twice. It appeared to be unstable about its fore and aft axis, and it required skilful handling near the ground, from which it would bounce twenty or thirty feet into the air at the slightest provocation.

Soon nobody ever flew the Venom, and Jeffrey took over the prototype Spitfire almost as his own private property. He used to come up from the Supermarine factory and airfield at Southampton to spend weekends at Weybridge, where he lived, and he commuted by Spitfire. He could do the distance in some seven or eight minutes, since this was a genuine 350 mph-plus aircraft, noticeably faster than the Hurricane. He would "announce" his arrival by diving low over the club-house at such a speed that the sound and the aircraft appeared together. Then he would point the Spit's nose up and execute a series of climbing rolls, often disappearing into the clouds thousands of feet overhead.

He also used to fly the big single-engined Wellesley bomber—a slow, but good load-carrying machine, with huge wings, enabling it to land about as slowly as our Tiger Moths. Once, in a strong, near-gale-force wind, Jeffrey carefully brought it down to land from directly overhead our club-house, descending the last thousand feet vertically and allowing the strong wind to make the actual touch-down a slightly backward one. He did this by keeping the speed of the aircraft just below that of the strong wind. The whole procedure took about four or five minutes.

These planes and the Blenheims and Fairey Battles, which also visited us, have all passed into history, and I regard it as a privilege that I was around when these famous test-pilots first put them through their paces. It was at Brooklands in 1937 that the first round of the Battle of Britain was fought, and it was people like Dick Reynell, Jeffrey Quill, Mutt Summers and their colleagues who laid the foundations of victory. In the short time I was there I saw the Hurricane undergo many improvements. The first version, with its fixed-pitch two-bladed propeller, could only just clear the Brooklands banking on take-off. By late summer the three-bladed variable-pitch version was, by comparison, rocketing out of our grass field, and it was obvious to us that the aircraft's overall manoeuvrability was constantly being improved.

Mutt Summers's Wellington, now with a strengthened undercarriage link, also won great honour and glory with Bomber and Coastal commands during the early war years.

To have turned down a chance to become a test-pilot and to be associated with the Blenheim, undoubtedly the most glamorous star of them all at that time, was a hard decision but, once up amongst the friendly Lancastrians at Speke, Liverpool, I never regretted it.

11: Liverpool—and the Thetis Tragedy

THUS ended a wonderful period in my life: exciting, absorbing and ever-active. I had the satisfactory feeling of "going places" and most certainly I was "doing things". Both in terms of time and money I was inside my target figures. I had acquired the essential flying licences in ten months rather than in the year I had set for myself.

There had been the one set-back, when I had first failed the B licence tests, but this was now a thing of the past and my mood of optimism was such that I was almost impervious to the events which were overhanging the world in 1938. Yet I had been given a pointed warning.

One day all the RAFVR trainees in the London area were summoned to hear a speech from a high-ranking RAF officer. This man did not mince his words. He told us bluntly that war could come at any moment and that we would be flung into the thick of it, whether fully trained or not. If we were to be given orders to bomb a town then we had to do so, and he sensibly advised us that if such a thing was not acceptable to our way of thinking, the honest thing for us to do was to say so now and to get out of the RAFVR whilst it was relatively easy to do so.

I was still at heart, though somewhat vaguely, pacifist, and I turned over these words in my mind during several restless nights. It had seemed that the RAF officer had been speaking directly to me. I had, by then, got all I had wanted from the RAFVR in flying hours and I could now easily quit. But I hated the idea. Part of me wished to fulfil my part of the bargain. Also I argued that not every pilot in the RAF would be asked to bomb cities. Many piloting functions had nothing to do with mass slaughter. I even saw myself as the daring pilot of an unarmed ambulance plane (shining white in my day-dream) flying through hell fire to glory!

But basically it was as inconceivable to me as it was to almost every other Briton, be he Cabinet Minister or brewer's mate, that there *could* be another world war involving Britain. Only "wild publicity-minded" orators such as Churchill or Lord Vansittart seemed to think otherwise.

Anyhow, what with now having a fiancée and with an ever-growing love for everything to do with the air, I wasn't in the mood to worry about war or such unpleasant speculations. Life was beginning afresh on a glorious note. Thus, I conveniently forgot about the Air Marshal and his sombre warnings.

I can't remember taking any holiday prior to driving myself up to Liverpool to start my first flying job. My fiancée had departed with her parents to pass the winter months in their beautiful retreat at Cagnes-sur-mer, near Nice, and my ambition was to earn some real money so that we could fix the wedding date.

Right from the start I loved Liverpool. The flying club was excellently run, the people there made me—a southerner—feel absolutely at home. I loved their directness and felt more kinship up north than I had ever done behind the lace curtains of the Sussex town where I had lived for so long. I was shocked to note the appalling poverty around Bootle and behind the dock areas. I remember, too, being shocked at seeing the women breast-feeding their babies on the busy city trams, but the fine mettle of the people enormously impressed me, and I was happy to be earning excellent money for carrying out a job which I loved under a man I came to regard with the same admiration and affection as I held for my father.

Geoffrey Clapham became, in fact, a second father to me, as my parents had, meanwhile, departed to live in Jamaica. He was at least twice my age and in every respect mentor, confidant and friend as well as being my Chief Instructor.

The Liverpool and District Flying Club divided their activities between two airfields opposite and within sight of one another on either bank of the broad Mersey. The main buildings were on the Speke or Lancashire side. Here the aircraft were housed, and here, too, stood the recently rebuilt club-house. At Hooton Park, on the Cheshire side of the river, there was only a typical flying club-house—a large, untidy room, mainly used as a bar lounge.

Geoffrey looked after flying at Speke and took me under his wing.

The No. 2 instructor, called "Buster" Heaton, was in charge at Hooton. "Buster" was as bright and cheerful to look at as his near namesake, Buster Keaton, was long-faced and glum. No matter what happened, Buster's cheerful face always radiated optimism. He never revealed any great psychological depths, but it was impossible not to be cheered up by his zestful approach to life. He looked about thirty but was at least ten years older.

I found myself a one-room bachelor flat in a nice part of the big city. It was quite modern, in that the bed folded up into the wall when not in use. I still had my 500 cc Fiat Topolino, and I rapidly fell into the flying club routine, which was almost the same as that which existed at Brooklands. I was on duty six days a week from 9 a.m. until flying ended for the day. All instructors worked Saturdays and Sundays but each took one day off during the week.

The flying was divided between regular club members, who paid thirty-five shillings per hour solo and two pounds per hour when flying with one of the instructors, and the new recruits for the Civil Air Guard Scheme. For both purposes we used the same aircraft. These were, once again, Tiger Moths. The club owned four or five of these, and Buster, with his new assistant, took two of them over to Hooton immediately upon arrival each morning.

The club members varied in their flying experience. Some were pupils who had yet to go solo, others were veteran pilots who had been flying for years. These latter only occasionally requested us to fly with them, but some did so in order to improve their aerobatics or navigation, or because they were experiencing some difficulty. Geoffrey and I were never really busy that winter of 1938-39, but one of us always had to be there to decide if the weather was OK for the various types of club flying. Also, we had to act as our own time-keepers. Many of the older members booked to take a lesson or two from the new "lad from the south". I think now that they were just checking on me. At the time I thought they were genuinely seeking to improve their flying, and since in many cases this had become rusty, I didn't hesitate to be critical about their habits. The club's chairman was one who was made aware of his faults in this manner! This frank treatment didn't upset the good people of Lancashire who, to a man, are almost totally lacking in "side".

Between our neat little club-house and the big airport buildings

(Speke, at that time, was the biggest airfield in Britain) lay the wooden huts of the Auxiliary Squadron. This was one of the week-end Reserve Squadrons of the RAF, and 611 was as famous up north as were 600 and 601 Squadrons around London. The Auxiliary Squadron had just been equipped with new Fairey Battle bombers, and one of these Battles had recently run wild without a pilot on board, doubled back upon its tracks and, as if drawn by a magnet, taxied itself at high speed into our new club-house, demolishing half the main lounge. A well-known aviation wit, Sydney St Barbe of De Havillands, promptly sent us a telegram "regretting that he had not been able to be present at the reopening of our new premises".

I owed my job to the decision of the club to take part in the Civil Air Guard Scheme, and the events at Munich had added urgency to this task. The Czech crisis had put Britain within hours of being at war with Nazi Germany. Like everyone else I had cheered our Prime Minister when he triumphantly brought back his famous piece of paper signed by Hitler. Like most other people I was absolutely astounded when Winston Churchill, still without office and barely recognised by any political party, stood up in the Commons with the cheers for Neville Chamberlain still ringing in his ears and bluntly stated, "We have suffered an unmitigated defeat—the whole of Eastern Europe now lies within the Nazi orbit—this is the beginning of a dark era and none can say where it may finish."

But as I see it now the "bit of paper" became the yardstick by which Britons henceforth would measure Hitler. The German dictator had signed an undertaking that "he had no more territorial claims in Europe". Now it would be easy to see whether he was a man of his word. And when he seized the rest of Czechoslovakia the following spring, the people of Britain, Chamberlain included, suddenly awoke from their long slumber.

The five-shillings-per-hour Civil Air Guard pilots came in great numbers, having first passed a stiff medical examination. They were clerks, delivery boys, engineers, farmers, lorry drivers, students, and they were bound by a common desire to learn to fly. For the first time ever, this ambition had been put within the reach of the ordinary people of England. It was impossible to find keener material, and I was eager to teach. The good instruction I had but recently received at Brooklands was still fresh in my mind. Both consciously and sub-consciously much of Ken's technique had rubbed off on to me—even to his casual "old boys" which had so reassured me during my first efforts.

One strange feature of our partnership at Speke was that never once did Geoff and I at any time fly together in an aircraft. He took me on trust when first I flew to Liverpool looking for a job, and we worked together in close harmony throughout. But he never tested me. After a while I began to sense how Geoffrey flew, as we were constantly flying with each other's pupils and I learnt to detect an infinitesimal difference between his teaching and my own. With his greater experience he obviously learnt about me, too, but he never once suggested that my small deviations from his methods should be changed.

Buster's pupils, over the river, were, much more obviously, differently taught—not that this is a criticism. No two people, I suppose, ever give instruction exactly alike. But Geoff and I came very close to doing so. He would take one pupil and I the next, and we would more or less stick to our own pupils till about four hours had gone by. After that we passed them back and forward for "second opinions". Geoffrey had the sole right to decide when they were fit to fly by themselves, but I was allowed to work my own pupils to the point when I would say to Geoff that they were ready to go solo. After this he personally tested them and decided whether he agreed with me or not.

The Civil Air Guard Scheme was not "money for old rope" to the flying clubs, as we had to produce good results or else lose money. After about five hours with each pupil we had to decide whether or not the pupil would be able to fly solo by thirteen hours. *All* flying up till five hours was subsidised by the government, which later paid us up to thirteen hours provided the pupil eventually learned to fly solo. After that each pupil qualified for a grant enabling him to fly a few hours each year. Throughout we were limited by the amount of subsidised instruction we could give. The scheme produced air-minded amateur pilots rather than fully trained airmen, but at Liverpool we got them flying solo by the hundreds in the end. Apart from the very few who couldn't take to flying on account of nerves, air-sickness or obvious temperamental instability, we trained them all to fly. It was to our advantage that they were young, fit and keen as mustard. They must have learned something, as not a single Air Guard pupil damaged any of our planes in the slightest way though we trained more than any other Flying Club in the whole country.

To me this was thrilling work. I found it impossible not to be infected by the fanatical enthusiasm of these pupils for whom the scheme literally opened up a new vista.

Rather exceptional weather conditions must prevail for all *ab-initio* flying instruction, and in winter, along Merseyside, these conditions were seldom present. The high, swirling winds made it impossible to attempt to teach landings, and the bumpiness often put the pupil off by upsetting his stomach. In the usual stiff north-westerly winds which howl down the Mersey, the Tiger Moth would buck wildly, and it needed surer hands than those of a hesitant pupil. When it ceased to blow it often turned to fog, and a Liverpool fog is every bit as thick, chemical and unfriendly as the better-known London variant. However, if we could possibly see enough to get our planes in and out of Speke's vast greenness, a fog provided near ideal teaching conditions aloft. Fog is a phenomenon which hugs the ground. At two to three hundred feet the aviator bursts forth into calm air, blazing sunshine and into conditions which provide a perfect horizon with the sky and cloud divided as if by ruler and paint-brush.

On one occasion, after departing in thin fog and conducting a successful first lesson above the clouds with the usual keen young lad behind me, I headed back towards Liverpool to find it completely blotted out. I couldn't see a trace of the Mersey or any other familiar landmark. All I could see was a carpet of purest cotton wool. I made two probes towards where I knew Speke must lie, but the risks ahead were not worth taking.

To the south most of Cheshire was still visible, so I selected a golf course, and after making a dummy-run down to five feet or so to check that no hidden undulations or drains were in the way, I landed on a long fairway. I have a clear picture of noting a foursome on a tee almost alongside the landing spot I had selected. I suppose I landed about fifty feet to their right. By the time the Tiger had come to a standstill a few people appeared from nowhere. One of the first on the scene was a gardener who lost no time in telling me that he had been with the RFC in the First World War. He suggested I taxied my plane close to his master's garden. He was sure "they will look after you" as they were "nice people". This seemed friendly advice, so I carried out his instructions after telling him to hop onto the wing and show the way. Apart from everything else this got the plane off the fairway which it was blocking, and I wasn't sure that Lamps would appreciate "damage by golf-ball".

We used the telephone, were entertained by a mother and two pretty daughters about our own age, were given lunch and were almost sorry to depart when, after lunch, another phone call brought the information from Geoff that the fog had lifted a little. All this time the gardener had guarded the plane and kept the curious sightseers and golfers from climbing all over it. However, when we came to depart, I couldn't locate him. This meant that we would have to start the plane ourselves. I dared not allow the pupil to swing the propeller on this, his very first lesson, as prop-swinging was a tricky business at the best of times, and had resulted in quite a few "lost" hands over the years. Since I hadn't any aircraft chocks with me I also did not dare to start the engine with no one on board, as initially some engine throttle is required, and if I were to set this too far forward the plane would be liable to cut its way forward, through my person, as soon as the engine's cylinders fired.

There was nothing for it but to put the pupil in the plane and instruct him most carefully what to do with the magneto switches and with the throttle lever. Luckily he was an intelligent lad and he carried out his part of the starting drill to perfection. If, for example, he had opened the throttle instead of closing it as soon as the engine fired, he would have gone waltzing off with the aircraft, leaving his instructor decapitated and himself aloft on his first and obviously only flight. We returned safely. My trust in pupils was confirmed. . . .

I had become aware of, and was fascinated by, the psychological effect that piloting a plane had upon these young people. All were affected. The extroverts quietened down and the introverts opened up.

If there was a typical air-guard pupil it was the nineteen-year-old lad who had left school at fifteen and was now some kind of ill-paid assistant earning, perhaps, thirty shillings a week, yet having to contribute to the family income. He would arrive by bus or else on his one cherished possession, a bicycle, occasionally even by motorcycle. He wore either an ill-fitting suit or some kind of cheap, loose jacket. His hair would be literally glued back in a slick style. His equivalent today is the leather-jacketed motorcycle youth—the "ton-up" boy or the tough, near-Ted with long hair, drain-pipe jeans and pointed shoes. But in those days, before the affluent society, although the same individualistic spirit was there, lack of material means compelled the pre-war youth to cut a sorry figure. He gave the impression that life had already got him down, and, in defiance, he assumed a brash manner belying the lack of self-confidence he really felt. But there was some spark deep inside him. The Civil Air Guard Scheme helped his confidence to grow, and turned the spark to flame.

Flying is a mental and physical release, also a mental and physical challenge. It demands much and gives more. I like to think that every pupil felt what I myself felt. At times I would get lost in the wonder of it. I would become aware that we were apparently alone in the vast empty chambers of space, above the grime and noise and nerves of the city. The engine's steady drone would be sounding endlessly into eternity—into infinity—like the ripples in a pond after a stone had been dropped. At these moments time would stand still and I felt that I was the first person in all creation about to alight upon an earth still warm from birth.

"Shall I do another turn, sir?" would bring me back from such daydreams.

Whatever the "magic" was, I am convinced that these pupils underwent important changes. Their backs straightened, they lifted their chins a little higher and a new gleam came into their eyes. After they had achieved a little mastery of the Tiger Moth they ceased to look upon life as a hopeless, losing struggle against forces beyond their control. In flying they found something new and challenging: something different from their normal pleasures of beer, football, fags, smuttiness and grub.

Days, weeks and months went by. I was made welcome again and again by the kind people of Lancashire, and when I went off in April to France once more, this time to get married in the tiny English church at Nice, the club gave me a week's holiday and sent one of those enormous telegrams full of good wishes and double meanings. It bore the stamp of having been composed at the bar by a group infused with good ale and inspired by Rabelais. My wife was made welcome at Liverpool, and back at the flying club life resumed its former routine.

War was threatening once again, and as I flew over the countryside I saw much evidence of late preparation hastily undertaken. Huge shadow aircraft factories, including one on the edge of Speke itself, were being assembled, and whole hillsides were being removed so that vast underground bomb-proof fuel storage tanks could be installed. New bomb storage areas with each enclosure insulated from the others by rectangular earth mounds were also easily recognised from aloft.

Italy had seized Albania and the Rome-Berlin axis was now fully operational. Czechoslovakia had been completely swallowed. Hitler's arrogance had little to contain it. In desperation the awakening British government had given categorical guarantees to go to war if either Rumania or Poland was attacked; and income tax soared to an unprecedented peacetime rate as defence estimates doubled and doubled again.

Much of this was over my head. I felt so good. I had a job which I loved. I was working for a man I deeply respected and who was friend, counsellor and daily companion. I was twenty-two, just married, living in my first-ever own home—a flat within Sefton Park; I was with my lovely young bride and summer was in the air.

I remember once arguing in a friendly way with Geoff and saying that "it didn't matter to me if the Germans did take over all Europe including England". My point was that they would still need pilot instructors and that they were basically of the same Saxon stock as ourselves. How little did I know! I blush now at my own naïveté. One's judgment is fickle when full of the springtime of happiness. I was, when I thought about it, still a conscientious objector of sorts, and I was troubled by my past action in having joined the RAFVR. When I tried to get out of this Reserve I found it now wasn't easy to do so. So I didn't press my withdrawal efforts.

My most unforgettable day at Liverpool was that following the *Thetis* disaster. HMS *Thetis* was a new type submarine which disappeared whilst on a commissioning trial. It had on board not only its full naval complement but almost as many shipyard workers, officials and ceremony celebrators. Nearly a hundred men had disappeared under the waves.

Someone got me out of bed early to take part in the big air search which started at first light. The submarine had last dived not far away from Liverpool, somewhere off the Cheshire coast.

By the time I reached the airfield the news had come through that *Thetis* had been sighted by a passing airliner partially submerged offshore near Anglesey. A couple of men had managed to get out via their escape apparatus but the rest were still trapped, as only the tip of the sharp-edged bow now protruded above the sea.

Speke airfield was alive with journalists, photographers and the like, and I set forth with a photographer on board and my head full of conflicting reports as rumour and fact tumbled over each other. The BBC had given "off Anglesey" and thus it was to Anglesey on a misty morning with visibility in yards rather than miles that I first flew. I flew high, keeping well clear of the haze below, and noted that I could just see through the greyness, provided I put the sun behind me and provided I looked straight down vertically. Slant-angle visibility was zero.

Over Anglesey the mountains of the Isle of Man were plainly visible in the distance and I flew towards these. As luck would have it, I happened to glance seawards at a time when a destroyer was producing a creamy wake. This, at least, was something of interest and was definitely photogenic. I took my passenger down to investigate, and whilst trying to pick up the trail of the destroyer, I came right upon the thin black pencil of the *Thetis'* bow gently bobbing up and down in the water looking more like a marker buoy than a stricken submarine.

There was absolutely no sign of life, nor at that time was there anything else in sight. The scene was eerily placid. Having no radio, we had no means of knowing if the survivors had all been taken out. Visibility was very poor, and as I circled round I felt singularly useless. We took photographs and raced back to Speke.

It took about half an hour to return and I told all concerned of what I had seen. Geoff at once sent me out again with a different cameraman. Using the same tactics and having now the knowledge of how far away from Anglesey the *Thetis* lay trapped, I again managed to find the submarine, but only after three or four attempts. The visibility was now better and this time I saw at least one destroyer and several longboats standing by. There was also a man astride the sharply angled dark nose and he was wielding a tool of sorts. This was a cheering sight. We speculated with each other wondering if he was passing an air hose, tapping a message, securing a hawser or what?

We circled for about ten to fifteen minutes, coming down to within a few feet of the waves to take pictures. We waved encouragement and felt light-hearted and gay in the knowledge that so many lives would now be saved.

We were amused when a particularly big movement from below caused the man to leap off his precarious perch into the water. Apparently *Thetis* had bobbed down for a moment. Back again we raced to Speke and there we assured all that the rescue was properly in progress. Our guess was that a line was in the process of being secured to the submarine's nose, and that the destroyer would somehow draw the submarine alongside and would either cut a way in or would pass an air-line and then take *Thetis* in tow, possibly to the nearest beach only about a dozen miles away.

I made two or three other flights the same day, but in the failing visibility could see nothing other than an occasional glimpse of a rescue vessel, as there were now at least half a dozen or more in the area. *Thetis* had been pin-pointed and the navy were on the scene. This meant that urgency had lessened. I went out again near dusk in the club's Leopard Moth with two or three Press men on board, but again drew a blank. This was not really surprising, as almost no one else had seen the submarine all day—although our apron was full of planes which had poured in from as far away as London. The *Thetis* disaster was the biggest home news of that year. And disaster it turned out to be. Though the thought never for an instant crossed our minds at the time, the photographer and I had been, in fact, the last people to see the ill-fated submarine. When the rescuer jumped, and we had laughed, the *Thetis* had gone down to her watery grave.

Weeks later they located her, salvaged and beached her, and undertook the grisly task of removing the ninety-odd bodies still entombed.

12: Navigation Instructor

DURING the long days of summer, 1939, we worked harder and harder. Every evening the local pupils were free to come and we had difficulty in preventing them, whether they were booked for a flight or not. First solos were happening almost daily, and the club headed the list published in the *Aeroplane* of new A licence holders for the whole country. Sometimes at week-ends Geoff, Buster and I worked seven or eight hours a day, and despite the strain it was most satisfying and rewarding. The club was considering an expansion. There was talk of buying half a dozen of the latest trainers, the economical Moth Minor monoplanes.

Happy as I was, a gnawing restlessness gradually began to overtake me. The club committee once irked me because, at a time when Geoff was sick, I had taken it upon myself to send a pupil solo without his prior consent. Geoff knew it was all right and he wasn't annoyed. I suppose the club chairman was unaware of how closely we worked together. There was, as was natural, a bit of feeling that both Geoff and I spent too much of the club's time teaching the Civil Air Guard recruits to fly. It was useless for us to point out that, financially, we were giving the club a sounder balance sheet than ever before and that we always left one aeroplane free for club members. Their club was changing and the old members didn't like it.

The shadow factory at the far end of the airfield had by now completed its first Hudson bomber, and Geoff managed to get a flight in it. It flew easily enough but the modern array of instruments in it had somewhat bewildered him. Aviation was growing apace and this small incident reminded me that I was not, in the aviation sense, acquiring new knowledge. And not to be learning was, in a manner of speaking, the same as losing ground in such a fast-developing industry as aviation. Also I asked myself what had happened to my ambition to become an airline pilot?

In this mood I found a Board of Trade instructor who *guaranteed* to get me through the visual signalling and semaphore tests which alone stood between me and my 2nd N navigator's ticket. I went to him for about ten lessons in the evening and then applied to take the test. To my surprise I found that my tutor and the official examiner were one and the same man! I passed, applied for my licence and in due course received it. With this in my possession I knew my earning potential to be beyond the £350–400 that I was currently receiving.

I knew also that I lacked twin-engine experience and that every worthwhile airline would require me to fly larger aircraft. At about this time I heard that there was a government scheme which necessitated twin-engined night-flying and pilots were urgently wanted for this. The object was to provide a target for the searchlight teams which were rapidly being formed as an additional defence measure. Since the target aircraft had to fly over the city where the searchlight batteries were, it was a stipulation that the target aircraft had to have at least two engines.

"Army Co-op" work was the semi-official title of this scheme, and I learnt that pilots could earn at least £1 per hour for taking part. I checked with Geoff that I had the club's permission to fly for money at night and he put me in touch with Mrs. Ann Davidson who had a lien of sorts on a twin-engined GA Monospar. It was probably the smallest twin-engined type in the country but it seemed huge by comparison with the Tiger, Leopard or Fox Moths.

Ann Davidson was an unusual woman. She scorned make-up. She was quite young and businesslike and only too happy to be paid for giving me an hour's instruction in her Monospar. I was much looking forward to these Army Co-op exercises as they would benefit me threefold. They would line my pockets handsomely; they would give me the twin-engined experience I needed and they would give me night-flying experience as, apart from my one official B licence night flight from Croydon to Lympne, I had never flown at night. I was slightly put off this last when an experienced airline pilot, known to us all at the club, hit a tree one night coming in to land at our large airfield. He was badly hurt and the aircraft was wrecked. Nevertheless

I was preparing to try my hand at this Army Co-op exercise when other events intervened. I suddenly got myself another job.

I don't remember how it all started. Maybe Geoff suggested it to me or, more likely, Brooklands wrote to me to see if I was interested—or I let them know that I now had my 2nd N.

At any rate, Brooklands became my new employers and my job was to train RAF navigational pupils at the Brooklands-owned RAF Flying Training School at Sywell in Northamptonshire. I would be teaching navigation and would be flying the twin-engined Anson. The pay was £600 pa plus extra for night flying, free life insurance and other fringe benefits. This was riches indeed. As a job it was also in line with my airline ambitions. The requirements happened to be what I now had: a B licence, the 2nd N licence and membership in an RAF reserve. The terms were so good that many well-established airline pilots had given up their jobs to join this CANS or Civil Air Navigation School. Eric Starling, he who had landed in the streets of Calais, was one of these. He had surrendered the position of Chief Pilot of a small Scottish airline (Allied Airways) to join the CANS. And it was here that our long lasting friendship first started.

This mixture of civil and military flying training was an unusual but very practical one. The RAF were keen to see if pupils could learn their trade but were not so keen to welcome them to their ranks unless they were teachable. They solved this problem by accepting recruits on a trial basis and by sending them to a civil flying school where they were either taught to fly at an EFTS (Elementary Flying Training School) or to navigate at a CANS. The planes belonged to the RAF but the maintenance of them, the instructors, and the classroom work were all in the hands of civilians. Neither pupil nor instructor wore RAF uniform, although the pupil held some quasi-RAF rank such as pupil-pilot. The atmosphere was semi-military, in contrast to the complete informality of the flying club.

It must have been late July or early August 1939 when I moved down to Sywell near Northampton. This member of the Brooklands family was several times the size of the parent body, for not only were there about ten Ansons in our CANS but there were 20-30 Tiger Moths belonging to the companion EFTS. It was probably the largest flying training unit in the country.

I was lucky to find a few friendly faces. One was Bertie Smallman, an occasional visitor to Brooklands, and it was he who taught me to fly the Anson. I had described myself as a twin-engined pilot, somewhat glossing over the details of the hour I had spent with Ann Davidson and ignoring the fact that I had never flown her Monospar solo. I went along with the well-known belief that the Anson would prove to be "a piece of cake" to fly until I realised that I was expected to climb into it and fly it without any instruction whatsoever. At this I balked and rather grudgingly Bertie gave me one circuit before leaving me to "make a few landings, etc".

The aircraft seemed as big as a cathedral and it had many devices completely strange to me. To start with it had differential air brakes, an artificial horizon, a directional gyro, wing flaps for additional lift during landings and take off, and a retractable undercarriage. It was also the first aircraft I had been inside which had a proper door, rows of windows, a control column instead of a joy-stick, a radio set, a clock, an instrument panel and engine gauges.

Another new instructor was engaged at the same time. He, too, had never flown anything resembling an Anson. Cooke was his name and I never did find out what his flying background was. I suspect it was even less comprehensive than my own, which was limited enough. There was a long pause after Bertie got out. Neither of us was exactly anxious to take over the vacant pilot seat. Taxi-ing back for the first take-off was a nightmare, as the asymmetrical use of the engines and the fierceness of the hissing air brakes caught me completely unawares. The aircraft flew easily enough but we approached to land at a flat angle, as we were hesitant to use the flaps. The airfield was ample and we each managed to get the Anson up and back a few times although we didn't dare to retract the undercarriage. It seemed altogether wrong to think of winding this up. Suppose we couldn't get it down again?

Not till I had been working with pupils for a couple of days did I dare to seize the handle and winch up the wheels. Personally I never did it again, as there were 144 stiff turns to be made: this clearly was a pupil's job!

I was now doing something completely different to what I had been doing in Liverpool. Instead of flying around the circuit most of the day, talking, teaching, persuading and trying to imitate Ken Waller's calm casualness, I was doing cross-country exercises across England.

I flew one "sortie" in the morning, another in the afternoon, each lasting about two hours. These pupils didn't have to know how to fly. They were there to learn to navigate by use of compass, drift sight, map-reading, course computing, DR plotting and wind computation. As I remember it, each pupil was given about fifteen such exercises interspersed with ground-school training on alternate days, and at the end of four to six weeks, depending on flying weather, the school said that they either would or would not be acceptable material for full training in the RAF.

A few were perpetually airsick. A few couldn't add up fast enough. Some didn't seem to know their left from their right and a few would not get down to hard work, but about 80 per cent passed. We flew fairly low under the clouds so that they could get accustomed to picking out landmarks on their maps. It was frequently bumpy at this height and at least 50 per cent were airsick on their first flight. But this usually wore off.

We took two pupils at a time, enabling one to plot on the chart whilst the other studied the maps and took drifts from the drift sight. The art of this kind of navigation is to ascertain the wind speed and direction and to find out by how much it affected the aircraft's track and speed. The drift sight enabled this angular displacement to be measured. Like a boat crossing a current, the 120 mph Anson in a wind would point in one direction but get blown off track. The wind also materially affected the speed of the aircraft over the ground, a fact which still confuses the air traveller today—who is often mystified to learn that whereas the Atlantic can be crossed in seven hours East to West (into the prevailing wind) it takes only five and a half hours coming back with the wind more or less behind the plane.

The navigator's key instrument is his watch. The aircraft's instruments enable him to tell with accuracy the air speed; time multiplied by air speed provides him with his mileage, leaving only the wind vector to be added. Directionwise the compass is all important. The aircraft's track is a result of compass heading plus or minus wind drift. By being able to recognise his position on the map, and knowing the heading and speed which have been flown since the last such "pin-point" position, a back calculation can be made to ascertain the wind speed and direction. Computers enable this to be done rapidly. Alternatively, triangles of velocities can be plotted on the chart itself. Quick thinking and quick arithmetic are the essential requirements, but without a sense of the obvious, or, common sense, no amount of quick responses can produce a satisfactory navigator. As with the Civil Air Guard flying pupil, so with the RAF navigation trainee—the human factor was all important.

In a week or two I got properly on top of this new job and was soon absolutely *au fait* with the dear, safe, wallowing Anson, possibly the most viceless aircraft ever designed. I had also leased a pleasant, detached house, bought myself a Rover car, bought a houseful of furniture, had carpets and curtains fitted, etc, hired a good servant and was settling down into a highly-paid interesting way of life when on September 1st, 1939, Hitler marched into Poland; and the world as I had known it flew into a million pieces.

13: The "Phoney War"

MUCH has been written about the rape of Poland, about Hitler's pitiful attempts to make his carefully prepared blitzkrieg look like a "defensive measure", and the subsequent struggle in which so many millions of people, and half the cities of Europe, were destroyed. But comparatively little has been written about the extraordinary "phoney" war which lasted until the time of the German attack on France through the Low Countries during the spring of 1940.

This six-month interlude was one of the strangest and most eerie periods in my life. War, however, touched me personally right away, as during the first few hours of war on the very first RAF raid (on the Kiel Canal) a Littlehampton friend of my own age was killed. Dick Vaughan-Williams was a young officer in the Wellington Squadron which got mauled by the hitherto little-known German fighter—the Me. 110. Casualty and death were then strange phenomena to both sides, and Dick was buried by his adversary with full military honours. Years later, when night after night sometimes hundreds of Allied airmen were to die over German soil, they were lucky to get buried at all.

But I am jumping ahead. When Poland was attacked on September 1st, Neville Chamberlain gave Hitler a 48-hour ultimatum. "Withdraw or else. . . ." No rational person expected a withdrawal, and since it was believed that the much vaunted Luftwaffe would promptly flatten London and our other cities as soon as the 48 hours expired, these two days were amongst the busiest in British history. Literally millions of children were evacuated to country areas; in the cities slit trenches were dug almost everywhere and anywhere, every kind of reservist was called up, the BBC filled the air with advice, warnings and instructions: the railways and postal services must have eclipsed all previous records. We were unprepared in detail, although to most of us the actual blow was not totally unexpected and we were reconciled in spirit that "this was it". No other honourable course was possible. Hitler had revealed his true self in full war-paint. That "bit of paper" which our Prime Minister had waved so triumphantly when returning from Munich the year before had categorically stated that Hitler had no more territorial aspirations in Europe. Now his armies were pouring across the Polish plains.

At 11 a.m. on September 3rd, 1939, Britain stopped whatever it was doing to listen to the voice of Neville Chamberlain on the radio. I shall never forget the sad, thick tones as he said, "This country is at war with Germany. . . . Now may God bless you all. May He defend the right. It is the evil things that we shall be fighting against—brute force, bad faith, injustice, oppression and persecution—and against them I am certain that right will prevail." Until the last shot was fired, I always remembered these words.

For our part, we at Sywell spent the first two days of September making our own preparations. We had learned that the very first raids the Luftwaffe made were directed at the training airfields in Poland. We were a training airfield—probably the largest RAF training unit of its kind—and it was our proud boast that our lovely white-painted club-house could be seen on a fine day from thirty miles away. Indeed, our pupil navigators spent much anxious time searching for it at the end of those exercises which terminated back at base. One of the first things we did was to start camouflaging the club-house.

The Brooklands organisation, by pre-arrangement, had agreed to concentrate its entire training empire at our airfield at Sywell, with the result that old friends like Duncan Davies himself, Ken Waller, dear old Brem (he who had sent me off into those scurrying clouds), little Pashley from Shoreham (even then about the oldest flying instructor in the country, who went on instructing for fifty-two years) and others poured into Sywell. Leslie Cliff, the elegant but aloof instructor-cum-skater, also arrived, and since he had no place to live, I was able to let him have our spare room which he shared with his beautiful wife and several large pedigree dogs.

Tiger Moths arrived from Brooklands, Shoreham, Blackpool, Storrington and Lympne until the airfield was a crowded and gay sight. Ex-RAF instructors on various Reserves also joined us.

Dispersal of aircraft became an immediate problem and our solution was to arrange for each instructor to take a Tiger Moth and fly it into a near-by field at the first warning that the enemy might be approaching. This was not practicable with the much larger Ansons so it was arranged that we would taxi these planes to the various edges of our airfield.

Thus it was that I never quite heard the end of Neville Chamberlain's most famous of all speeches. The air-raid siren abruptly finished it for us. To this day I have never heard an intelligent explanation of why it went off as it did almost all over the country a bare ten minutes after having been told we were at war, but the effect was electric. We seemed like actors in a movie as, in perfectly serene surroundings, we all abandoned the club-house lounge and rushed for our planes. The scene had an air of unreality. I felt that if I pinched myself hard I would wake up.

Tiger Moths were soon taking off in all directions and could be seen circling around looking for suitable fields not already occupied. Anson engines cannot be started by hand-swinging the propeller and it was some time before we had all found mechanics to hand-crank laboriously each of our Cheetah IX power horses. When under way I tried to hide the large, clumsy plane under the branches of a tree which stood on one side of the airfield.

After that there was nothing to do but wander away with my ground team and sit in the stubble of a corn field and smoke cigarettes, feeling a mixture of ridicule and desperation. I had been at war forty minutes during which I had undergone nearly the full gamut of emotions, pricked by occasional recollections that, as a conscientious objector, I shouldn't be there at all!

Uniform and rank created other problems. At 10.59 a.m. on the day the war started we had been a flying club. Ten minutes later all was changed. Mackenzie was our manager. His right-hand man was called Goldsmith. Bill Heywood was chief Anson pilot, and the civilian instructors at Sywell were divided between full-time Tiger Moth EFTS instructors, week-end, part-time EFTS Tiger Moth instructors, the Shoreham, Brooklands, Blackpool, Storrington and Lympne purely civil instructors, and ourselves, the CANS Anson pilots.

All the EFTS and CANS pilots were known to be on some sort of Reserve list, as such was a prerequisite for obtaining their jobs;

however, there were many kinds of RAF Reserves in those days, some of which required a uniform and others not. My RAFVR had never provided me with a uniform although I did have the rank of sergeant simply because everyone in the RAFVR who was a pilot had the rank of sergeant. We acquired this rank the day we were accepted. Luckily Mackenzie, as befitted the No. 1 man of the place, held a high-ranking Reservist title and he appeared as a wing-commander—a half stripe ahead of the next ranking man who happened to be a part-time instructor with a recent, distinguished RAF career. Duncan, the real boss of the whole Brooklands empire, could only muster the two stripes of a flight-lieutenant. Goldsmith, the Sywell No. 2, appeared as a flight-sergeant.

Some of the civilian instructors belonged to no Reserve so couldn't appear in any military guise. We found an RAF unit near by and, with others, I duly collected a sergeant's uniform. As I climbed out of my car, I happened to see Duncan—resplendent as a flight-lieutenant. I sprang out of the Rover and saluted as best I could. Duncan roared with laughter. This was not what I had been led to expect from my OTU days at Charterhouse, and I soon abandoned all attempts at saluting my new officers. The elongated Ken and rotund little Pashley were both roped into the RAFVR and they, too, soon appeared as sergeants.

But, in truth, we were, militarily, a shambles with rank all in the wrong places, and some instructors still wearing sports coats and grey trousers. Very few of us had actually passed the RAF wings exam, so strictly speaking we were not entitled to wear pilot's wings on our uniform. The position of flying instructors without wings was incongruous, so one day a strange, colourful character known as Blisso, one of our Anson pilots and an ex-British Airways airline pilot, went into town and simply bought about thirty pairs of wings which we all promptly had sewn in place. Some two years later I was informed that the *Gazette* had promulgated notification that Acting Flight-Lieutenant A Spooner, then on his second tour of operations, had officially been granted his wings!

About a month later by which time our CANS had become an (RAF) AONS (Air Observer Navigation School), by common consent, we all abandoned the idea of uniform and went back to our sports clothes. But not before we had given Air Chief Marshal Sir John Steel one of the most curious days in his career.

Sir John was one of the chiefs, if not the No. 1 of Training Command, and we were now part of his rapidly expanding organization. We were, in fact, by now wholly absorbed into the RAF. Hence his visit of inspection. For obvious reasons we could not provide him with any guard of honour or line of troops to inspect because we had neither. We had pupils and instructors who flew with them, and we had little else. To complicate matters Alex Henshaw, known to many of us as a celebrated racing and record-breaking civilian pilot, chose this same morning to visit us. This excellent amateur flyer had been snapped up by the Vickers-Supermarine group as an additional test pilot and had, in a very short time, come to be known as an exceptional Spitfire operator. There were already friendly arguments about who flew this fine aircraft in the more spectacular manner, Alex Henshaw or Jeffrey Quill.

Whilst Mac was entertaining Sir John Steel in the office, Alex announced his own arrival by a low-flying, high-speed "beat-up" of the airfield, flashing overhead at roof-top height. After spiralling upwards in a series of climbing rolls he appeared once more in another screaming dive, but this time in the inverted flight position, and as Sir John and Mac stepped out to see what the rumpus was all about, Alex flashed across the field so low that I thought his Spitfire tail had actually touched the grass. He was upside down doing about 250 mph.

These kind of manoeuvres were not normally carried out at any of Sir John's other training fields, and most certainly not on inspection day, when all was spit and polish and when flying was conducted strictly in accordance with "the book"!

As it was now nearing lunch Mac and Duncan Davies guided the rather irate Air Marshal towards our bar in the club-house. Here we were all having the mid-morning beers which we habitually enjoyed between flight sessions. This perfectly normal flying-club habit obviously appalled our visitor, accustomed as he was to the maxim that flying and alcohol didn't mix, and, indeed, were especially not to be mixed in the presence of pupils. However, he soon had a tankard of beer thrust into his hands, and "Skipper" Duncan was calling for his usual Haig and Haig Black Label. He also began to introduce Sir John to the various instructors who were chatting around. I was with Ken Waller and another intent upon solving the *Daily Telegraph* crossword.

"Meet Ken Waller," said a voice.

"Ken—Sir John Steel." The languorous Ken uncoiled and with his usual affability grinned his shy smile. "Pleased to meet you, old boy. . . . What'll you have?"

This was almost the last straw. Ken was, like myself, in a sergeant's uniform and his habitual "old boy" form of address was not that which the Air Marshal was accustomed to hearing from sergeants. He just about exploded and left the mess with Duncan and Mac in tow.

Later came the Orders. Officers and sergeants were *not* to mess together. Instructors were not to drink alcohol between lessons. Pupils were to be provided with one mess, sergeants with another, officers with a third. Nor could we even eat together. I don't know what he said about the Alex Henshaw Spitfire interlude but I expect it was uncomplimentary.

We were wondering how on earth to fulfil these orders when two things happened. First, we were all abruptly returned to civilian clothes and civilian rates of pay! (Upon mobilization I had abruptly dropped from a princely £600 pa plus benefits to a sergeant-pilot's 12s 6d per day.) And soon after this the Anson flight was detailed to fly up north to Blackpool, there to continue as an autonomous unit.

In those days we had to pinch ourselves to realise that a war was being waged. Poland was slaughtered so rapidly by the German war machine and invaded by Russia from the rear that in a matter of a very few weeks it had ceased to exist. Russia and Germany were left glaring at one another across a hastily drawn frontier dividing the old Polish state. No bombs fell on England and no enemy plane had even remotely approached us at Sywell. For a week or two we faithfully rushed to the airfield whenever the alarm was sounded and each took his plane to his favourite farm. We soon established personal friendships, and in farms all around Sywell, whenever the siren went, farmers' wives would put on the kettle, certain in their knowledge that within minutes a Tiger Moth would come in to land or, in my case, a familiar pilot would come striding across the field separating their land from the tree under which I now regularly dispersed an Anson.

Initially there had been other shocks, too. On the very day that war was declared an efficient RAFVR office machine had correctly located my address and sent me a posting notice directing me to attend as a pupil at a Tiger Moth training school near Newcastle. In their books I was a certain sergeant who had done some forty or so hours at the Fair

Oaks, Chobham, RAFVR School, and I was material for further rapid training. I took the notice to Mac who calmly told me to tear it up and forget all about it. Perhaps this was the start of the long administrative muddle which followed me until war had ended. I never seemed to have just *one* number. As a sergeant I started off as 740824 and soon learnt to bark out "824 Sir" on Fridays in order to get paid at the archaic, time-consuming pay parades. I also learnt that a sergeant is not allowed to pay his wife an allowance. This is the state's prerogative. So added to my own pay of 12s 6d per day, my wife had to collect so many shillings per week by cashing an official draft at a Post Office.

One day she said to me, "Isn't your number 740824?" When I nodded she then asked, "Why is it that they pay me my allowance as the wife of Sergeant Spooner, A, 740827?" I couldn't answer. I attributed the discrepancy to an obvious clerical error and was sufficiently amused about the possible marital complications which could ensue that I mentioned it to one of the officer instructors during a morning beer session. He had been an officer for some years and wisely advised me to write up and do something about it. The immediate result was that my wife now started getting *two* allowances, one as the wife of 740824 and the other still as 740827. This led to further correspondence which got more and more involved and which was only settled in June 1940 by the RAF's decision to grant me a Commission. Until that date, the extra allowances arrived as fast as I could send them back.

I was clearly *very* honest in those days!

On thinking back to those first few months of war I chiefly remember the idyllic autumn weather. Never could I recall a fairer October. Clear, brilliant days, with the fine white tracings of the fighters wheeling in practice overhead, were followed by star-filled nights and the enormous harvest and hunter moons. England never seemed more fragrant, more peaceful or more lovely.

On the ground we were like actors playing out some weird unrehearsed masquerade as we attempted to sort out our uniforms, our "wings" badge, our mess problems and the like. Rationing was virtually non-existent, though petrol had begun to be a problem.

The principal change in our duties was that we kept away from the North Sea coast and arranged all our flights to start west. Otherwise we had the same pupils, the same aircraft and the same syllabus. We were not actually expecting to meet the enemy in the air over Britain at that time, but we were scared, and rightly so, of our own Fighter Command defences. The balloons, too, began to rise around key railway junctions, aircraft factories and the like, and we viewed these strange monsters with trepidation and suspicion (as did every RAF pilot throughout the war). No one knew exactly what would happen if we flew into the invisible trailing cables, but I, for one, had no intention of risking the encounter. The Anson's wings were all wood and were obviously not made for such an engagement. But we were even more frightened at the prospect of being shot down by our own forces. Somehow this seemed the most futile and ghastly fate of all: but it was very likely to happen if we strayed too near the prohibited areas, which grew like a rash, making red blotches all over our aviation maps. One of our ex-Brooklands colleagues, a person known to us all, Tony Reid, if my memory serves me correctly, was shot down by our own Hurricanes *twice* before the end of 1939.

The first time he was flying a Hampden and the second time a Lockheed Hudson. The second occasion was hair-raising. He was unable to get out and thus was prevented from using the parachute which had saved him earlier. As the burning plane plunged earthwards the fuel tanks eventually exploded with such force that the aircraft disintegrated in mid-air, solving Tony's urgent problem of how to escape. He survived, but I did hear that he lost his enthusiasm for flying for quite some while.

14: Blackpool 1940

IN all I spent nearly a year in Blackpool. We and our Ansons were now based on an airfield hastily prepared out of the old racecourse at the south end of the esplanade. This was renamed RAF Station, Squire's Gate.

During the year I spent there the "phoney war" gave way to the real thing. Russia tested her might against tiny Finland. Quisling betrayed Oslo and Norway fell to the Germans. The ill-fated Narvik expedition followed.

We had little time to digest this lesson before the enemy struck at France through the Low Countries. Chamberlain, the man of peace, fell and gave way to a National Government, which put aside party differences to serve under Churchill's dynamic leadership. The "impregnable" Maginot Line was turned and then overrun; the BEF, our new Model Army in France, was thrust aside; Belgium capitulated, and with unbelievable swiftness France, and her huge land army, which had fought so long and hard in World War I, collapsed from within. Dunkirk followed, and as the last of our depleted forces staggered ashore in tatters the skies over southern England became filled with the roar of Heinkels and Dorniers, Junkers and Messerschmitts.

The RAF alone stemmed the tide, and with their victory over Goering's greatly feared Luftwaffe our spirits revived and we listened spellbound to frequent doses of Churchillian prose with which the radio filled our homes.

Down came the bombs, on our ports, our aircraft factories, our airfields, and then upon the capital itself. Day after day, week after week, London became the objective of the enemy's frustration and rage, and as the Londoners withstood the onslaught and the people of

Britain rejected Hitler's "last plea to reason" the shock wave of our resistance began to travel around the world. America still sat on the fence, but she now watched us with a growing admiration and a new awareness. She did what she could to help without actually committing herself. The grey waters of the Atlantic had become the graveyard of hundreds of Allied ships, and Roosevelt reminded his people that these same waters washed America's eastern seaboard.

Whilst these terrible and tragic events were shaping human destiny practically nothing happened to change the even tenor of our lives at the RAF Station, Squire's Gate, Blackpool. We were now designated No. 2 School of General Reconnaissance, and with this change we learned that we were in Coastal Command. We went back into uniform and reverted to Service pay on January 1st 1940.

Our unit grew in size, doubling itself again and again. We acquired an Establishment and we observed with wonder the influx of cooks, orderlies, drill-sergeants, store-keepers, parachute-packers, MT drivers, guards, airfield defence personnel, clerks, WAAFs, armourers, fitters, riggers and the like. Men began to stamp around drill squares and we learned to throw salutes at each other in passing. But for all this, and for all the world-shattering events taking place around us, we, the original dozen civilian instructors, just kept on doing exactly as we had done before. Now our navigational exercises took us over the Irish Sea and we taught our keen young recruits the arts of navigating over sea as well as over land. We flew more often, too.

We all lived away from the station, as the old grandstand which served as our Station HQ provided no sleeping accommodation. At first we gathered ourselves together with our families in one or two small but pleasant seaside hotels on the South Shore district of the famous resort. From here we were within five minutes of our airfield. This was a great asset as strict petrol rationing was now in force.

One day a Commissioning Board arrived and I was detailed to appear before them. Henceforth I wore the smoother blue of an officer and the half ring of a pilot-officer (acting) on my sleeve.

Blackpool without its crowds is a pleasant place to live, especially as at this stage it had never witnessed an air-raid. My wife and I left the convivial atmosphere of the hotel and moved to a pleasant house just behind the South Shore funfair. The funfair was still open for business and at the Casino restaurant nearby we could still eat well.

My life assumed a regular pattern. I cycled or took a tram to the airfield, arriving there at 9 a.m. I flew a morning detail, came home for lunch or sometimes joined the others in a nearby pub. I flew an afternoon detail and I was home again soon after 5 pm. Occasionally, a particularly fierce north-westerly gale would keep our aircraft on the ground, otherwise we flew every day, and not until a week in August, when the Battle of Britain was at its very height, was I given any leave. Then, unexpectedly and almost apologetically, we spent a quiet but wet week in a peaceful fold of the Westmorland hills. Here an RAF pilot was a rarity, and since RAF pilots were already the glamour boys of Press and radio I was treated as a hero, although I had never seen an enemy plane, dropped a bomb or heard one drop, fired a gun in anger or done anything radically different from what I had been doing before the war began.

As summer faded and the long evenings began to draw in, the daylight attacks on Britain began to peter out, and the night raids upon Coventry, London and elsewhere took their place. It was then that the original group of ex-civilian pilots at Blackpool began to break up. We were by now in a minority, as dozens of regular RAF pilots had since come to join us. Two of our number were posted away for night-fighter training and I applied to join them. This task seemed to demand qualities which I possessed and I liked the idea of fighting in defence of a burning, blasted London. Also I still held qualms about dropping bombs. I was, of course, incensed by the enemy raids upon London, Coventry and elsewhere, but if these were the acts of butchers and murderers as the papers claimed, what did that make the pilots of the RAF when they did likewise? What was Essen other than the Coventry of Germany? Why was it a crime to bomb London streets, but not a crime to bomb Cologne?

Nothing came of my application and it began to appear that the rest of us would continue as instructors, though no longer at Squire's Gate. An aircraft factory had sprung up at the inland end of our airfield, the famous Lytham St Anne's golf course had been requisitioned and Squire's Gate Airfield, a small, narrow grass field, as we knew it, was to be put to other uses. Our unit, now a huge one, was to be split into two, with one half moving to George, at the tip of South Africa, and the other section moving to Prince Edward Island, Canada, in the mouth of the St Lawrence River. I was secretly informed that this latter was to be my destination.

During the busy weeks that followed we packed our belongings, obtained a release from our house contract, sold the Rover car, enquired about Canada, and, learning that we could both go, obtained the necessary visas, inoculations, permits, passports, etc. Whilst awaiting details of our passages from Liverpool my posting was abruptly cancelled. I never found out why, but it could have had something to do with an incident at the airfield which happened at about that time.

I had the misfortune to knock my Commanding Officer into some very wet mud! I was landing in pouring rain, peering through the wiperless glass screen, when I spied a figure taking a short cut across the grass. This was dangerous and strictly forbidden. To teach the miscreant a lesson I side-slipped the Anson directly at the figure, kicking off rudder only at the last split second. This had the desired effect. The man broke into a hasty run, slipped and fell. The pupils and I enjoyed this spectacle as the grass field was a quagmire. I felt grimly pleased with the practical lesson I had handed out until summoned to appear before the CO "at once". He was a fierce-looking ex-World War I regimental sergeant-major, commonly called "Woof-woof" from his habit of barking at people in gruff stentorian tones.

"Come in!" he roared to my knock on his door.

As I entered I knew the worst. The wing-commander was plastered with mud. I was a very junior officer and I don't think I helped matters by telling him that it was all his own fault and that he was courting disaster by walking across the landing path under such poor visibility conditions.

Three days later a posting notice arrived. A young flying officer called Sandy and myself were to proceed at once to No. 10 OTU at Bassingbourne in Essex, where we were to learn to fly Wellington bombers prior to joining PRU.

Since Sandy was a non-smoking, non-drinking, conscientious Scot who never did anything wrong, it was hard to equate his posting with mine, if mine was, in effect, some kind of punishment. Also Eric Starling and Blisso received posting notices at about the same time. They, too, were to go to a Wellington Operational Training Unit, but not for PRU purposes. The cause for the posting must remain a matter for speculation. What was certain was that my wife and I were definitely "off the boat". We were no longer bound for Canada and, ominously, I was to learn to fly a bomber.

I had to ask a dozen regular RAF officers before I could find one who knew anything about PRU. The unit was new and rather "hush-hush". The initials, I eventually learnt, stood for Photographic Reconnaissance Unit. Its pilots flew over enemy-held territory in unarmed Spitfires specially prepared for height and speed, qualities which alone protected them.

"PRU," my informant told me, "doesn't fly Wellingtons or anything remotely like them. It must be a mistake. Or," he added as an afterthought, "they are working upon something entirely new."

This news cheered Sandy and I a lot. We liked the idea of taking part in something new. "But what?" we asked one another. Our first theory was that the PRU would arm Wellingtons to the teeth and, protected by extra guns and encased in armour, we would have to blast our way through to photograph objectives. This was a grim prospect. But we later thought it far more likely that our Wellingtons would be used only at night, when presumably we would take photographs by the light of some enormous flash bombs.

Although I didn't much fancy our chances if our first theory was correct, I was, on the whole, pleased, as I could now safely dismiss my earlier fear that I was to be trained for Bomber Command. PRU, I had been assured, was an off-shoot of Coastal Command, in much the same manner as was our school of general reconnaissance at Blackpool.

The Wellington, with her slightly old, ambling sister the Whitley and the smaller, less commodious Hampden, was then the backbone of our growing night-bombing forces, which were already hitting back at enemy towns and targets. The large four-engine bombers, the Stirlings, Halifaxes and Lancasters, were not yet delivered in any great numbers. I didn't mind, as I felt fairly at home with the idea of flying the Wellington, since I had watched her early development at Brooklands two years earlier. Nor do I recall feeling upset at being removed from the Prince Edward Island list.

I think I had begun to feel myself a bit of a fraud wearing RAF wings, yet remaining in comfort far removed from the real theatres of action. Churchill had built up my morale from the low ebb to which it had fallen when France collapsed. Within limits, I was eager to join battle with the foe. I had taken the epic feats of the RAF to heart and I was proud to wear their pilots' wings. Though I couldn't conceive how it was at all possible to win the war, since Hitler now held all the aces, I was, nevertheless, in full agreement with the Press, the radio, and the people of our islands that Britain must fight on alone until somehow "right would triumph". The "evil things, the bad faith and the brute force" which Chamberlain had told us about were now in plain evidence. We knew about the refugees. We had seen Hitler's treachery unmasked. We had an inkling of his tyrannical aims and we were beginning to understand what bestiality his "final solution" to the Jewish problem involved. I wasn't dead sure what I was fighting FOR, but I had no doubts at all as to what I was fighting AGAINST. Hitler and his followers were a stain on civilisation and one that somehow had to be removed.

Britain, in spite of shortages, discomforts, bombs and defeats, was a splendid place in which to live in 1940. There was a purpose and zest in the air, and the more that Hitler and Goering threw at us from the air, and from their U-boats at sea, the more determined and more closely-knit did we become. It is true that I had been on "easy street" throughout, but this was not from choice. The abrupt change in my plans fell like seed upon fallow ground. My own "phoney war" had gone on for too long. I was fit, and I was ready to fight on a personal basis, and it was my private prayer that when my moment of truth arrived I would not be found lacking at a time when others in air force blue were winning the acclaim of the free-thinking world.

15: Strange Happenings and Postings

AFTER receiving the posting order I had to undo the departure arrangements I had previously made for my family. I decided that my wife would remain in Blackpool whilst my training courses took place, especially as no one could tell me where next I would be sent.

It so happened that Eric, Blisso, Sandy and I all left Blackpool together. None of us knew what lay ahead. But we all knew that we would be getting closer to the real shooting war. The journey southwards confirmed this. The crowded train had stopped at a little known junction in the Midlands on a winter's evening when we heard "All change".

So out we trooped to learn that all the lines to London were blocked and that no more trains would be going that way that evening. The blitz had played havoc with the railway system.

We ascertained that "There *might* be a train for Derby: there *might* be a train for Northampton later on." It all sounded very vague and uncertain. Northampton suited us fine. None of us had visited Sywell since we had departed there a year before, but we knew several pubs where we could be sure of a bed and a good welcome. However, the railway staff were not able to say definitely if a train would be going there and, if so, at what time.

"What about this little chap?" said Eric, pointing at an ancient, tall-funnelled engine with a single carriage behind it.

"He can't go no place tonight, 'cause the driver's based here and he would have to pay for his night's lodgings elsewhere."

"Suppose we paid for it," persisted Eric, now more serious, "would he then take us all to Northampton?"

In almost no time it was arranged! We would pay him 22s 6d. In return he would drive us in his little train to where we wanted to go. I was flabbergasted, I couldn't help but wonder how it was that such a private deal could be made without risk of head-on collisions. Central control of the railways had almost ceased, so great was the damage around London. Local control was in force and somehow goods and passengers were kept moving towards their destinations without catastrophe.

Our triumph was, however, short-lived, as a larger group wanting to reach Leicester "outbid" us for our special train! But we did eventually get to Northampton that night, and there we duly drank away the memories of the day's frustrations.

It was late next evening by the time Sandy and I arrived at the railway station nearest to the RAF Station, Bassingbourne. We were now a further day late, so reported by phone to the Adjutant and begged transport to his station. Sandy and I also duly reported at his office wearing our "best blue" by 9 a.m. the following morning.

He had never heard of us. He didn't know what we had come for. He didn't have facilities to train us. He had never even heard of PRU. We hadn't thought to bring our posting notice with us so were almost persuaded that we had read it incorrectly. By that evening we were on a train again, heading towards London, but this time we carried a copy of the order that Bassingbourne had given us. We were now going to a Wellington OTU at Lossiemouth, far, far away in the North of Scotland.

The train stopped some twenty to thirty miles from London and we soon saw why. The sky overhead was criss-crossed with searchlight beams and pock-marked by the bursting of AA shells: and the glow of huge fires on the ground lit the horizon. With the dawn our train probed its way slowly forward to St Pancras, where a great job of clearing up was in progress. The glass roof was full of missing panes, and a dirty, depressing drabness hung over everything. But the WVS women were busy passing tea around and, in spite of the rubble, which handicapped every endeavour, the railways were still carrying on. Before long we were again in another overcrowded train heading northwards for Edinburgh.

All war-time trains were stuffed to capacity with uniformed men, carrying arms, gas-masks and longrolls of luggage. These trains were invariably unheated and were as cold as a damp bog on a winter's night. The engines used inferior coal and the trains jerked and swayed alarmingly, giving the impression that all their experienced drivers must have been called up for other duties. A few of the passengers found seats; the rest squatted on their kit-bags. If eventually you gained a seat you slumped into it, inhaled the thick acrid tobacco smoke and soon fell into a series of disrupted cat-naps as the train jerked its way forward. The windows were blacked out at night and very seldom open at other times. The light bulbs had been "nicked" and the toilet was permanently in use with a fidgeting queue outside. For food we fought for tea, pies and buns on various platforms.

By the following dawn I had been in one such train or other for the best part of the four days since I had left Blackpool and I now possessed a corner seat and was in a deep slumber, when Sandy woke me up so that I could admire the Forth Bridge. He had, upon crossing the Border, reverted to a long forgotten Scottish accent and was in fine fettle. It was belting with rain and I had a retching feeling in my very empty stomach and a taste of butterflies fried in nicotine in my mouth. I cursed him hideously. Sandy dismissed the rain as an "Easterly haa", whatever that might be.

By nightfall after various transfers, we found ourselves on a Highland railway, some twenty of us squatting in a guard's van! A fur-clad lady of quality was bemoaning the fact that she had a first-class ticket! A tiny engine was labouring to pull several hundred of us up the steep gradients. It would have been possible to trot alongside so slowly did we labour. Eventually, the clickety-click of the wheel against the rail quickened and soon we were hurtling down the other side, gathering momentum in spite of the squeals and groans from the brakes beneath us. In the dead of night we arrived at our destination. Actually, it was 8 a.m., but by then the authorities were retaining Summer Time or Double Summer Time in the midst of winter, on the grounds that it worked wonders with the cows. It almost eliminated all morning light up in Scotland in December, one always had breakfast in the dark.

RAF Station Lossiemouth had never heard either of us or of the PRU. They didn't know why we had come; nor could they think what to do with us. They trained Wellington *crews.* A crew was a captain and five others. We were two—both claiming to be captains at that.

This time we had an order to wave at them, and we were not in a mood to be put off lightly. Sandy had come home to Scotland, and whatever else was in store for us, he intended to be trained there.

After much useless hanging about we were eventually put in charge of a Sergeant Instructor B. He was to teach us to fly the Wellington. This poor fellow had been hustled through various war-time training units at such a pace that he had found himself on operations against the enemy with only the haziest idea of how to fly any aircraft. The Wellington, in particular, clearly terrified him: so he had been posted from his squadron to the only post-operational job available. He was made an instructor at an OTU. Every operationally-expired pilot followed this same procedure. The theory was that if you survived flying against the enemy then you were the obvious person to teach others.

Sergeant B first told us that whatever we did we must *never* attempt more than a "rate 1 turn" by day and a "rate ½ turn" at night. These were such gentle manoeuvres as to be ridiculous, and since I had seen the early Wellingtons flung all over the sky even to the point of being barrel-rolled by Mutt Summers of Vickers, I was not impressed by this warning. Later, he demonstrated how to fly the aircraft. After his every landing, invariably made by motoring the aircraft against the flaps on a long, horrible low approach, the poor sergeant was bathed in perspiration.

Later Sandy and I were allowed to take an aircraft to the station's satellite airfield, called the Bogs of Maine, and there we gradually taught ourselves how versatile the Wellington really was. It was never lively, but it could be made to turn as steeply as most other aircraft. We found, too, that it would just fly on one engine alone, and that provided no attempt was made to motor it against a full flap setting, it responded and landed normally. We learnt that it would never be as simple to handle as an Anson, but we suspected that no aircraft ever would be. Finally, we got passed out by the squadron leader, who (rather late in the day), came to befriend us, and was at once delighted by Sandy's precise instrument flying.

After completion of the Wellington training at Lossiemouth, I was given a week's leave. We packed up the house at Blackpool, put our furniture into store for the rest of the war, and took ourselves to a hotel at Wallingford, the village nearest to the RAF Station at Benson—the home of the PRU. We were without a car. We proceeded there by train, changing stations for the last time at Reading, a detail which was soon to become significant for me.

At Benson I reported to my flight-lieutenant. He was an Australian called Daish, if I recall the name correctly, and I liked him at once. He was the first of many down-to-earth Australian pilots I was to meet during the next few years. He addressed Sandy and me.

"Where are you from?"

"No. 20 OTU—Lossiemouth." A frown creased his brow.

"No. 20 OTU, eh? What do they fly, Battles or Harvards?"

"Neither, sir, they fly Wellingtons."

"Wellingtons! Jesus wept! You two jokers know what you got to fly here?"

"Wellingtons?" we enquired hopefully, but without much confidence.

"No, son! Here, it's Spitfires all the way."

As Sandy and I looked at one another with astonishment Daish got down to practical matters.

"Now, let's get some facts down on paper: Your ages? How many hours? What types have you flown? Know anything about navigation, or photography?"

In about two minutes he had obtained our essential details. He swiftly made up his mind.

"You'll do," he said. "The Spit is easy enough to handle—the photography is child's play. You've got the essential navigation experience and you've bags more hours than anyone else here—including myself. So how about it? Want me to send you back or will you two jokers go along with me?"

His easy approach was impossible to resist. We became part of his team.

"Normally," he said, "I like to check out my new boys on our Harvard trainer, but in your case it wouldn't be fair, seeing as how you've never flown one at all—anyhow, someone pranged the Harvard last week, so that's that: I'll find you a Spit and let you try it out for yourself."

Thus it was that I found myself in a completely strange aircraft, utterly different from anything I had ever flown before, taxi-ing downhill through sticky mud with my head full of last-minute admonitions and instructions. I wasn't to taxi downhill too fast, or the nose would tip over. I was to watch the radiator temperature gauge to see that it kept below the red-line. The best climb speed was 140; the gear had to be pumped up with my right hand and this would mean changing hands after take-off. I had to watch for some take-off swing as the power from the Rolls-Royce Merlin was great. I had about one hour's petrol and the rest I would find "more or less obvious". I felt like a new boy at school, half-scared, half-excited.

By the time I had the Spitfire turned into wind the radiator temperature was way beyond the red limit mark and it showed no sign of cooling down. I was at a loss to know what to do. I chanced it and went. It was a shockingly bad decision, but luck was with me and the engine soon cooled off in the air as I had hoped.

The great surge of power and acceleration took my breath away as I had never before experienced anything remotely like this. After take-off, I changed hands and pumped the wheels up, raised the flap-lever, adjusted radiator shutters and oil-cooler doors, kept a good, fast climb speed, ran over the instruments once more and now, feeling slightly more at home, I glanced over my shoulder to see where I was, relative to the airfield. But this was no Tiger Moth, Anson or Wallowing Wellington, sedate aircraft which climbed away at under 100 mph and at less than 500 feet per minute. I was now in a Spitfire, doing 180 or more, and was soaring upwards at 2,500 feet per minute. With a shock I discovered that I was 7,500 feet above thin broken cloud, and there was no sign of Benson or of any other airfield. I was lost, and I realised with hot embarrassment, that I had no maps on board and had only the haziest notion of where Benson lay.

The next twenty minutes were agonising. First, I had to get underneath the clouds, then I had to find out where I was, and finally I had to find a way back to Benson. And all the time I had to keep the sharpest possible look-out for the dreaded balloon-barrages. Eventually, I located the main E-W railway lines out of London, and from these was able to pin-point the Huntley and Palmer biscuit factory at Reading—an easily recognisable mark I had learned from Brooklands days. From here I followed the branch line up to Wallingford, and just to make sure I flew as low as possible over this village and read the name of the George Hotel, where I was living. Thence I followed the road up to Benson.

Had I not gone to Wallingford by train I doubt very much whether I would ever have found my way back to base.

Apart from the fact that Sandy landed once with the wheels up instead of down, he and I took readily, both to the Spitfire and to the job, for which we seemed well-suited by virtue of our navigational experience. Daish proved to be a first-rate leader too. These particular Spitfires flew high and fast, having been completely stripped of arms and armour. With their high-speed they were reckoned to be invulnerable. They were painted pale green or deep blue, and were kept highly polished to give them extra speed. Not in a hundred years could I have found a job more suited to my training and personal inclinations.

Sandy and I had to have a pressure-chamber test at the RAF School of Medicine at Farnborough. Neither of us had ever used oxygen before, and as they pumped us to 40,000 feet at a rate of climb of 7,000 feet per minute, Sandy became doubled up with an attack of "the bends" and I passed out cold. We were both failed for PRU work. A kindly doctor told us how the release of nitrogen bubbles attacked our weakest points: "In Sanderson's case it attacked his stomach . . . in Spooner's case, his brain!"

But before we left Benson I had one more incident. I was asked to fly down to Exeter to pick up a PRU pilot who had been forced down there with a damaged aircraft. The only plane available was a Tiger Moth. After the Spitfire, this aircraft seemed almost stationary, but I eventually arrived at Exeter in appalling weather, only to learn that the pilot whom I had come to collect had sensibly departed by train, It was the kind of day when even the birds preferred to walk. After a hasty lunch in the mess, I departed back, but was soon forced by lowering cloud to "navigate" along the railway lines. This was a dangerous business in war-time, as the junctions were apt to be guarded by balloon barrages. However, in the rain and low clouds no other course was open. Once again I eventually located Reading, and then took the branch line northwards to Wallingford. It was now past 4 pm on the shortest and darkest day of the year. From Wallingford I set course for the three miles to Benson, but after about one minute I came to a point where cloud and rising ground practically met. I was flying dangerously low in gathering gloom. I hastily turned back. On a second attempt I tried to follow the road along which I daily travelled to work. Again I had to beat a retreat when within a mile or so of Benson. It was now almost totally dark, so with the last rays of light and still in pouring rain, I side-slipped the aircraft safely into a farmer's field.

I remember well the phone call which followed. I hadn't been able to contact Flight-Lieutenant Daish, so was put through to an officer of higher rank, who asked my name.

"Spooner, sir, one of the new PRU pilots."

"And you are where?"

"In a field, sir."

"Are your photographs OK?"

"I haven't got photographs, sir. I'm only flying a Tiger Moth. It's not damaged, sir."

"A Tiger Moth! What on earth are you doing in a Tiger Moth, and where did you say you were?"

"In a field, sir . . . one mile south of the airfield."

"ONE MILE away. Do you mean to say you couldn't fly ONE MILE?"

I had had about four or five hours in the air, in an open cockpit in pouring rain. I had been scared stiff on what turned out to be a futile errand. I was wet, frozen and depressed. I believe I told him to look out of his "bloody windows" before asking any more damn-fool questions, and hung up.

Next day I had to submit various reports in triplicate. Next day, too, the same senior officer elected to fly the aircraft home, but he had the misfortune to get the aircraft into an inverted flat spin. This is the one manoeuvre from which a Tiger Moth cannot readily be extricated. He had no option but to bail out at about 5,000 feet. He landed safely by parachute, the aircraft crashing near by.

What kind of reports in triplicate he then had to put in I don't know. But to have to explain why he bailed out at 5,000 feet during a flight of only one mile is not a task that I personally would relish.

After this incident Sandy and I just did nothing. We were awaiting yet another posting instruction. We had had the stigma of "failed" branded upon us. My wife and I spent a lonely Christmas in that Wallingford hotel. My future was clouded and unknown. We were far from friends or family. The war seemed interminable. The weather was wet and cold. Uncertainty and gloom hung in the air.

That Christmas 1940 was perhaps our personal "darkest hour".

16: My First Crew

SANDY and I didn't have to wait long for our next posting. We were sent to Bircham Newton, an established Coastal Command airfield on the East Coast of England, in the heart of the rich low farming lands that lie south of the Wash. Here we were to join 221 Squadron which apparently operated Wellingtons. The system had triumphed in the end: we had been trained to fly Wellingtons and, thanks to failing our pressure-chamber tests, we were now about to do so!

We were greatly cheered as one obvious implication of this posting was that Sandy and I were still regarded as operational pilots for all normal purposes other than the high-flying PRU.

RAF Station, Bircham Newton, was the most isolated place I had up to that time seen. The nearest town, Hunstanton, was a dozen miles away and King's Lynn was twice that distance. The mess was, as usual, fully occupied, but with many others living in digs or in abandoned houses in Hunstanton, a limited amount of transport was generally available.

It was cold, bleak and lonely for the wives deposited in Hunstanton or billeted in the other village communities dotting the countryside, and within weeks my wife had had more than enough. The London blitz was raging, and in her own way she, too, wanted to contribute to the struggle in which at that time Britain and the Commonwealth stood alone. My wife went to live with cousins in South Norwood, London, and was soon driving LCC ambulances. In that wonderful willing community of auxiliary firemen, air-raid wardens, rescue squads, ambulance teams, and the like, she found a satisfaction akin to that which we pilots found in our aircraft, our crews and our squadron loyalties.

221 Squadron was forming up. It was a new squadron, having been

no more than a cypher since World War I. It had a new task, too. It was to be equipped with a special kind of Wellington with which it could hunt U-boats day and night. Over the Atlantic our convoys were being decimated. In fact, isolation from supplies across the seas, so vital to our war effort, was Britain's most vulnerable point.

Our Wellingtons were to have hush-hush ASV, the CO told us. He was a youngish wing-commander, with very clean-shaven looks, fair hair, and built on neat, precise lines. We learnt that Sandy and I would both be made captains of aircraft, that we would each be given five crew members and we were to prepare ourselves to be operationally effective so that the squadron could go into action as soon as their "real" Wellingtons arrived—those fitted with ASV. Meanwhile, there were a dozen or so ordinary Wellingtons available for training.

"Any questions?"

I was born abundantly curious. "What, sir, does ASV stand for?"

He glanced carefully out of both windows and at the door before replying. "ASV stands for Air to Surface Vessel," and since we still looked blank, he added, "it finds ships."

My flight-commander, a friendly, but rather cadaverous looking squadron-leader, called Ian Brolley, was a little more explicit.

ASV was *supposed* to find ships. But no one on the station, excepting possibly the wing-commander himself, had ever seen it or knew what it did or how it did it. "Anyhow it's absolutely secret and is not to be discussed," he said.

The squadron-leader was quick to tell us that he was an ex-flying-boat-pilot and, by his proud way of saying "when I was on boats", we sensed that flying-boats would always be his first love.

This was rather an eerie beginning, but I was soon cheered to find that amongst the other new captains milling about finding their place and purpose in the Squadron were both Eric Starling and the enigmatic Blisso. They already had their crews.

Blisso, in fact, was having great fun with those large Verey light cartridges which, when fired, produced two large coloured flares. These were supposed to distinguish friend from foe and were one of the means by which we hoped to escape being shot down by our own forces. Blisso's great joke was to put them down the outside chimney of the solid fuel stoves which formed the focal point of our various hastily assembled Nissen huts. Since those nearest the stove usually had their feet resting on it and since the others would all be huddled around its warmth, the effect was electric. The cartridge usually blew open the top of the stove and scattered red hot coke in all directions. It also erupted with a shattering roar and its own red and green firework mixture added colour to the explosion and confusion.

I paid great attention to the crew I had been allotted. After all, they were the first persons I had ever commanded anywhere. Apart from the navigator they were all raw recruits straight from various training schools. My first surprise was to find that my co-pilot was not only a rank higher than I but a regular naval officer to boot. Not even a Reservist!

Lieutenant Davis flew with me for about three weeks before inexplicably and abruptly being posted elsewhere. He was a fine young pilot and I was sorry to see him go. In the air he called me "sir" and on the ground, if occasion demanded formality, I repaid him the compliment. On an early flight he saved the aircraft by being quick to notice a rapid fall in oil pressure. The Wellingtons we now had were armed with gun turrets and other war-like impedimenta, and they had lost their original ability to maintain height on one engine. Thanks to his timely warning I was just able to get back to Bircham Newton before the faulty engine totally failed. After his departure I then acquired a Sergeant Reason, a young-faced, sandy-haired sergeant-pilot, this being the minimum flying crew rank in the RAF.

The crew now became:

Captain	P/O Spooner
Second-pilot	Sgt Reason
Navigator-Observer	F/Sgt Wavell ("Chiefy")
1st WOP/AG	Sgt Terrington
2nd WOP/AG	Sgt Radford
3rd WOP/AG	Sgt Evans

and we sat thus:

The captain at the controls on the port or left of the aircraft the second-pilot alongside him on a collapsible seat. The navigator had a small desk behind the radio operator and a bomb-aiming couch under the pilot's feet. In front of this couch was the nose turret. The radio operator sat directly behind the captain with his racks of equipment forming a bulkhead between them. Some thirty or more feet to the rear and reached by a cat-walk was the tail turret. Both gun turrets would rotate, and a hydraulically operated control activated through a pair of motor-cycle handle-bars enabled them to be swung through a full semi-circle. The guns could also be swung upwards and downwards to a limited extent.

I found that Sergeant Reason's name was Dennis and that he had a bare 200 hours experience. But he had completed a Wellington course, and at an earlier stage had passed a GR course similar to the one which I had been teaching in Blackpool. He had a likeable, open face. He was about nineteen. The three wireless-operators/air-gunners (always called WOP/AGs) didn't have a hundred hours aloft between them. I had to appoint one to be the Senior WOP/AG, so chose the most experienced. Terrington had forty-nine hours flying experience only because he had gone sick in the middle of his final course and was consequently held back to complete the whole of the subsequent course. These three between them had to man the front and rear turrets and to operate the two-way radio set. The turrets each had a pair of .303 machine-guns. We never really understood the purpose of the front turret as the wallowing Wimpey (the nickname the Wellington acquired from the cartoon character Wellington J Wimpey) was incapable of overtaking any enemy aircraft. But the rear turret was our main defence against enemy fighters.

Early exercises showed all too clearly that the crew had been hastily trained. They were still pupil-minded. Their efforts were solely directed at passing the next exam. They did not regard themselves as part of an operational unit, nor did they realise that their lives depended on their skill. On one exercise the weather turned sour on us. We had no bad weather landing or approach aids and we normally relied upon maintaining visual contact with the ground. We had no other way of returning to base. If this failed the safety of the aircraft was placed in the hands of the person operating the wireless set. He would transmit a long signal and a direction-finding unit at the home station would sense the direction whence the signal came. This information would be sent back to my operator in morse.

I now asked Evans, who happened to be on the radio set at the time, to get me a series of QDMs as these guiding bearings were called. Provided I had these I could fly towards the station until, when over the station (where the bearings reversed their sense), I could fix my position and then get down through the cloud as best I could. Evans duly got bearings in a steady stream—but omitted to pass them up to me! Not until I had handed over the controls to Dennis Reason did I realise what had been going on. Evans explained it to me this way.

"Well, you see, sir, 'Daddy' Page insists upon neat logkeeping, so I gets a bearing, writes it down quick-like on a scrap of paper, presses the key for the next signal, copies the last bearing neatly in the log and have barely time to do this before the station comes back giving me the next bearing. So you see, sir, I really haven't time to pass them up to you!"

"Daddy" Page was a much feared warrant officer whose job it was to install discipline and method into the many raw radio recruits who poured into the station. I tried to explain that in the air Evans and the others were exclusively under my command and that I didn't care a row of figs for "Daddy" Page and his neat log-keeping. I just wanted to keep alive.

But months of being "at school" leaves its mark. All Evans could say was: "You haven't met 'Daddy' Page, have you, sir?"

In fact, I had never met any warrant officer. I had met flight-sergeants, and they seemed formidable enough. They were scarce and they seemed to know almost everything. Indeed, as a kind of excuse for the rawness of the others, much had been made of the point that I had been given a most experienced flight-sergeant navigator—"Chiefy" Wavell—and he looked almost old enough to be my father. He didn't take much part in the early exercise, when I was mainly concerned to re-learn how to fly a Wimpey, to find out what my second pilot could do, to find my way around locally by recognisable landmarks and to try to determine how best to employ the three "green" WOP/AGs.

Dennis Reason soon proved that he had natural flying ability and, once airborne, I could hand the controls over to him and see for myself what was going on in the rest of the aircraft. We only had one set of controls and the hand-over required some gymnastics, which started when the second pilot slipped off his folding seat, collapsed this, stepped forward on to the bomb-aimer couch in the nose, and then gradually slithered up and back into my seat as I edged my way diagonally rearwards into the narrow passage alongside the radio compartment. We had no usable auto-pilot, and this meant that the drill had to be performed fairly slickly.

Little "Chiefy" Wavell was a quiet, almost insignificant-looking man. Every time we went flying he would appear complete with a huge assortment of maps, pencils and calculators. He would also ensure that the huge, clumsy bomb-sight was in its correct position, though we never carried bombs and only used the drift-taking device attached to its top almost as an afterthought. At other times whenever we met he would stand to attention and enquire hopefully, "Your orders for the day, sir?" The only orders I could ever think of were to get him to make sure that the crew turned up at the right place and time for the next flight, but as these details were prominently posted up on Squadron notice boards this seemed rather superfluous.

Unlike my other aircrew sergeants, "Chiefy" punctiliously saluted all officers on sight.

Bircham Newton held several units. 500 Squadron, with their Hudson light-bombers, were the permanent residents, and their officers had secured most of the living quarters: however, being now in effect a single man, I managed to infiltrate into the mess, as other aircrew officers got themselves posted or killed—one was never quite sure which. The RAF's policy of posting crew members at unexpected but frequent intervals helped to mask the fact that some were being reported missing or killed.

Death stalks all pilots, and long before their training was complete, pilots learned to live with this. Death was invariably regarded as the deceased's own fault. Pilots were never killed: instead pilots "got themselves killed". More usually their loss was simply referred to as "old so-and-so has gone for a Burton" or "has bought it" . . . The way I looked at death in the air was that flying had opened up a new lease of life for me and if flying also brought my life to an end, I couldn't reasonably complain since, on the whole, the "awakening" was worth a few risks. The more poetic would explain that pilots had to make up their minds whether Death was going to be their Master or their Mistress—and if it was the former the sooner one gave up flying the better. No one, on the other hand, was opposed to a mistress, even if certain risks were involved. On an operational squadron, perhaps we did think about death more than other people, but such thoughts could usually be blotted out, if needs be, by a big "booze-up". Even on wartime beer it was still possible to get drunk, especially in the pubs, with their blacked-out windows, their crowds of perspiring bodies in heavy uniforms, their thick, swirling smoke and boisterous camaraderie. Here we could sing songs like "Roll me over in the clover" and feel just fine in a boyish, sweaty way, reminiscent of Rugby scrums or football crowds.

When our crew reached the stage of over-water exercises, I discovered with a rude shock that "Chiefy" had no idea whatsoever of how to navigate. I was still rather over-awed by his age and experience, but I had to tackle him about it. It transpired that after entry as a boy he had been trained as an armourer. He had, indeed, become an armourer first-class. From this he had progressed to become an air-gunner, and when the two-seater planes became larger, he had been made an air-gunner observer. In this role he had served with the RAF in a Fairey Battle squadron in France during the first year of the war. Since the navigation requirement in those circumstances consisted only of map-reading, no one had thought to give "Chiefy" an official navigation course, especially as his knowledge of guns and bombs had been of great use. But now he was my navigator, and we were destined to carry out long over-water patrols, requiring a high-degree of precision navigation.

At his suggestion I agreed to teach him to navigate, and to make sure that we didn't get lost too badly, I obtained for myself a Bigsworth plotting board, on which I could carry out a separate check upon our progress. This handy plotting board could be carried on my lap. It was a great help to discover, too, that young Reason, by virtue of his GR course, also had a fair idea of how to navigate. He was adroit at drift-taking. This was particularly valuable when out over the water.

My moment of near despair came when first we set out with live ammunition to carry out a target-firing exercise over the Wash. For forty minutes I flew over the target area whilst first one gunner then the other either failed to rotate his turret, failed to depress the guns or simply failed to get them to fire. Guns jammed and then took ages to be cleared. Since our large, slow plane was a perfect sitting duck for enemy fighters, this lack of defensive fire-power was alarming. Thoroughly depressed, I turned for home and, when over the land, was startled to hear a long rat-tat-tat from the rear. Through the intercom, which connected us all together, I learnt that it was a "runaway" gun.

Furthermore, it continued to runaway until all ammunition was spent, and the barrel was ruined by heat. We were lucky not to have killed some innocent farm worker below. By now I was hopping mad and I lashed into my crew with all the pent-up fury and frustration I had earlier felt. I was no gunner, but knew enough to realise that a runaway gun could easily be stopped.

So the next time "Chiefy" came to me and enquired "Your orders for the day, sir", I told him that I wanted him to get hold of the three WOP/AGs and at every possible moment have them strip guns and operate turrets until they could do it blindfold with flying gloves on. This last was not mere "bull", since at night in their frozen turrets this would be their very practical problem. I said that I wanted my guns to fire at a second's notice, and I wanted them to keep on firing, in the direction of targets. Furthermore, I added, that I never again wanted to hear the words "jammed turret", "jammed gun", or "runaway gun". And in the year and more that we flew together as a crew we never again had a gun failure.

I had discovered an unexpected virtue in having as a navigator a master armourer.

17: 221 Squadron

WINTER drew to its close and with its end came the completion of squadron training. An ASV expert appeared and lectured us in terms far beyond the understanding of most of us. We wanted to know what our secret equipment would do and how we must operate it. He told us the principles and history of the invention. An ASV "trainer" appeared too, but this seemed to be almost ridiculously simple. All radar devices work on the same principle. They transmit signals or pulses in a steady stream. These pulses radiate outwards into space at the speed of light, 186,000 miles per second. If they strike an object they bounce back, and the "echo", as it is called, is recorded in a visible form on a cathode-ray tube. Television is but a variation of this principle.

As someone said, radar is somewhat like throwing a golf ball about. If it hits something hard it comes back fast and you know it! And the nearer the object is the faster it comes back. By timing its return, a distance can be determined.

Eventually our specially-equipped Wellingtons arrived. We had never seen aircraft such as these. They were festooned with aerials: one row ran along the aircraft's spine, others were affixed to the sides and were suspended in rows beneath the wings. One glance was enough to convince even the most optimistic of us that these aircraft hadn't a hope of being able to fly on one engine. The additional aerials all meant additional drag. Also the neat nose line was no longer nicely streamlined, since it had to house the "dish" or spinner, from which the stream of pulses were radiated into space. A bulge now protruded beneath the front turret.

As soon as each crew received its aircraft, they set off to find out what the ASV apparatus, still labelled top secret, would do. And in the flight huts, far out on the muddy field, we compared the results of our various experiments. Over the land it showed us too much: over the sea, too little. In the former case the cathode-ray screen showed a clutter of echoes: in the latter case, it was only just possible to pick up well-defined targets such as coastlines. At all times the presentation was made confusing by interference.

ASV, in the form that it then took, helped us most when it came to finding the shore line. Modern radar now has a circular screen which virtually draws plan-view pictures of all objects ahead. All we had was a tiny screen on the centre of which a green vertical line would appear. If the set picked up anything at all the object so detected appeared as a small "tick" across the vertical line. Unless the object was dead ahead this tick would be longer on one side of the centre line than the other. By turning the aircraft towards the longer side of the tick until the two sides were of equal length, and noting the aircraft's compass reading, the direction of the object could be determined. The theoretical maximum range was a hundred miles, and there were three range-scales, enabling an accurate assessment of range to be made when running towards an unknown "blip", as the tick or echoing return came to be called.

The viewing end of the set was housed between the radio and navigational compartments, and since no additional crew member was supplied to operate it, and since it required continuous manning, we all handled it in turn. Initially, I think, Sergeant Reason, my second pilot, spent most time looking through the hooded visor, but he and I used to exchange positions frequently. The three WOP/AGs already had official positions in the two turrets and at the wireless operator's station respectively and little "Chiefy" was not the kind of person to thrust himself forward. He persisted in the belief that we were getting nothing useful out of the set. The rest of us let our imaginations rule our heads.

The squadron was now really at war. One crew got shot up over the North Sea by a Junkers 88. Luckily, it so damaged one of the Wimpey's engines that its propeller came off, which enabled the damaged plane to hold height on the remaining engine. The Luftwaffe was strangely quiet, and we carried out our final working-up exercises far out in the North Sea seldom encountering the enemy. However, they had a nasty habit of laying in wait for us around our airfields at night and then pouncing on our planes as they drifted down to the landing flare-path. We lost at least one aircraft in this way. Once they darted out of the clouds in broad daylight and flung a string of bombs across the airfield buildings, killing a few people and setting fire to our underground fuel storage tanks. These, greatly to our relief, merely gave forth smoke for an hour or so before ultimately snuffing themselves out.

Two charming young girls came and had tea with us in the mess one day. The younger one, Margaret, pranced about with obvious *joie de vivre*—the more serious, Elizabeth, then in her early teens, obviously knew what issues were involved and, like her Royal father, knew where her duty lay. But she, too, was fascinated by the Link trainers, those one-seater black cabins which were used for instrument flight training and which realistically produced the motions and behaviour of flight.

On another occasion Blisso worked out a lecture for us and persuaded the CO to call the squadron together. For nearly one hour he blinded us with scientific terms, of which he knew thousands. He hastily chalked up graphs on a blackboard and even more hastily erased them. He equated the wind velocity with engine pressures. The Greek terms mu, pi, rho and theta filled the air. And as the technical terms followed each other with frenzied rapidity we began to realise that Blisso was pulling off one of his celebrated stunts. When we heard him describe, in his machine-gun style, a parabolic curve as radiating in millocraps per kilo-turd, Eric and I just sat back and enjoyed ourselves. Yet, within this farago of nonsense, lay the germ of an idea, which was not to come to fruition until many years later—the idea of pressure pattern navigation, the art of translating drift into isobars and isobars into drift. Blisso was gravely thanked for a fascinating talk and as gravely acknowledged the bewildered applause.

We had two satellite airfields. The large one at Docking was seldom used by us. But the Germans dropped a huge bomb upon it one night. It was a new type of bomb. It didn't explode on contact, but it looked so ominous that they even stopped trains from using the main railway lines, which ran past the airfield. The entire area was evacuated. A naval bomb-disposal expert was summoned. He examined it, sat on it and hammered it, and just before departing remarked: "I've set it to go off in half an hour and it is liable to make an awful mess!"

The other satellite airfield provided the tragic setting for the first Polish effort to bomb Berlin. The thousands of Polish pilots who escaped back to Britain were fanatical in their hatred for the Germans. They knew their enemy far better than we did. One of their Wellington squadrons was detailed to make a night raid on Berlin—the first time the Poles had been given this long-awaited target. For some extraordinary reason they were detailed to depart from our small satellite field. From here, we used to carry out practice night-flying mainly in order to avoid exposing our main airfield and buildings to the lurking German night-intruders. This satellite was wet, muddy and of limited size. It had no paved runways. The Wellingtons of the Polish squadron were fully loaded with bombs and petrol. Of the first six to attempt to take off, only two actually got airborne and the sortie was then cancelled. But how those gallant Poles tried! One came to rest three fields away from the boundary fence, having hedge-hopped and bulldozed his way across field and farmland in the dead of night. Remarkably few were killed but their frustration and disappointment must have known no bounds.

On another occasion Blisso and I were told that we had to do some *official* night-flying. Officially, we hadn't been checked out at night. We both thought it rather pointless and foolishly made light of the requirement. We didn't take a tail-gunner, as we obviously should have done, and we elected to fly from Bircham Newton itself rather than from the satellite. Nor did we bother to draw parachutes or equip ourselves with maps, chart or instruments—a job which, in my case, was always done for me with punctilious efficiency by little "Chiefy". We were, in fact, piqued, and showed our disdain by breaking nearly every station regulation.

Blisso did his four landings and then we exchanged seats. We were using a glim lamp landing flarepath with low intensity light, and were operating without a ground floodlight. On my last landing I remarked to Blisso that the last of the eight lights had blown out. A bare fifteen seconds after touchdown the aircraft ran into such a thick fog, spreading so fast that we were not able to taxi the aircraft back to our squadron dispersal area. We had difficulty enough in even finding the control tower. This fog was completely unforecast, and it covered the whole countryside.

Unfortunately, it was a night when Bomber Command was out in full strength! On this terrible night of tragedy the RAF lost scores of the bombers they had despatched. There was no place for them to land. Planes were abandoned and crews bailed out in their hundreds. One obscure training airfield in Wales, unaffected by fog, saved more than fifty planes. The Control Officer on duty displayed great ingenuity in guiding the bombers there and landing dozens of these large aircraft, often simultaneously, and at speed, as their fuel reserves were fast running out.

One of our co-squadrons, with whom we shared the airfield, the Hudson Squadron 500, had five planes out that night, laying mines off the Dutch and German coasts. They were diverted northwards to North Coates, in Lincolnshire, but the fog got there before them: northwards again to Newcastle, thence to Dyce, near Aberdeen. Each time the fog arrived first. Finally, they were diverted to Wick, near John O'Groats, but none of them ever reached this haven. Their fuel was now spent.

Many familiar faces were removed from our mess, and for once we knew for certain that they had "got themselves killed" and had not been posted. Blisso and I walked around in chastened mood. None knew better than we the truth behind the saying, "And there but for the Grace of God go I."

Soon after this our squadron was also engaged upon night patrols of the enemy coastline. We even got shot at by German batteries at times, although, with our secret equipment on board, we were not supposed to cross the enemy shoreline. ASV operation had now been taken over by the WOP/AGs, leaving the nose-turret empty. We still kidded ourselves that we could "see things" on our ASV screens, but all we ever saw for sure was an approaching coastline. I navigated with the Bigsworth board on my lap, and "Chiefy" kept a parallel plot. Dennis Reason took the drifts, and occasionally relieved the WOP/AG on the ASV set, enabling one gunner to serve the coffee from the flasks. We were becoming a team.

Then, one day, Pat Green, an auxiliary squadron flight lieutenant and a personal friend, and I were summoned to the CO's office.

The German battle-cruisers *Scharnhorst* and *Gneisenau* had been bottled up in Brest on the French Atlantic coast, for some months. Intelligence reports had just come in that they were preparing for a "break-out" that very night. The weather was foul and the Navy were not sure that they would be able to head off this move. 221 Squadron had been asked to send two of their ASV planes to the area. We were to be nightwatchmen. Our ASV serving as "night eyes", we had to be ready to fly to St. Eval, in Cornwall, within an hour.

By nightfall we were both out over the Bay of Biscay, keyed up with anticipation. We were patrolling some twenty or so miles off the French coast. It was real "break-out" weather and our aircraft was being tossed about in the low clouds and swirling rain. Luckily we were not an air-sick crew. We had no means whatever of accurately maintaining our position.

In war-time all coastal lights and light houses were doused, and in this kind of weather night-drift taking was a problem beyond solution, as the flame floats we used to assist us in this purpose disappeared in the murk as soon as we launched them.

After some six hours of this, when we were all feeling truly battered, we turned for home, and on the way came to an almost rigid alert when the WOP/AG on the ASV set announced over the intercom, "Skipper, I've got a 'blip', it's twelve miles and almost dead ahead." We barely had time to prepare a signal in code and have this sent out over the radio. I had to get the "ops flash" out whatever happened, yet I was terrified that we would lose the blip if I turned aside. We flew towards the target as slowly as I dared, whilst fumbling with the awkward "Sy-code" machine on which we were obliged to code all our messages.

I had to make absolutely sure that I had indeed discovered the fleeting German battlecruisers so, brought the aircraft down to what I judged to be about 300 feet but the aircraft lacked a reliable altimeter. At three miles I still saw nothing, and the intervening space ticked off with agonising slowness. At this distance the ASV invariably lost contact with the echoing returns, as the clutter from the big waves tended to obscure all objects at close range. A beach flashed by and a cliff top reared up before me. Furious spurts of gun-fire followed. We had located and "homed" upon the defended island of Ushant off the tip of the Brest peninsula.

I left the area as fast as I could, and hastened to correct my "ops flash" and coded messages. I realised that my first signal must have alerted half the Royal Navy and aroused Ministers from their beds. I felt thoroughly ashamed. One fact stood out above all others. I realised that if the ASV could only detect the large island of Ushant at a paltry dozen miles range, it would never be able to detect the German battle-cruisers for all their 30,000 plus tons—and that I hadn't a hope in hell of ever finding U-boats. And this in spite of the fact that this was the purpose of all our squadron-training and, in fact, the reason for ASV's very existence!

Next day it was announced that the whole exercise had been a "scare". The big enemy ships were still at their usual anchorages and Intelligence now no longer thought it likely that they would emerge. Pat Green and I were free to depart back to base station at our convenience.

However, we had been talking amongst ourselves, confessing our inabilities and sounding out other pilots of a Hudson unit which carried an even earlier type of ASV. One of them recommended that if we wanted to know how best to work ASV we should go to a RAF station in South Wales called St Athans.

St Athans was secret and it took some time before we could find out where it was. But Pat and I both flew there in the end. They welcomed our unofficial visit as they hadn't seen a Wellington equipped with their special apparatus before. They took us out in their special ASV Anson and showed us how to use this detecting device effectively. The "interference" which we had been at such pains to reduce to a minimum was, we learned, essential to effective performance. This gave the set its required degree of sensitivity. We ran up and down the Bristol Channel and were able to home on to tiny Lundy Island from a range of thirty to forty miles. Also we detected isolated ships. Detecting by ASV is always difficult as the interference tends either to mask real blips or to create false ones.

Also to watch so much "fuzz" oscillating in a continuous manner is a great strain on the eyes. We realised that ASV was going to require intelligent interpretation and extreme watchfulness. We hoped that the experts were right when they told us that experienced operators developed a sixth sense, and that they could detect blips from the most unlikely looking collection of interference and clutter.

We hastened back to Bircham Newton to spread this new gospel.

We didn't find any enemy capital ships, but on the whole we had not journeyed to Cornwall and Wales in vain.

18: Northern Ireland—
and Atlantic Patrol

EARLY in 1941 the squadron moved to Limavady, a recently-created RAF Station lying alongside Loch Foyle, twelve miles east of Londonderry in Northern Ireland. We shared the airfield with a Whitley Squadron, No. 502, also newly equipped with ASV. Both types of aircraft had about ten hours maximum endurance, and our task was to find and sink enemy U-boats, and to shadow and protect the incoming convoys during the last 700 miles or so of their Atlantic voyage.

Ian Brolley was an easy-going flight-commander and his deputy, whom I shall call Appleton, was certainly no disciplinarian. He was an eccentric character—a great party man and a person with a magnetic attraction for the other sex.

Bircham Newton and Limavady are isolated airfields in the wilds of farming country, yet within days of arrival at both, Appleton had acquired girl friends of outstanding charm. These women would patiently wait for him outside the camp gates in their own cars—usually Jaguars! His habit of firing his revolver through his ceiling late at nights was upsetting too—especially for those living above. He was seldom seen before 11 a.m. and even at party time he retained his sleepy eyes and manner. But he had a fast-moving brain and a natural flair for arranging intricate details, such as the squadron flight roster.

For £5 I bought a Ford 8 from one of his rowdy friends. The car had to be driven even in the winter cold with the windows wound down, as oil fumes poured up through the floorboards. Oil and petrol consumption were approximately equal. I had a new engine put in and spent another £15 on much needed tyres, after which it gave no trouble. In fact my wife and I used it for the rest of the war and then sold it for £150 in 1946!

Although we were miles away from the enemy and had no fear of German raids, the station, like all new ones, was laid out for war-time dispersal of aircraft. This meant that the aircraft were kept on individual concrete stands far away from the mess and that apart from these, the taxi-tracks, some hastily erected hangars, and the ugly Nissen huts, the squadron lived in a sea of mud. The amount of time we spent cycling to and fro or awaiting decrepit squadron buses was fearful to contemplate. My car was most useful, especially after I discovered that my ground crew, quite unasked, would fill it up with petrol whenever I went on an operational trip. I didn't ask where the precious fluid came from; indeed I thought it best not to notice what was being done for me.

As a crew we flew our hardest. We sharpened up our intercom drill, since in action this would become our one common link. We practised gunnery with enthusiasm. We dropped as many practice bombs as was allowed, and the WOP/AGs became as expert at interpreting ASV information as had Sergeant Reason. I even spent some time aboard a Polish submarine in Londonderry in order to see the enemy's viewpoint. We rearranged crew duties so that one of the WOP/AGs was always on the ASV set: another monitored the radio set and the third kept a watchful eye in the tail turret. We sometimes manned the nose turret too.

It was arranged that if it were empty when we sighted a submarine either Reason or "Chiefy" Wavell would at once man this position, whoever was nearer. Both were now practised at doing so, although neither was officially an air-gunner. "Chiefy" and I both kept independent navigational plots, he at his station amidships; I on my portable board. Soon we were splitting hairs about the aircraft's exact position. Sergeants weren't supposed to handle coding, but young Reason relieved me of part of this duty, too. I kept the crew busy changing positions at least once every hour, as the ASV operator would become mesmerised and sleepy after even one hour spent gazing at his tiny screen and its constantly confused oscillating patterns. Along with others in the squadron, we invented better ways and means of doing our job. To solve the problem arising from the fact that we had no accurate indication of our exact height over the water we experimented with a long, weighted length of wire affixed to a simple bell. This warned us when below 100 feet. We also had difficulty in taking drifts over calm, featureless water. We solved this by arranging for the front gun to fire a burst vertically downwards. The person lying in the bomb-aimer's position in the nose would then be able to take a drift reading from the disturbance artificially created below.

We also learned that the most accurate drifts could be taken by the tail-gunner lining-up his guns on flame-floats or markers dropped from the aircraft. These drift angles were given in units as small as a half-degree. My friend Eric Starling and his navigator, a pleasant officer called Edwards, became experts at reading the wind by visual inspection of the sea. They noted the visible wind-lanes and applied correction for altitude. Reason and I tried this, but we didn't find ourselves able to get reliable and accurate results.

Whole groups fiddled with the ASV trainer, and under the guidance of a brilliant young officer named Wiseman, we stripped this rather useless device of most of its valves and re-built it into something more like our airborne apparatus. We were all quick to realise the value of ASV as a navigational aid. An ASV "responder" beacon was installed at the station and we could detect this unmistakably clear blip at ranges up to seventy miles. We also learned to equate certain types of weather with relative ASV effectiveness. Eric and I worked out a descent-through-cloud procedure, using the station's ASV homing beacon as a reference point. This was of great safety value, as Limavady lay between two hills and was a dangerous place to have to seek in bad weather.

There was much truth in the local saying, "If you *can* see across the Loch it is a sign that it is shortly going to rain. If you *can't* see across the Loch it means that it is raining already!"

We were trying to establish contacts across the border in Eire, so that we could secretly install another ASV homing beacon on or in the chimney of a house in Tory Island—a lonely island in the Atlantic some dozen miles off the north-west tip of Ireland. I am certain that this would have saved lives, as it was fairly common to get lost over the Atlantic, and I felt that some of the aircraft which never returned from sorties were not shot down but were simply lost. Wireless security prohibited them from receiving adequate radio assistance, and apart from drifts we had little or nothing to guide us. Our compasses needed to be deadly accurate too, which was why Reason, "Chiefy" and I used to check ours on the station compass base at least once every month. We carried out "in flight" checks too, though with rather inadequate equipment.

We did get lost one particularly foul night when cloud clutter reduced ASV efficiency to almost zero. Fifteen minutes after the coast of Ireland should have appeared we still could see only water beneath us. Rather than blunder on and risk colliding with the Glasgow balloon barrage, I had Reason carry out a square-search pattern so as to hold our position in space whilst "Chiefy" and I checked through our navigational plots. I then climbed above the cloud for better radio reception and told the wireless operator to open up his set and to get us whatever bearings he could from anywhere. After an anxious thirty minutes of this loitering above the clouds we were made sufficiently sure of our approximate position to set a positive course for Limavady. Along with others, I had been practising certain methods of operating the engines for optimum fuel economy, and on this occasion I was grateful for the hidden reserves that these methods produced.

Ice was our great enemy, as the planes had virtually no protection against this great natural hazard. Whenever possible and in spite of the bumpiness of the air, we flew beneath cloud. Here we were unlikely to get iced-up. But at times the weather was such that it was dangerous to fly so low, especially with our unreliable indication of height above the sea. There was on issue a chemical paste for spreading over the forward-facing part of the wings and tail surfaces. It was reasonably effective at preventing ice formation but rain was apt to wash it off. The propellers collected ice easily, and all we could do was to make violent alteration in the rpm hoping to dislodge the ice by vibration and centrifugal forces. The engines, too, would collect ice in the carburettor throats. When this happened we could either try a full-power climb through the cloud to the clearer air on top or, as a last desperate remedy, we would switch the ignition off—then on; the monumental back-fire which resulted would, with luck, clear the carburettor throat. But we had no means whatever of preventing our rows of ASV aerials from icing up. We used to hear them "singing" as they vibrated under the uneven ice loads.

The Bristol Pegasus engines which powered the Wimpey would

take unlimited abuse, and they proved wonderfully reliable work horses. As far as I knew no engine ever failed—a splendid testimony to the devotion of both manufacturer and ground crews.

Inevitably the squadron lost aircraft and crews. Robinson flew into one of the hills which stood sentinel over the airfield. A Whitley pilot, Dixon, flew into the other one, but most of our losses remained unexplained. Other crews went out and simply "failed to return". Perhaps an engine failed? Perhaps they got lost? Perhaps they flew into the sea deceived by their altimeters? Perhaps they got iced up, or ran out of petrol fighting engine ice? Perhaps even the enemy shot them down as they dived on submarines, or engaged the big four-engined long-range German Focke-Wulf Kondor aircraft, which at that time were almost as damaging to our shipping as were the U-boats. But losses due to enemy action were unlikely, as in the first place it was obligatory to send an immediate "ops flash" signal as soon as any enemy sighting was made, and also because the sad fact was that neither 221 nor 502 Squadrons were *finding* the enemy, except on very rare occasions—and when they did sight a U-boat it usually was able to dive under the waves before the crew could drop their load of depth charges. We could hardly fight Kondors, as we lacked the speed to catch them.

Our results, in fact, disappointed me. The squadron had no single official U-boat to its credit. Yet by now we and the others thought ourselves to be efficient crews. We stayed out longer than we were supposed to. We scanned the oceans continuously. We manned the ASV assiduously. We managed to keep a good idea of our position, as was proved by our good record of finding the convoys we were sent to escort. We were well practised in gunnery and bomb-dropping. Yet apart from the comfort we must have brought to our harassed ships (which, not then being accustomed to seeing any planes other than German Kondors so far out in the Atlantic used to open fire on us at first), and the possible effect of causing U-boats to dive as they sighted us, we were achieving very little at a huge cost of fuel and manpower.

We increased our effective range by flying patrols to Iceland soon after that island had been occupied by British forces as a precautionary defensive measure. It was obvious that we, the invaders, were not welcome in Iceland, but the airfield at Reykjavik was a boon to us. Also the Icelandic people were critically short of vegetables (in which Ireland abounded), and they apparently had all the cigarettes and ladies' stockings in the world, whereas we had strict rationing. So a natural exchange, cabbages for cigarettes, developed, with our squadron acting as the carrier and our mess—a big old country house—the principal gainer. In Iceland we saw at first hand how very close the USA had come to war. Their planes were now openly patrolling the Atlantic alongside ours, even using the same "colours of the day" Very-light signals. But we still sighted far too few U-boats, and those that we did see we located by eye rather than by ASV.

A great man descended upon us. Sir Henry Tizard was a civilian scientific adviser to the Cabinet. He came to see how ASV was being used. After official talks with our commanders he asked to see some of the regular pilots. He elected to see those who had done the most flying. Eric and I were always competing for this role, and with two or three from the other flights and squadron we were detailed to attend.

He rapidly cross-examined us. "How long have you had ASV?" "How many U-boats have the squadron sighted?" "Only about six, eh?" "How many were attacked?" "How many were *first* sighted by ASV?"

When we had to confess that the answer was "none or possibly one", the great man, keeping a straight face, innocently proposed: "Then I suppose you would all like to get rid of the apparatus?"

The howl of protest which greeted this remark set the meeting going. We started to tell him that without ASV we couldn't be sure of finding Limavady or Ireland. That without ASV we wouldn't dare stay out so long. That without ASV we wouldn't be able to find the convoys we were now daily escorting home. That without ASV we would have no safe aid for bad-weather approaches. We even told him of experiments we had been making, linking the interference appearing on our screens with possible naval radar, thus allowing us to home on to our convoys via their naval escorts from longer ranges than the twenty or so miles which was normal. This really shook him, as he saw at once the supreme danger of a situation whereby all naval ships using radar were possibly transmitting an indication of their position continuously, making a mockery of the strict radio silence rules in force.

He summed it all up for us. He accepted the fact that our ASV was invaluable to us as a navigational, homing and bad weather approach aid. ASV, as he saw it, could locate surface ships with their large superstructures either by day or by night in any sea, at ranges from about twenty-five miles downwards, depending upon the state of the sea and weather. However, it was not likely to locate a submarine unless both weather and sea were calm.

He departed leaving us all with the impression that in one short meeting he had obtained a complete grasp of the situation, and that he would somehow use this knowledge intelligently.

The other great event which happened during the six months whilst I was with 221 Squadron in Limavady was that the *Bismarck*—the great German battleship—broke out into the Atlantic, sank the *Hood*, damaged the *Prince of Wales* and attempted to escape back to Brest. This was a terrible blow to our national pride and naval prestige. The *Prinz Eugen* had been with the *Bismarck,* but the two ships parted company after their successful engagement. The order had gone out that the *Bismarck* had to be stopped.

221 Squadron was ordered to detach about six planes and fly them to St Eval at once. Six volunteers. I forget who told me that I had "volunteered" but I was certainly on the list.

St Eval had been crowded at the time of the *Scharnhorst* and *Gneisenau* alarm but now it was packed. We soon received our orders. We were to have our planes fully refuelled and to have them at immediate readiness with 500-lb armour-piercing bombs loaded in the bomb bays. "Chiefy", as usual, carefully double-checked this latter. Contact with the *Bismarck* had been lost but it was believed to be beyond our range. As soon as contact was regained we were to fly out, bomb the *Bismarck* and sink it. If we hadn't enough fuel to return, we were to land alongside one of the naval units which would be in the area giving chase. The *Bismarck* had to be stopped at any price.

It was quite outside our imagination to see how our slow, wallowing Wimpeys could possibly sink or seriously damage the largest, best-protected, and most heavily-gunned fighting ship afloat, but we were not invited to reason why. There was tremendous excitement in the mess, with pilots crowding around the radio sets listening to every news bulletin. The bar was doing great business, too. I had previously made my Will and lodged it with a Liverpool friend, so I could think of nothing better to do than to spend an hour or so in the intelligence office studying pictures of the *Bismarck* and of the many other British ships which were likely to be in the same area.

Next morning we learned that a Swordfish—an ancient stringbag biplane—from a carrier had immobilized that vast German ship with a torpedo hit on its rudder, after which she had been pounded to pieces by our battleships' guns and finally sent to the bottom by further torpedoes. Then the bar really did record business, and no one was drinking with more relish than I.

I was nearing the end of my first operational tour. I knew that after forty or fifty trips I would be given a rest, during which I would become an instructor once again. I knew, too, that the crew was top-line and fighting fit.

The London blitz had died down and my wife and I were living on a farm a few miles from the station. Hitler had attacked Russia and his war-machine was again sweeping all before it. Only in the Middle East, at night over Germany, and over the Atlantic were Britons engaged with the enemy. In the Western Desert the tide of war swayed back and forth. First one side then the other would sweep forward hundreds of miles, only to be stopped by determined resistance and the complications of an extended supply line. Rommel's Afrika Korps and our Eighth Army were well-matched foes fighting a comparatively straight-forward tacticians' war. Malta remained a thorn in the side of the Axis powers. But her strategic position athwart the shipping lanes connecting Italy to Tripolitania, was daily being neutralized as the Luftwaffe and Mussolini's much-publicised air force pounded the tiny island incessantly. The defence of Malta had caught the imagination of the British people. Its invasion was thought to be imminent.

I personally had tried and failed to stem the Nazi successes in the Atlantic. As a crew we flew more than any other, but no U-boat ever came within our sight.

Suddenly, an alternative opportunity presented itself. 221 Squadron was asked to supply three crews to be sent to Malta as an autonomous unit. They were to go there for "Special Duties". The CO asked me if I would like to be one of them. But it was made plain that I could back out. This was not a compulsory call for "volunteers". I elected to go, with the one proviso, that if my wife was against the idea, I would like a chance to reconsider my decision. Life in the ration-free Irish countryside was almost unrealistic after the action she had seen in the London blitz. It was a time for decisions and we made them. I would go to Malta as the junior of the three crews; she would return to London.

The CO offered me another officer—a gunner or a navigator—"to strengthen my crew". I looked at him in surprise. I had thought that everyone must have realised that I now possessed the "best crew in the world". Such are the dreams of young men, on the eve of departing on a modern Crusade—the defence of the island of Malta—an island under such fire as it had not seen for four hundred years, when the original Knights of St John so valiantly put paid to the plans of Barbarossa and the all-conquering Turks.

In 1941 the new Knights of Malta defended from the skies, as I was soon to learn.

19: Malta—Early Days

SINCE Reason, Terrington, Evans and little "Chiefy" were also approaching their operational rest period, I gave them all a chance to withdraw. They were all prepared to "give it a go"; the new young WOP/AG who had taken Radford's place in the crew—a fresh-faced bright-eyed fair-haired young sergeant called Haynes—was obviously raring to go.

We added two additional members to the crew. My wife's little Dandy Dinmont chose this moment to present us with nine puppies, the outcome of an unscheduled liaison with the big collie which belonged to the farm where we lodged. I soon learnt to say "they are Collie-Dinmonts" with such casual authority that others started to tell me that their aunts used to breed them! We decided to take two of these three-week-old puppies with us. They were obviously not house-trained, which probably accounts for the names they acquired. Bronco and Harpic were, however, healthy playful pups, of original but not unattractive appearance.

We went to an airfield near Cirencester to collect a new ASV Wellington VIII and, after a test flight or two, flew this to St Eval, whence we were detailed to depart for Gibraltar, on the first leg of our flight to Malta.

We chose to fly a track which took us across the Bay of Biscay sufficiently far from enemy fighter patrols, but near enough, we hoped, to surprise a home-coming or an outward bound U-boat. With this in mind we also loaded up with ammunition and depth charges. We loaded all our personal possessions—including "Chiefy's" heavy trunk full of books—and the two puppies, and set forth on a warm day in late September.

Three-quarters of the way across the airfield I began to sense that due to our excessive weight, the Wellington wasn't going to rise. I knew the "feel" of the aircraft, and I realised that it would be suicide to attempt to pull her off the ground at the wretched speed we were making. Yet the far hedge was coming at me at an alarming rate. I spied a concrete taxi-track only about twenty degrees to our right and I managed to swing the aircraft towards this. We were still firmly on the ground when we crossed the airfield boundary road, and not until we had careered about two hundred yards into the heart of a dispersal area did my hands get the right responses from the controls. My last glimpse of England for a year or so was of a startled airman diving for cover and hastily dragging his bicycle out of our path as we finally lifted off.

Adieu to England: and very nearly goodbye to everywhere!

The flight to Gibraltar was without further incident, and after a night or two there we joined the other two aircraft and set forth for Malta, flying in loose formation, as the previous delivery aircraft over this route had been shot down. Enemy submarines were not expected in the Mediterranean, so this time we decided to leave the depth charges behind. We arranged the long flight to Malta—over ten hours—so as to arrive at night, as we had been advised that enemy fighters were liable to be swarming around the island during daylight hours. And when cloud was at hand we kept close to it.

We kept about a mile apart except when we spotted a Me 110 (or something similar). Then we closed up with all guns poised. But the aircraft sheared off. Later we also sighted a Caproni 310 twin-engined torpedo-bomber on a lonely patrol. We were prepared to tackle this, but he headed rapidly away, and as it was nearing dusk and we were beginning to worry about our fuel situation and how to locate tiny Malta we didn't give chase.

Land appeared on our ASV screen at hitherto unattainable ranges due to the calm sea and the uninhibited visibility. In due course we arrived over the blacked-out RAF station at Luqa, landing on a runway barely delineated by a very inadequate flarepath.

In Malta we were known as the Wellington SDF (Special Duties Flight). We consisted of the Unit Commander, a newly-promoted squadron-leader, a flying-officer and myself and our crews. We were not there to find and sink submarines nor to escort friendly convoys. We were there to find enemy surface shipping and we were soon put in the picture strategically.

All enemy supplies for the Italian-German North African armies were shipped through two ports, Benghazi and Tripoli. These supplies either came through the Straits of Messina or around the west tip of Sicily. Either way the enemy supply ships had to pass within flying range of Malta. These ships had been attacked in daylight by our Malta-based Bristol Blenheims and some Maryland light-bombers of 69 Squadron. This was why they now routed themselves so as to pass by Malta at night. German and Italian fighters from Sicily would protect them during the evening. Likewise, fighters from Cyrenaica and Tripolitania would protect them next morning. Our job was to intercept them at night and either attack them ourselves or else summon someone else to do it. The job was new; we were, in fact, the first ASV-equipped RAF aircraft that Malta had seen. Tactics would be developed in the light of experience. But first we had to establish the fact that we had the ability to locate enemy shipping at night.

Our aircraft attracted great interest. No one in the island had seen anything like them, with their rows of aerials. We in 221 Squadron had come to refer to them as "Sticklebacks", but for some obscure reason they came to be known in Malta as "Goofingtons". The mechanics of another Wellington unit on the island, 37 or 38 Squadron of Bomber Command, were detailed to maintain our planes.

A glance at the map shows that Malta could hardly have been more awkwardly placed for the enemy, and it was obvious why their bombers were reducing the place to rubble. Already it had suffered over eight hundred air raids, mainly directed at its three airfields, its harbour, its submarine base and the oil supply dumps. The see-saw desert war had reached a temporary stalemate situation in the vicinity of Tobruk, some four hundred miles east of Benghazi. Crete and Greece had fallen to the enemy. Only forces based in Malta could harass the enemy's vital supply routes. The Italian Navy had been drubbed at the battle of Cape Matapan and had been raided in Taranto harbour itself. Although they had a preponderance of battleships and cruisers and although our nearest capital units were a thousand miles away at Alexandria or Gibraltar, the Italians were not prepared to force convoys through under the guard of their big, fast ships.

Our first sortie was a search for an enemy convoy believed by our intelligence services to be running the gauntlet to Benghazi. We saw nothing. Was our Limavady lack of success going to continue? A few nights later we again drew a blank. Reason had gone sick with "Malta Dog", a local variant of the better known "Gyppy Tummy", and, to my surprise, a Squadron Leader Lowery from headquarters had asked to accompany me as co-pilot. He didn't fly Wellingtons, but I could hardly refuse such a senior officer.

On the way home at night—all my operations from Malta were flown at night—we were nosing about the Maritimo Islands off the west tip of Sicily, still seeking the convoy, which was supposed to have been heading out of Palermo, when young Haynes, on the ASV set, said that he thought we might have a "blip". With so many small islands in the area I didn't see how it was possible to interpret the overcrowded patterns on the screen with any certainty, and I asked "Chiefy", who was behind him, to have a look too. The whole crew had developed an uncanny sense at picking up objects on the ASV. I spent about five minutes above thin, scattered cloud, turning this way and that as the two of them tried again and again to re-tune the set so as to give optimum results.

"Yes, Skipper, we think there is a ship or two between the islands. If you could approach from the mainland it might become clearer."

This suited me as it meant that I would also be running towards the setting moon. We fused the 250-1b bombs we were carrying, setting them to explode 11 seconds after a strike. When attacking at sea-level height an exploding bomb would destroy the plane that had dropped it unless a time-delay such as we had set was put upon the fuse. We opened the bomb-doors, manned both turrets, dropped down to a few hundred feet, and began a cautious run-in as directed by Haynes, who had decided to remain on the ASV set. Evans was in the rear turret. Terrington took over the nose turret. Haynes curbed his excitement and went through the drill like a veteran.

"ASV to Skipper."

"Answering."

"They are definitely ships, sir, and there are at least two—five miles almost dead ahead."

At three miles I could see a large hull shape crossing the broad, silvery moonlit path. I had prepared for such an event for the best part of a year. I knew the obvious error to avoid. At all cost I must never drop my bombs at the middle or towards the rear of the ship as the forward movement of the ship could easily result in a miss astern. I shifted the aircraft to aim at or ahead of the bows. "Must drop early," I was muttering to myself. This would give us a double chance over the calm sea, since, provided the aircraft was very low and on a level keel, bombs so dropped would skip or bounce along the flat surface of the sea. Also the fatal underwater hits can only be achieved by an early bomb release.

We flashed over an accompanying destroyer at less than a hundred feet. Still not a shot had been fired at us, and as my finger trembled on the bomb-release button, I realised with horror that I was going to pass too far in front. I kicked furiously on the rudder and flung the aircraft at the ship which I could now see was of large proportions. But this banked the plane so steeply that my bombs could only fall outwards and away from the ship's bows. With our bomb load still on board and the aircraft standing on one wing, we swept over the ship's bow. Still in this banked and turning attitude I passed over another destroyer on the far side of the main target—after which all Hell came up to meet us. The gunners of the three vessels were blasting away, furious at having been caught napping, and now it was I and not they who was silhouetted against the bright Mediterranean moon.

Lowery, the squadron-leader, was saying something. Evans was firing back from the tail. Everyone was shouting at once on the intercom. A wild fury gripped me. By my stupidity I had fouled up a near perfect surprise attack. All I now wanted to do was to get back quickly before I lost sight of my target. With throttles wide open I hauled the aircraft round in a violent rate 4-plus turn, and sped back towards the target, being guided to it by the wild firing from all three ships. Only one gunner, in the bows of the big vessel itself, was at all near the mark, the tracer bullets of the rest were merely illuminating the scene for me. This time I never let the big bows out of my sight.

I was a bare fifty feet above the calm sea and was almost staring upwards at the vessel's high bows when I pressed the bomb-release and heard "Chiefy's" matter-of-fact voice report, "All bombs gone, sir."

I kept low and flashed below and ahead of the deck of the target before turning and twisting my way out of the area. The smell and smoke of cordite from my own front turret filled the plane. But we didn't seem to have been hurt. Nor, alas, did the enemy. I was yelling at Evans.

"Skipper to tail. Do you see anything? Did we hit her? Did you see anything? Did you see anything? Can you hear me? Did we hit her?"

The horrible dull certainty of failure was beginning to overwhelm me when suddenly Evans erupted into a garrulous garble of "Yippee, wow, boy oh boy!" I could get little sense from these ecstatic rantings, but it was the noise I most wanted to hear and it instantly calmed me.

"I gather we hit something," I remarked to the squadron leader beside me. We turned the plane to see what we could see. I had dropped all eight bombs and Evans now was telling me of at least two terrific explosions. All enemy firing had ceased and *we* now had *them* exposed in the moonlight once again. We had climbed to about 2,000 feet and the last we saw of the scene, some ten minutes later, was that the big ship had stopped: it was listing with a cloud of billowing smoke pouring out of it. One destroyer had pulled alongside. This would have made a sitting and rewarding target for another bomb run, but we had expended all our bombs on the one attack. My blood was still boiling and I was all for going down and attacking the stationary ships with both turrets. Gently and deferentially Squadron-Leader Lowery dissuaded me.

"Is it really worth the risk, Skipper?" he sensibly enquired. "At best you could only kill a few more. You can't sink ships with machine-gun fire." Reaction was now setting in and I found my hands trembling and I was suddenly eager to set course for home. October 8th, 1941 and one ex-conscientious objector was at war.

Two nights later I was out on patrol again with a young officer from another squadron deputising for the still-incapacitated Reason. We located a convoy east of Sicily shortly after it had passed southwards through the Straits of Messina. We had Flying-Officer Glazer, an ASV officer on board, and by arrangement we attempted to guide a Swordfish squadron from the neighbouring Fleet Air Arm base at Hal Far to the ships we had found. The ruse worked, and an hour or two after sending our first sighting report, and whilst we still shadowed the enemy by ASV, the old "stringbags" arrived in formation and fired their torpedoes with such success that at least three ships were hit. The escorting Italian destroyers darted to their assistance, their creamy wakes being easily discernible in the bright starlight.

I now attempted to guide a force of Bomber command Wellingtons to the same target, using this time a continuous radio transmission.

This too succeeded, and the Wimpeys carried out some medium-level bombing. For this attack I had dropped by pre-arrangement a line of two of parachute flares in an attempt to illuminate the area better. I was about to tour the area for a final assessment of damage before returning home, when I received a wireless signal ordering me to keep shadowing. We did our best, although the enemy was now split into at least two groups and some had stopped altogether. Several hours later the Swordfish squadron returned and dropped another salvo of torpedoes. In all at least two ships were sunk and others damaged.

I had been in action over ten hours, and I had to break the rule forbidding heavy aircraft to return to Malta in daylight—luckily without being intercepted.

Another long sortie followed two nights later. Again the accuracy of the intelligence reports, plus the effectiveness of our ASV, under warm Mediterranean skies, enabled us to find the enemy convoy. Lowery again opted to fly with us, although I also had the co-pilot of our SDF squadron-leader's crew with me. The ships ran for safety into the Italian harbour of tiny Pantellaria before I could summon any attacking forces from Malta. Pantellaria is a companion island to Malta, about one hundred and forty miles to the west-north-west. The island put up a heavy barrage of flak and searchlights as we flew over the harbour and aimed our bombs at the port into which the convoy had scuttled. There was too much smoke and cloud for us to see if we had hit anything of value, and we turned for home rather than expose the aircraft further to the enemy's fire.

I now had had only two night's sleep in the last five. I was also aware that I was doing more flying than the other two crews put together. But I was finding the targets. However, I was dead tired. The island was being raided, chiefly by Italian planes, at least four or five times per day, making daylight sleep spasmodic at best. The bad winter weather was beginning and with clouds nearly at ground level I had the utmost difficulty in getting the plane down safely, due both to weather and the almost pitch dark state in which the airfield had to remain. I walked into the underground operations room and, as usual, was almost blinded by the sudden light. Everyone there was standing up. Rather stiffly someone said, "This is Pilot-Officer Spooner, sir."

I was still festooned with flying clothes, boots, gloves, helmet, goggles, intercom, and was too tired to take careful note of the situation. As my vision improved I could pick out an officer wearing more stripes and medal ribbons than I had ever seen before. He had an abrupt, direct manner, a fine head and piercing eyes. He strode towards me.

"Congratulations, Spooner," he fired at me, fixing me all the time with a penetrating gaze. All at once I felt better. I had never before met any officer of such high rank, and it pleased me to discover that instead of sitting in his fine safe office or sleeping in his comfortable bed, he could be found at five o'clock on a wet and miserable morning at the heart of an operational station, apparently taking an interest in incoming crews.

He listened whilst I went through the debriefing, and when this was complete, he again stepped briskly forward. He held out his hand.

"We haven't met, have we? I am the AOC—Lloyd. Air Vice Marshal Lloyd."

This was news indeed. Air Vice Marshal Hugh Pughe Lloyd was not just the Air Officer Commanding RAF forces in Malta. He was also a much-discussed personality. Some held that he was too brutal and unrelenting: others swore by him, declaring that he was the finest leader we could possibly have. None was negative about him. He wasn't that kind of man. At that time I imagined that all Very Senior Officers lived in comfort whilst being waited upon hand and foot by pretty little WAAF's. Later I was to learn that this particular officer slept, when he did sleep, in a hole in the ground with the Admiral on one side of a partition and he on the other.

He had won my support simply by being there at that ungodly hour, and I really warmed to him when he said that he had been studying the weather and that he realised how "damned difficult" it must have been to get down safely.

"You were out two nights ago, weren't you?"

"And two nights before that, sir," I shot back.

"Aren't there three of you—three crews?"

"Yes, sir."

"What are the others doing?"

It was on the tip of my tongue to say "precious little", but I refrained. My silence was probably as informative as anything I could have said.

"Oh, I see. Now, Spooner, I want you to get a good rest for a night or two. I'll see you aren't disturbed. Then come and see me in my office. I am not entirely happy about your ASV. Maybe we can put it to better use, eh? Come and see me in a day or two. Ring for an appointment first. Now off you go to bed. Well done. Keep up the good work."

It was machine-gun talk, but I welcomed its directness. The man was impressive, too. He had a fine head, strong mouth and smoked dramatically from a long black cigarette-holder. He didn't want to see my squadron-leader. He didn't want me to report to my Luqa Station Commander. He wanted to know about ASV and he wanted to hear this directly from me. I was eager to tell him, too, as already I had noticed that others at the station were, in their complete ignorance of the apparatus (an ignorance I wasn't permitted to dispel for reasons of security), expecting things from our SDF unit that clearly weren't possible. Some seemed to think that all we had to do was to switch on, point the aircraft approximately in the right direction and then be able to describe in detail the number and types of ships we could "see".

When I phoned for an appointment I was put through to Hugh Pughe himself.

"Spooner. Someone else wants to see you first. Go and see Captain Agnew on his ship the *Aurora*. Tomorrow at 4 pm, OK? Then report back to me. All right?"

I was about to ask who Captain Agnew was, how to find the *Aurora* and to enquire what I was to see him about when he rang off. I had barely had time to say, "Yes, sir."

Thus it was that the following afternoon I reported in my best blue uniform at the naval dockyard at Valetta and told a curious marine, "I've come to see Captain Agnew . . . I believe he is expecting me."

It sounded unconvincing and I was asked to wait. I still had only my one half stripe of a junior officer, and if challenged I had no idea what I had come for. I had never had any connections with the Royal Navy and frankly I was a bit scared.

And what was I doing there? Why wasn't my squadron-leader there? My thoughts were interrupted by a voice saying, "Come this way, sir. Please follow me."

20: With the Navy—Force K

I FOLLOWED my guide through the bowels of the ship, envying him the dexterity with which he negotiated the ladderways.

Captain Agnew's cabin was a pleasant surprise. It was large and well-appointed in the style of an English country house. There was a chintz-covered settee, easy chairs, matching curtains, shining silver vases and framed family portraits.

Captain W G Agnew was tall, straight and lean, with balanced features and the easy gait of the natural athlete. He spoke quietly and had an economy of movement and gesture. Here was a shy, diffident man, who nonetheless commanded in an easy—if aristocratic—manner. He reminded me of the Edwardian characters I had read about until, from out of the blue, he would relax the controlled muscles around his jaw and expose a mischievous schoolboy grin. Then and only then was I aware of the generosity of his mouth. And as suddenly as it had been turned on this light would be switched off, and his "manner" would return.

A white-coated orderly brought the silver tea things. The cups were bone china, of course.

We chatted: I learned about his family, his home and his animals. For a few golden moments I was transported back to the English countryside—far removed from the clanking steel ship in the bomb-pocked harbour where we actually lay.

"Now, if you don't mind, Spooner, I would like to get my radar officer to join us?"

"If I didn't mind!" This man, apart from being vastly my superior officer (and in the Senior Service at that), had already won my affection.

"Now, Spooner," he continued, when we were all together, "I want you to tell us in the simplest possible language what it is that you have on board your aircraft and what it will do. I am not a scientist and I shall probably interrupt you"—his smile flashed—"especially if the talk becomes technical."

This was music to my ears. Someone at last wanted to know both the potential and the limitations of the device my plane carried.

He listened and he asked a few direct questions. I was left with the impression that during the next fifteen minutes he mastered all that I had ever learnt about the use of airborne ASV.

He, in his turn, then launched into a concise and clear description of his purpose on that bombed and battered island. He was the commander of Navy Force K. This consisted of four ships—two destroyers, *Lance* and *Lively,* and two light cruisers, *Aurora* and *Penelope*. His job was to sink the ships supplying Rommel and his Italian and German armies in North Africa. Both RAF and Naval Intelligence were first-rate, and word of intended departure of these ships from Naples or Palermo was often forthcoming or could be deduced from photographic reconnaissance. But he was not allowed to risk his ships in daylight in an area where the Italians had battleships and heavy cruisers and where Italian torpedo bombers frequently swept the seas.

A brief but brilliant history of naval actions fought at night followed, ending with: "So you see, Spooner, there has rarely been a naval engagement at night in which ships didn't fire at their own forces or in which ships failed to fire at enemy forces for fear they might be firing at their own.

"However," he went on, "I am allowed to leave harbour one hour before dusk and I am supposed"—the broad grin flashed for an instant—"to be back in port one hour after dawn, and it is just possible for me to reach their lanes in this time."

The time-scale allowed to him prohibited any search. By the time he reached the area where his prey might be, he was obliged to return.

He then explained his ideas to avoid the confusion which had so plagued previous night engagements. Force K steamed and fought *as one ship*. They steamed throughout at twenty-eight knots, at close stations, always keeping in each others wake.

If they got into a scrap they were thus at liberty to fire at *everything* not dead ahead or dead astern. It was as simple as that.

..... Enemy (Axis) supply routes.
– – – Enemy (Axis) supply routes adopted after December, 1941.
Benghazi had very limited port facilities. Tripoli was the enemy's

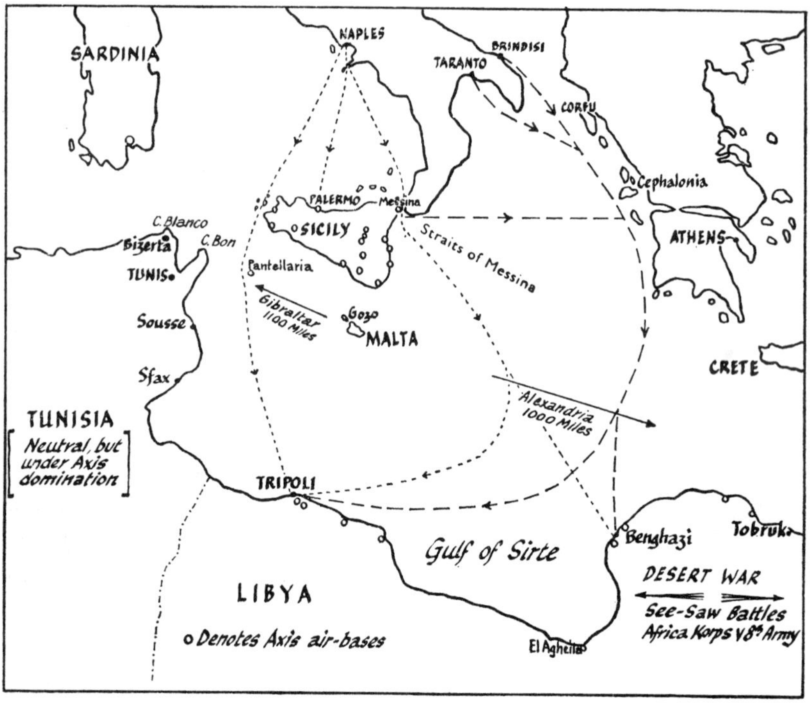

only proper supply base. Apart from Tunisia (neutral) all else shown was in Axis hands. The Desert Eighth Army briefly advanced to Benghazi, but soon fell back some 400 miles beyond Tobruk. Gozo was 43 miles from Sicily.

They were confident of success, but first they had to find an enemy to fight.

"So go home, Spooner, and think carefully over what I have said. Feel free to contact me if you require further information. Meanwhile, we here will be thinking, too. Let us meet again, say, in three days' time? I feel that between us we may come up with something useful, eh? This has been a most interesting afternoon."

He held out his hand. The tea party was over.

Events now followed each other swiftly. My squadron-leader was sent to Egypt as an instructor; the other aircraft captain was grounded. I found myself in charge of the unit. Hugh Pughe promoted me to flying-officer. A week or so later he added another stripe and made me a flight-lieutenant. I discovered that one of the second pilots had flown in command of a Wellington on a few occasions before. He was David Beaty, later to become known as a best-selling author.* Without further training he took over one crew. The other co-pilot, a young Scot called MacDougall, joined him. David henceforth became my right-hand man. If a third crew became necessary I knew that Sergeant Reason could manage on his own. And 2nd pilots could always be found on the island, which abounded with men whose own aircraft had been destroyed on the ground.

My ASV officer, a keen and scientifically gifted young Canadian by the name of Al Glazer, was soon hard at work with the Navy, and in no time they had rigged up an ASV beacon on top of *Aurora's* masthead. With this we would always be able to tell friend from foe, as the "blip" that *Aurora* now produced would appear on our ASV screen in a special shape. Also, it could be picked up at enormously enhanced range.

On another occasion Captain Agnew, his signals officer, and I sat down and in less than twenty minutes produced our own private wireless code. It was christened by Captain Agnew "the SAIR" code (SEA to AIR code). It reduced all signals to six or seven messages, each prefixed by SAIR and a coded Christian name, thus: SAIR GEORGE: SAIR EDWARD: SAIR WILLIAM: SAIR HENRY: SAIR ROBERT and SAIR CHARLES, if I remember it correctly now. These few words would tell what we wanted from the other. They also

**The Donnington Story, The Heart of the Storm, The Proving Flight, The Cone of Silence, Wind off the Sea, and a dozen other books.*

solved our separate navigational problems, as it was agreed that in guiding his ships towards the enemy I would pass him only *relative* bearing and distances. We chose to use one or two easily-remembered radio frequencies such as 8888 cycles. With our communication link established, we were now ready to embark upon an experimental form of air-sea co-operation. Within the next six weeks we were able to sink many enemy ships, and the only damage to our forces was one shell splinter in *Lively's* funnel. In fact, Captain Agnew and his Force K, of which we now proudly considered ourselves to be a part, virtually stopped all supplies going to the Afrika Korps at a time when they stood poised perilously close to Egypt. The biter had been bit. The insignificant dot on the map called Malta, surrounded and cut off and under constant siege, had successfully severed the enemy's African armies from Nazi-dominated Europe—their sole source of supply. Our submarines and strike aircraft had always harried this supply line but never before had our surface Navy dealt with it with such devastating success.

Let the enemy tell their own story of this success.

These are the words of the German Vice-Admiral Weichold: "In October, 1941 the African convoy tonnage dropped to 50,000 tons—a third of the monthly average of the past seven months. Of this, almost 63 per cent was either sunk or damaged; in the whole month only 18,500 tons of shipping space arrived safely in Libya. On the night of November 9th an Italian convoy was attacked by surface craft and almost destroyed. One destroyer alone survived.

"In November the total tonnage used fell to 37,000; of these, 26,000 tons were sunk and 2,100 tons damaged. This was 77 per cent—the highest percentage of tonnage lost and also the remaining 8,400 tons was the lowest monthly delivery . . . the battle for Cyrenaica (Western Desert) was not decided during a month of actual land fighting, but rather by these external factors. The battle had already been lost by the Axis months previously through the British mastery of the sea and air."

How were these actions fought? And why were they so startlingly successful? In writing down details I am conscious of the fact that from the RAF point of view these tactics have *never* previously been disclosed. They were worked out at two or three short meetings with Captain Agnew: and I certainly kept no minutes. Flying-Officer David

Beaty and Sergeant Reason rapidly picked up what we were doing by flying a sortie or two with me. The fact that we carried Naval signalmen in our planes also helped those at sea understand better the problems of the air. The system worked largely because we each understood the other's limitations and we grew to think as one.

A typical sortie worked like this: It would start when the Navy received an intelligence report or was passed one of Warburton's famous low-level photographs that a supply convoy was due to pass through the Straits of Messina or was to leave Naples or Palermo on a certain tide. Naval navigators would then work out where the enemy was most likely to be at various times during their passage to North Africa. These calculations indicated where Force K was most likely to be able to attack at night. One hour before dusk Force K would leave Grand Harbour, Valetta, and, in their line astern formation, would head towards where they hoped the enemy would be. At much the same time we, too, would head towards the area of probable interception. Our ASV Wellington would be loaded with fuel and flares. Sometimes, as night fell, we would pass over Force K. It was a thrilling sight to see our ships in a long straight line of foaming wake heading at speed away from the island.

We were "their aircraft". They were "our ships". Captain Agnew had this kind of effect on us all.

We would hasten to the "most likely interception" area, and there commence the long-drawn-out ASV search for our probable foe. Sometimes the ASV was first-rate; at other times, in poor weather, the best ranges we could obtain would be less than fifteen miles. With winter approaching, air-frame and engine ice menaced us whenever weather conditions forced us to fly in cloud. Usually the search area would be 150-200 miles or so from Malta.

Sometimes the enemy wasn't there at all, but if they were we usually found them in the end, even if it required several hours of search. We would make just one run over the ships to get a better idea of their numbers and size. If we suspected that the convoy escorts included battleships or heavy cruisers we knew that Captain Agnew would wish to be informed at once. At all times he wanted to know the enemy's approximate number (SAIR WILLIAM 7), approximate course and speed (SAIR EDWARD 190 degrees—I2) and the approximate number of their naval escorts (SAIR CHARLES 3). We would endeavour to get this information during one straight run over or alongside the enemy.

Thereafter we would shadow by ASV, keeping at least twelve miles away out of sight and beyond earshot in order to lull them into a false sense of security. I am told that aboard Force K ships' companies would cheer when the news was given that their "Goofington" had located a prey. Next, we would turn back towards Malta carefully plotting our time, course and speed until, at about ninety miles, the big special blip reflected off the ASV beacon we had affixed to *Aurora* would make its welcome appearance on our tiny screen. And when Evans, Terrington or Haynes would shout, "I've got them, Skipper!" it was our turn to cheer. Some quick plotting then had to be done on the Bigsworth board I still carried for this purpose, and in a few minutes I was able to pass to Captain Agnew his direction and distance relative to the enemy. This was our key SAIR message—SAIR HENRY 128-140 ie, "You are 128 miles away, and the enemy bears 140 degrees from your present position."

Back we would now turn to relocate the enemy and, as soon as we had positively done so by ASV, we again reversed course in Captain Agnew's direction. SAIR HENRY 104-160: "You are now 104 miles and he bears 160 degrees from you." As the night wore on and as I shuttled between the two groups I would eventually get to the position where I could get both sets of blips on my ASV screen simply by turning my aircraft through 180 degrees. At this point I would have undoubtedly got myself into the classic "night fighting muddle" had not the *Aurora* blip been of such distinctive size and character. As it was, friend and foe were readily recognisable. In the final stages Captain Agnew would begin to work Force K into a position from which he would be able to launch his attack into the bright Mediterranean moon. Using his superior speed he could manoeuvre his fighting ships so that they would not only be sure to intercept and engage but that they would be able to do so *on his own terms;* he could silhouette them against the moonlight whilst himself remaining hidden in the darker segment of the sky opposite.

And if there wasn't a moon, we would make one! "SAIR GEORGE 5" sent to me meant that I was to drop parachute flares (on the opposite side of the convoy to where Force K lay) in five minutes' time. I would drop these so that they drifted slowly down about two or three miles

24. A group of Fleet Air Arm Pilots. Lt. Bibby (cap under arm), Lt. Pain centre of group.

25. H.M.S. PENELOPE—damaged by mine and bomb blast. This earned her the nickname of H.M.S. "PEPPERPOT".

26. Christina who served the R.A.F. so well and was decorated for her work in Fighter Control.

27. Nelly Galea—barely 18. Her tireless work for the A.O.C. included saving the author's plane on one occasion. A Maltese to be proud of.

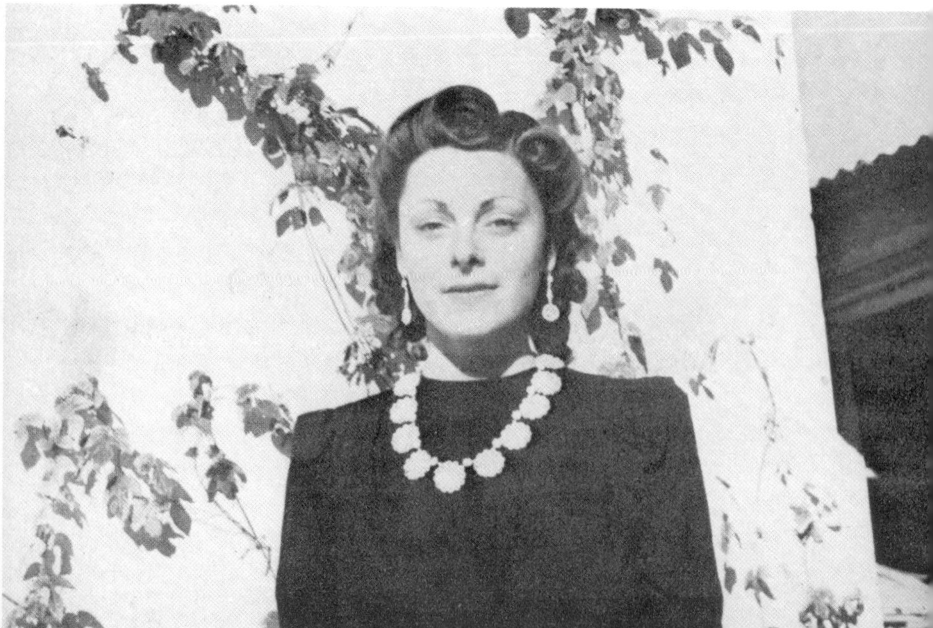

28. *Adrian Warburton. Individualist, Iconoclast, Ace.*

29. *A Maryland reconnaissance plane of 69 Squadron. In "Warby's" hands it became both bomber and fighter.*

30. A.V.M. Hugh Pughe Lloyd and Vice Admiral Ford.

31. M.V. TALABOT—hit abaft the funnel at No. 6. Buoy, Grand Harbour, Malta, 1942.

32. *Aerial photograph of Malta and Gozo. Hal Far is in the foreground. The two natural harbours of Grand Harbour and Sliema can be clearly seen on right of picture.*

33. *Wreckage of Junkers Ju 88 shot down over Malta.*

34. Building an anti-blast pen from empty petrol tins filled with earth—60,000 tins to protect each Wellington. The Army helped enormously.

35. Beaufighter on fire at Luqa Airfield caused by slow-burning incendiary bullet.

36. *On average this kind of thing took place 7 or 8 times per day during the author's period in Malta.*

37. *The tanker OHIO, badly damaged, is towed into Malta.*

38. *Many priceless tons of oil were pumped from the BRECONSHIRE before the Germans again set her on fire.*

39. Rockall—a bare rock several hundred miles out in the Atlantic. At the O.T.U. in Lamavady in 1942 we used to send advanced pupils to find and photograph it.

40. Ballykelly—from where the author set forth on several U-boat attacks. At this Coastal Command Station the runway was extended over the main railway lines.

41. Attack on an enemy submarine (coastal command at its best!).

42. At this time S/Ldr. Spooner was regarded as an "anti-U-boat Ace"—having attacked more at night than any other R.A.F. pilot.

43. 53 Squadron crew. Left to right: W.O. Ware; F/O Moore; Author; F/O Wilkinson, D.F.C.; F/Lt. Wells, D.F.C.; F/S Mills, D.F.M.; F/S Bayley, D.F.M.; F/S Thomson, D.F.M.; Sgt. Hinchcliffe; F/S Barnes, D.F.M. This crew gained 1 D.S.O., 2 D.F.C.s and 4 D.F.M.s.

44. This U-Boat was attacked by day. The author's night attacks presented photographic difficulties. This underwater explosion was near enough to be lethal.

from the enemy—again with the intention of keeping Force K hidden in the dark whilst silhouetting the ships it was to fire at.

Laying a stick of flares at the right place, angle, distance and time was by far the most difficult job we had to do. In my aircraft "Chiefy" Wavell looked after the actual flare launching, and each parachute flare, weighing about twenty-five pounds, had to be hand-launched through a small chute from a blind and draughty part of the fuselage. Naturally the flares opened and floated down far behind my plane and considerable anticipation, tight manoeuvring and liaison between ASV operator, pilot and flare dropper had to be employed. Foolishly, the enemy would often fire at these drifting flares, achieving nothing of any value but unmistakably revealing their position to the ships swiftly bearing down upon them from the dark of night.

Whether using nature's moon or "Chiefy" Wavell's version, the enemy never knew what hit them. It would all be over in minutes. Captain Agnew was an expert gunner, and by the time Force K opened fire every major gun of each of his four fine ships would have been trained and steadied upon an unsuspecting enemy. Their ships burst into flames as they were hit and they went down like ducks in a shooting gallery. More than once Force K sank all the supply ships and most of the destroyers too—but invariably their own ships emerged triumphant without a single serious shot coming their way. Each action would end with the laconic SAIR ROBERT—the signal for "search for survivors".

I have partially forgotten the christian names we used, and actual connotations we gave to each. SAIR EDWARD, SAIR GEORGE, SAIR HENRY,were, I believe, three of the groups we used, but the other names might have been SAIR ARTHUR and SAIR DONALD as easily as SAIR CHARLES and SAIR ROBERT. Nor do I now pretend to remember which name signified which message. What is certain is that we produced a code containing, at most, seven groups and that it sufficed for all our needs. Using Aldis flashlamp and the expert naval signaller carried by us, we would, on some occasions, fly back to Captain Agnew's Force K and pass supplementary information as we circled his ships.

We had become experienced at achieving petrol economy for various purposes. Whilst shadowing we virtually loitered with less than 100 mph on the clock. Range and endurance were major problems at times. On one night we located the enemy in a position only eighty miles from Benghazi. Force K was gamely ploughing along, but was still some way behind us and the night was drawing to its close. With the first rays of dawn lighting the eastern sky I received a brief message over our private frequency. "Go home," it said. We sadly abandoned the quarry which had occupied us for the past eight or nine hours, and as we flew past the Force K beacon on our way back to Malta we didn't go down through the clouds and circle. We were short of fuel and we realised that "our" ships were even shorter of hours of darkness.

Had we gone down to flash code at each other we would have been heartened. Captain Agnew had *not* turned back as I had imagined. He and his ships were still steaming into the rising sun although already a couple of hundred miles or so away from the protection of Grand Harbour.

The next twenty-four hours for Captain Agnew must have been among his most memorable. First, he caught up with our quarry in the clear, cold dawn and sank all three ships, including what I had thought was one tanker. At the time he was right on the edge of the minefield guarding the approaches to Benghazi and almost within sight of that port. Captain Agnew decided to make maximum use of this rare excursion into the daylight. The previous day a Blenheim from Luqa had damaged an enemy merchantman to the south-west of Malta. This had been reported and an Italian destroyer was thought to be attempting to bring this damaged ship into Tripoli. So instead of turning north-north-west and running back to Malta, Captain Agnew now led his force due west across the Gulf of Sirte in broad daylight. All day he was within range of at least half a dozen enemy airfields.

Naturally he was spotted, but his signals officers had acquired such a good working knowledge of the enemy codes, frequencies and procedures that they managed to jam each reporting message and even to invent false ones. At one time, when no less than three enemy planes were circling his ships, signals officers managed to keep up this subterfuge by ordering the circling enemy in the name of their base stations to keep radio silence! And all that day neither the enemy's naval forces nor his many torpedo bombers came to contest Force K's exposed position. By dusk Agnew had come upon the damaged merchantman and its destroyer escort. The latter fought bravely, but was no match for the superior guns of *Aurora* and *Penelope*. Soon *Lively* was busy with her customary task of picking up survivors. Only then did Captain Agnew turn his ships for home.

Some days later I asked him why he had ordered me home so soon. His answer was typical. Unknown to me he had obtained details of my aircraft's performance, and, not aware of the petrol tricks we had learnt, he had calculated that I must have been critically short of fuel!

When congratulating him on his success, I enquired how it was that he had been able to stay out in daylight contrary to what he had explained earlier. He gave his most disarming smile. His blue eyes twinkled. "You do realise, I hope, that I *did* get back to Malta in darkness?"

His look of innocence was such that I deemed it best not to ask him what had happened to the whole day he had somehow "lost" in between. As I drove home I recalled that Nelson, too, had known the waters surrounding Malta.

21: Successes—and Tragedies

CO-OPERATION with Force K was but a part of my assignment in Malta. For every sortie with them I flew two or more with the Fleet Air Arm. The Navy in one form or another kept me fully occupied. This had the effect of separating me from the RAF at Luqa. Our SDF was still based there, our Goofingtons were maintained there and from time to time the crews lived in quarters there. And, of course, we were still in Royal Air Force blue. But the unit had ceased to be an appendage of any Wellington squadron, and the group-captain in charge of this RAF station was my CO in a nominal sense only. I now reported directly to the AOC at his office underneath the viaduct connecting Floriana with Valetta, and from there I went across to Naval Operations room near by. After a while the Navy claimed my services to such an extent that I received an official signal from them ordering me to attend daily at Naval Ops room at 11 a.m. for a pink gin session! Another signal at that time from AOC Malta (Hugh Pughe Lloyd) directed me to patrol an area in the Adriatic using my "Bloody Instrument". On an earlier signal he had referred to "my ASV" and in the politest way I had had to tell him that these initials were secret and should not have been used.

The Fleet Air Arm squadrons with whom I co-operated were 830 and, more latterly, 828. The former flew Swordfish aircraft that would not have seemed out of place in World War I. They were wire and fabric biplanes with open cockpits entirely lacking in streamline or style. They rightly earned their nickname of "stringbags". They had an early mark of Pegasus engine of inadequate horsepower. They were tired and hopelessly out-of-date. Yet in the hands of the Fleet Air Arm they achieved miracles. A year previously they had crippled the main Italian battle fleet in its home base at Taranto. Also I am convinced to this day that I owe my life to the Swordfish pilot who disabled the mighty *Bismarck*. Their chief value was that they could (just) carry a torpedo. This weighed nearly a ton and the saying was that with the torpedo on board the aircraft would take off at 75 knots, climb at 75 knots, cruise at 75 knots and land at 76 knots!

Like Captain Agnew and his Force K this Swordfish squadron was willing and able to sink enemy ships, but its planes hadn't the fuel or range to search for them. Our job, in the SDF, was to find the enemy and to arrange matters so that the Swordfish could deliver an attack.

As before, with Force K, the night attack was only attempted after we received from Intelligence news that there might be a quarry within Swordfish range. Whilst our Goofington flew to the likely target area and began its long search for the enemy (who might or might not exist and whose position, course and speed was at best only inspired guess-work), the Swordfish remained on the ground at Hal Far, a naval airfield connected to Luqa by a long and tortuous taxiway. Upon finding a target we would transmit the normal sighting reports, telling them our estimate of the number of the enemy, their size, direction and speed. On receipt of this the Swordfish, *flying in formation at night,* would take off and head for a likely point of interception. They flew in formation because, incredibly, only one of them carried a navigator and proper navigational equipment. This crew also had the only plane to be equipped with ASV. The rest each carried a torpedo. The Stringbag's performance was so inadequate that it couldn't carry both a torpedo and a navigator with an ASV set.

My ASV officer, Al Glazer, again rose to the occasion, and this time produced an ASV beacon which he fitted to our plane. Our role henceforth was simply to keep in contact with the enemy. As before, we endeavoured to shadow our foe whilst keeping at a distance, hoping by this to lull him into a false sense of security. The leading Swordfish could, under good conditions, pick up our ASV beacon on his set, and so home on to us, at a good range. When they neared the target his crude set would detect the enemy, too. The leader would then manoeuvre his flight to the best attacking position. If he wanted us to illuminate the enemy ships he would send us a signal to commence flare-dropping, and, in just the same manner as with Force K, we would do our best to silhouette the targets. This was even more difficult as we had no means of telling, other than by an attempt to "read his mind", the direction from which the Swordfish leader was planning to attack. We would have agreed beforehand that if asked to supply flares we would lay them "away from Malta". This saved precious Swordfish petrol. Lieutenant-Commander Howe was their brilliant leader.

Apart from the obvious danger of having to drop torpedoes at defended convoys from aircraft which were painfully slow and vulnerable, the Swordfish pilots and observers had to fly at night in formation over an area plagued by ice, cloud and storms in winter. And their petrol reserves were so limited that they considered themselves lucky if they had ten gallons left upon arrival back in Malta. Communication between their planes and ours was never good. A modern VHF radio-telephone link would have made all the difference. As it was, we used wireless HF, and were obliged to employ complicated RAF and naval codes. In an endeavour to improve the situation we took to carrying one of their officers with us on each sortie. Their new acting CO, a hearty, bearded lieutenant called "Panco" Paine, flew with us more than once.

The spirit of co-operation could not have been greater. The pilot who often led the Swordfish was a Lieutenant Bibby who, by a lucky coincidence, had been one of the experienced amateur pilots at Liverpool during my time there as an instructor. Even in those days he had been an outstanding pilot. He was a Quaker, and thus a non-smoker who never touched alcohol, but he was as sociable as he was competent. I admired him greatly, and we became friends as well as key figures in an experimental form of co-operation between the FAA and RAF. I cannot recall any occasion when the Swordfish failed to hit at least one ship with their torpedoes during attacks. But there were occasions when they had to turn back due to engine trouble or lack of petrol or when I failed to guide them to their target for one reason or another.

One night I found them a small convoy beyond Pantellaria, and after sending the usual signals we remained around the enemy for hour after hour. Eventually we had to return to Malta, although no attack had been launched. I had left myself a reasonable petrol reserve, which was fortunate as it took me over half an hour longer to reach Malta than I had anticipated. Clearly the wind had changed direction.

Only when we had landed back did we learn that four of the seven

Swordfish, including that of their Commanding Officer, which had been dispatched to attack had mysteriously failed to return. The other three had returned earlier with mechanical faults. Various possible explanations were proposed. I was sure in my mind that the change of wind that had taken place had defeated them and that they simply ran out of petrol. I also believed that if we had been able to establish a readily workable communication link, I might well have been able to prevent this tragedy. This was a great loss to us all. By now, both David Beaty and I knew many of their pilots and observers.

At times the SDF, in spite of the frequent bombing of Luqa, was able to produce two serviceable aircraft, and on these occasions I might set forth in one direction, operating with Force K, and another crew under David Beaty or Dennis Reason would go off elsewhere to work with the FAA. Pilot Officer MacDougall was also "given a command course" by the only expedient open to us, that of taking him on a trip and telling him to land back! The vulnerable Wellington was not supposed to fly in daylight as enemy fighters were liable to patrol over our airfields. Even at night this ruled out normal training procedures.

Later 828 Squadron also came to Hal Far. They flew Albacores—a slightly modernised version of the Swordfish. They had less restrictive weight snags and were a little faster. Lieutenant-Commander Langmore was the CO and again a good measure of cooperation resulted in many enemy ships being damaged or sunk.

I shall always remember with pride my association with these FAA flight crews. Their morale was inspiring. Their feats were outstanding. At times they would land agents in the desert behind the enemy lines south of Tripoli—and once with a bicycle strapped on the side of the Swordfish. They hadn't the fuel capacity for such a two-way journey. They therefore loaded their cramped, open cockpits with spare four-gallon petrol tins and, after night landings behind the enemy on lonely roads, they calmly set about the laborious job of refuelling their ancient biplanes by hand.

One FAA officer who flew with us two or three times was Lieutenant Stevenson. And we were helping the FAA on an attack when "Steve's" own Swordfish was shot down. We got word of this and managed to locate him in the water. However, the remains of the convoy went steaming away, abandoning him in the dark waters a hundred miles or more from any possible aid. It was sad that all we could do for this brave and likeable man was to fly low over the sea as slowly as we dared and to attempt to drop through our hatch a few supplies and a Very light pistol and cartridges wrapped up in our Mae Wests. We had earlier flown alongside an enemy destroyer and tried to get this to turn back and go to Steve's rescue by dropping flame floats in a line. Not surprisingly, the destroyer merely fired at us.

All in all, November was a very active month. It was the month when I officially took command of our little unit, and, in addition to my two promotions and twenty-fifth birthday, I was also awarded the Distinguished Flying Cross. But it also became a month of deep tragedy.

It all really began when a decision was made to reinforce the naval strength at Malta. This must have been a very secret move. Certainly it was unknown to me. I was by then on friendly terms with Captain Wadham, Commander Martin Evans and the rest of the Naval Operations room. I first learned about this reinforcement in a curious manner. Sergeant Reason had taken my crew to search for some enemy ships believed to be attempting to run from Sicily to Tripoli by hugging the French shorelines around Tunis. In the area between Cape Bon and Cape Blanche, the corner of land north of Tunis itself, his ASV picked up some blips. They were so close to the shore that he dropped flares in order to verify the sighting. Later he sent radio signals to Luqa calling the Swordfish and Albacores to the attack. Very shortly after transmitting this report, and long before any plane could possibly be expected to arrive, flashes could be seen below and soon flames and a pall of smoke rose upwards. Some kind of battle was clearly taking place. At about the same time the Cape Bon light went out. This latter normally was a great help to us. Since French territories in North Africa were still technically neutral it was in order for their lighthouses to continue to operate, although no other navigational lights burned for hundreds of miles around.

We only learned what had happened the next day when the local radio urged the citizens of Malta to go to Grand Harbour to cheer the victorious destroyers as they steamed in.

As I now remember it, four of our destroyers bound for Malta from Gibraltar were passing Cape Bon when, aided by the Wellington's signals, they virtually ran into the enemy. This consisted of two Italian light cruisers carrying a deck cargo of petrol plus a few other ships and escorts. The use of cruisers as petrol carriers shows how desperate the enemy now were. Our destroyers were so close to the French shore that they barely had room to turn their ships in order to fire their torpedoes. The two Italian cruisers were both set on fire and believed sunk. The startled enemy, attacked by an invisible force, could only see the Cape Bon lighthouse and, in panic or desperation, they shot this out! The destroyers involved were *Sikh, Maori, Legion* and the Dutch *Isaac Sweers* in what proved to be a David and Goliath battle. The Navy made out that the engagement was an unplanned but happy coincidence.

At about the same time some larger cruisers also came to Malta. These joined the latest destroyers and became Force H. But when operating with Agnew's Force K, the combination was called Force B.

The Navy in Malta had been reinforced in order to pursue the tactics that Force K had proved so successful. However, I rather resented the fact that we of the RAF were not taken as fully into the Navy's confidence as had been the case in the past.

One of their big cruisers was the *Neptune*. The others were, I think, the *Ajax* and the *Sheffield*. This latter was the leader and carried a rear-admiral in command.

Captain Agnew and I were both told that we could no longer use our private SAIR code. Apparently our few simple messages had been intercepted by Navy monitoring units both in Gibraltar and Alexandria, and decoding experts had been trying to break our code and to determine whence these strange signals came! I also learned that such a large force wouldn't be able to steam in one straight line. All in all, our established simple patterns suffered many changes.

In due course we learned from Warburton or from the Intelligence of a target, and I set off knowing that the naval forces behind me now consisted of about four cruisers and six destroyers. They expected the enemy to have larger escorts and they were prepared for major naval actions if needs be. We did find a target, but the handicap of not being allowed to use SAIR code proved formidable. We had to fly the whole way back to Force B and pass our sighting report with signal lamp. With such a large naval force to circle this was more difficult than before. Some confusion resulted, and after many rather frustrating hours of shuttling, we were delighted to observe that our home forces had split into two. The newcomers were returning to base leaving four familiar ships in a long white line heading towards the enemy. We cheered aloud. We were once again alone over the sea with "our" Force K.

A big naval victory luncheon was arranged a few days later, and I was invited. My car broke down on the way and I had to thumb a lift on a Maltese donkey cart. This caused me to arrive at the Customs House steps half an hour late. A naval sentry informed me that "the Admiral's barge would return for Flight-Lieutenant Spooner shortly". We were to lunch on the island fortress of St. Angelo.

My embarrassment when I finally arrived was great. The rest had nearly finished eating. At the table sat Vice-Admiral Ford (VAM), Rear-Admiral Rawlings, Captain Wadham, Captain Nicholls (*Penelope*), Captain Agnew and several other captains unknown to me. Only Commander Martin Evans had less than four thick gold rings on his sleeve. By the time I had hastily gulped down the best meal ever put in front of me whilst in Malta, and after the third or fourth passing of the port bottle, I was less self-conscious of my inferior rank. In fact, I was in a friendly argument about the merits of Socialism with *Neptune's* magnificently Irish Captain, "Rory" O'Connor. Wine, food and port were having their effect. I heard Captain Agnew's controlled voice saying: "Let's ask Spooner. After all, he represents the RAF here."

He was at the far end of the table with the admirals. He gently explained to me that they had been discussing the thorny problem of whether or not Coastal Command, "the eyes of the fleet" as they had been called, should be directed by the Royal Air Force as at present, or, as they were contending, by the Royal Navy as in the past. I told them that I had served in Coastal Command and that I agreed with their contention that Coastal Command and the Navy should be partners. However (and here the port rose to the surface), I had one small difference of opinion. "I maintain, sir," I said, "that Coastal Command should take over the Royal Navy."

There was a horrible hush as the six or seven captains and the two admirals first looked at one another, then at the flushed face of the acting-flight-lieutenant speaking. Luckily I had often drunk pink gin with Vice-Admiral Ford, the senior officer present; luckily, too, he had a sense of humour!

The incident was relayed back to Hugh Pughe, my AOC, and I gather that he enjoyed my rallying to the defence of the RAF.

This luncheon might well have been the start of greater things. But luck now turned against us. On the very next sortie with this large naval force, tragedy struck. In the first place, the Goofington was unable to pick up the now familiar Force K beacon. Unknown to Al Glazer it had been shifted from *Aurora's* to *Neptune's* mast. Here it failed to work. The task of guiding this sizeable force on to an enemy became immeasurably greater, and long before any such link could be established Force B, with *Neptune* leading, ran into a minefield, and only the four ships of Force K were trailing paravanes—the anti-mine cables designed to touch off mines before they came too close. *Neptune* hit mine after mine and sank in about three minutes with the loss of nearly all her 560 officers and men. This left Captain Agnew in command. He despatched the destroyer *Kandahar* to go to the aid of *Neptune*, but mines were now exploding all over the place. *Kandahar*, too, was mined and had her stern blown off. Captain Agnew, to save further losses, ordered "about turn" and so took the rest to safety out of this highly lethal area. It was an unenviable decision to have to make. He and Rory O'Connor had long been together, and were old friends from Dartmouth and Whale Island days. But Rory O'Connor in *Neptune*, together with all her company, and *Kandahar's*, too, had to be abandoned to the sea in enemy waters at night.

Aurora and *Penelope* were both damaged, as their paravanes had touched off several mines. Force K and the remains of Force H limped back to Malta at reduced speed.

Captain Agnew was standing and staring at the walls of his cabin as he told me about the action. His face was half turned away from me. His voice told me of the strain.

"You understand, Spooner," he said, "that I had to give the order to withdraw." There was no doubt in his voice, only a deep, echoing sadness.

Neptune and her crew were gone. But we bucked up a lot next day when first we received a message from a patrolling aircraft of 69 Squadron that *Kandahar* was somehow still afloat. She had lost forty-three feet of her stern, but skill and craftsmanship in her making and the calmness and discipline of her crew had somehow enabled her, or two-thirds of her, to keep above the surface of the sea. She was over a hundred miles from Malta and obviously immobile. She had no engines, no power, no fighting value. She could send no signals. She was such a sitting duck that our hopes soon fell. It seemed certain that during the day an enemy plane or destroyer or even an MTB would be sure to apply the *coup-de-grâce*. Either that or she would sink without further attack.

The destroyer *Jaguar* and, I believe, the *Isaac Sweers* were ready to put to sea again, and a plan was swiftly prepared. These ships would go out that night and would try to get close enough to the sinking *Kandahar* to pick up those of her crew who had not been killed. It was hoped also that a few of *Neptune's* survivors might have been able to get aboard *Kandahar*. Would I go out and help?

The ASV beacon we had made for the Navy had gone down with *Neptune* so the task wasn't going to be at all easy. I enquired from my friends in Naval Operations what the chances were. They said it was 10-1 against *Kandahar* even being afloat. We only had one plane serviceable, and I decided to send Dennis Reason, who hadn't flown for a week or so. He had been training a second pilot to our specialised work, and he had told me that his crew were now capable of carrying out any job. I regarded this rescue attempt as no more than a training exercise for Reason (flight-sergeant now), as I had been assured that if she wasn't already sunk the Italians were certain to send *Kandahar*, powerless and stationary, to the bottom as soon as darkness fell.

As it happened, Reason found *Kandahar* still just afloat. She was listing and low in the water. He radioed this news and hastened back to make contact with the onrushing *Jaguar* and to guide her to the right position. Also, on his own initiative, he carried out a search to the south, from where enemy forces would most likely be coming. To his dismay he located a force of MTBs on their way. They were closer to *Kandahar* than was *Jaguar* and would clearly get to the stricken ship first. At this point he displayed a touch of greatness. He had observed that the enemy torpedo boats were slightly off-track and would, if they held their course, pass to one side by a mile or so of *Kandahar*. Could he, he wondered, get them so far off track that they would miss altogether? It was the only hope. He thereupon flew back to *Kandahar* but to one side and, when about thirty miles distant from *Kandahar*, he proceeded to put up the best pyrotechnical display he possibly could. He jettisoned his drift-taking flame floats and left them bobbing on the water; then, climbing high, he launched flare after flare, and as these drifted down he dived down to go skimming over the water firing all his guns upwards. Tracer bullets thus flew upwards as flares drifted down.

The ruse worked. The enemy boats altered course and sped towards the display. And by the time they realised their error, Reason had guided *Jaguar* alongside the stricken *Kandahar* and, in a flurry of frenzied activity, *Jaguar* safely took off all 173 men aboard her. A few minutes later *Kandahar* rolled over and sank.

When the survivors reached port almost the first action they took was to ask the Goofington crew to visit them. The party was to be held on board one of the naval cruisers. Reason and his crew were all away from camp. "Chiefy" gave me some clues where they might be, and the Navy set forth to round them up. One by one they were located: all except the principal guest. Eventually they found Dennis Reason emerging from church as it was now Sunday. I kept well clear but I gathered that the party was a vast success. One twenty-one-year-old flight sergeant and his crew were chaired, fêted, feasted and cheered. When it was all over I gave them all a few days leave and they went off to Gozo, the smaller island to the north of Malta.

I was absolutely elated at Reason's great success. We had flown together for nearly a year, and we had done over fifty operational flights sitting inches apart. I felt entitled to regard him as a protégé. Also, I now knew for certain that in him I had another first-rate crew. This was good news, too, as David Beaty and I had carried almost all the load to that point.

A few days later Reason took his crew on a search for enemy ships and had the FAA torpedo-carrying biplanes at Hal Far at readiness. He and his crew went out in high spirits. They never came back. It was less than a week since he had saved 173 men. And we never knew what became of him. Was it our old enemy ice? Did an unkind fate decide to burden him with a faulty engine? Our Wellingtons wouldn't fly with one inoperative. Did the lack of an accurate altimeter lead him into the waves as he searched low? Did the absence of any proper weather report lure him to his destruction? Or did he and his crew die gloriously attacking the enemy?

All I know was that an unbelievable event had happened; that my eager, young, fresh-faced companion-in-arms was gone. And I felt as empty within as Captain Agnew must have felt when forced to abandon his old shipmate to his certain death.

Flight-Sergeant Dennis Reason, from somewhere in Stafford, I salute you. Before you died you proved yourself.

22: Malta—Darkness and Light

MY worst moment in Malta came at the time when we had driven the enemy to seek longer convoy routes. They now passed their ships, whether Benghazi- or Tripoli-bound, by a circuitous route which hugged the Albanian and Greek coasts and almost went as far east as Crete.

On one such sortie our Wimpey and all its aerials became iced up. This was not unusual, but this time it was especially bad. However, after some hours of search, a large blip appeared on our ASV screen at a range of forty-one miles.

"Must be an island," I told the WOP/AG who had given me the report.

We had never had a ship or convoy blip beyond about thirty-five miles even in good, cloudless, dry weather.

I had very little idea of where I was. We had been searching the sea for hours either in or below cloud. I thought it just possible that the island could be Caphalonia or Corfu so I altered course to home on to it. It might tell me where I was.

"Skipper, it's definitely a convoy with at least one huge ship in it."

Although I was flying with Beaty's crew, using MacDougall as co-pilot, I knew that the ASV operators were experts. Their interpretations of these tiny green blips, "ticks" no more than three-sixteenths of an inch long, were positively uncanny.

What kind of ship was this?

In the dark of the night we tried to get positive identification, but our ASV was behaving oddly. The patterns on its screen kept changing range abruptly. Whenever we tried to home onto them, they disappeared. It was the devil's own job to find the enemy at all. Several times we picked them up *after* we had passed by them. As we homed in towards them they would move farther away. Ice on every aerial hummed with vibration and was causing the set to work in reverse. It was a long, painstaking process, and when we did manage to get ourselves over the ships, all I could see was the unusually broad wake of just one.

"Christ!" I yelled. "It's a ruddy Eye-tie battleship."

We tried again and again to regain contact but the weather was appalling, and for once the enemy didn't give away their position by gunfire.

Another crew member was quite positive that as well as the battleship, if indeed it was one, there was another huge liner in the convoy. "Big enough to be the *Rex* or the *Contessa de Savoia*." This was indeed news. These two ships were crack Italian 50,000-ton liners. The presence of a battleship now made better sense. Normally, these speedy heavyweights of the Italian Navy kept to their ports. Certainly we had never seen one. But if the *Rex* or the *Contessa de Savoia* was at sea, their presence was likely.

The large ship was later reported to be the *Vittoria* of 24,000 tons. It was hit and sunk by bombers and torpedo planes from both Malta and the Middle East.

Finally we transmitted a guarded radio signal reporting that we had found a large cruiser or battleship, a 25,000-ton liner and about five other vessels or escorts. We were beyond Swordfish strike-range, and beyond Force K range, too. We only had the haziest idea of where we were, but we did our best to give an approximate position. We tried to find a better fix by flying towards Greece and Crete but, with our ASV behaving so erratically, I did not dare to wander far for fear of losing all contact with the convoy. We had no idea what forces of ours were available to tackle this formidable foe. Our radio also became iced-up, and for long periods we lost all contact with Malta.

Except when using a burst of full power to fight off carburettor ice, we exercised maximum fuel economy. We also made several attempts to climb through the weather into the clear sky above, where we could attempt to fix our position by reference to the stars. All night long we struggled to remain in contact with the enemy; to find out where we were; to get our radio to work, and to combat the various effects of engine, aerial, airframe and propeller ice. We had our hands full. In case British submarines or fleet units from Alexandria or from Malta were being dispatched we wanted to remain over the enemy as long as possible. We were half expecting some special instructions. But none came.

Finally we turned for home. The weather had improved a bit. Under these conditions our ASV ought to have been able to locate Malta at about eighty miles. The navigator said that Malta should be "close to us", but as we still had nothing but sea showing on ASV, I became anxious. We climbed above cloud and saw the sun rising in the east. The need to be back before daylight was the least of my worries. Above all else I wanted to know in which direction Malta lay. If, by chance, I had already passed over it, then every mile I flew farther west spelt disaster as petrol was dangerously low.

I got MacDougall to fly the plane on an economical square search for the island. This more or less kept the aircraft where it was at minimum cost of petrol. Whilst he was doing this and using the Bigsworth board, which I still carried, I attempted a complete replot of the hundred or more courses we had flown during the night. From the various drift readings (on nights like this we would launch up to sixty flame floats for drift-taking purposes) I tried to calculate both where the winds had been and to draw up an isobaric weather chart to tell me where the wind now was. It was eighty per cent guesswork, but at least it was better than doing nothing or flying aimlessly on.

It took me nearly half an hour. Finally I came out with some kind of position. All that could be said for my efforts was that I figured with some certainty that I had not yet overflown Malta. I now turned the plane north towards Italy. The chance of being able to find Malta itself was remote. If I could locate Italy and recognise where I was, I still might have a chance to reach Malta before all petrol was gone. The aerials began to thaw out in the clear morning air above the cloud and I eagerly requested the wireless operator to get me a series of a homing bearing. This was something we seldom did as the enemy had the habit of intercepting these requests and of supplying false information. A station replied: "Unable to read your signals. Signal strength too weak for any bearing."

With still no sign of land on the ASV, and with no radio assistance and precious little petrol, I was in real trouble and knew it.

"Captain to radio."

"Radio answering."

"Send out an SOS."

Now, not one radio officer in a hundred is ever asked to send out this famous distress signal. You could hear the awesome hush throughout the plane. Every crew member had heard my order via the intercom which connected us all.

"SOS, sir?"

"Yes, tell them we are lost and are running out of petrol. Tell them our special equipment is on the blink. Tell them anything, but keep transmitting in the hope that someone, somehow, can give us a bearing. Try one frequency, then another, and keep pumping out SOS. Use plain language, if you think it will help them to understand."

Meanwhile I kept flying towards where I hoped Italy or Sicily lay.

"Radio to Skipper."

"Go ahead, radio."

"I've a funny kind of message here, sir. It's from Malta, I think. They suggest that we might be eighty miles away on a bearing of 095 degrees from them."

"Did they tell you what class of bearing?"

"No, sir, it's a very odd signal. Not their usual one." It certainly *was* odd. Malta didn't, indeed couldn't, offer us distances, only bearings.

Was I walking into an enemy trap? Were they trying to lure me over their land? At all cost I knew I had to crash into the sea. The secret details of the ASV equipment on board had to be preserved. Even if attacked we had to stay over the sea.

"Well, at least it's something. OK, I'll steer 095 degrees. Check your chutes. We may have to bail out approaching their coastline. Check the dinghies, too. Get someone in the nose turret, too. Everyone look out for fighters."

This was a sensible precaution, in any case, as it was now broad daylight in an area dominated by the enemy air forces. There were between 400 and 500 German planes based in Sicily alone at that time plus many more Italian planes.

At twenty-five miles a land blip appeared on the screen.

"Looks like Malta, Skipper," said a happy, confident voice.

And so it was. But twenty-five miles seems an awful long way for a dead tired crew in an aircraft, with every fuel gauge reading zero or below. Also, I asked myself, suppose an enemy raid was in progress? Would I try to land in spite of the attack or would I be better off ditching when within sight? We radioed for the Air Sea Rescue

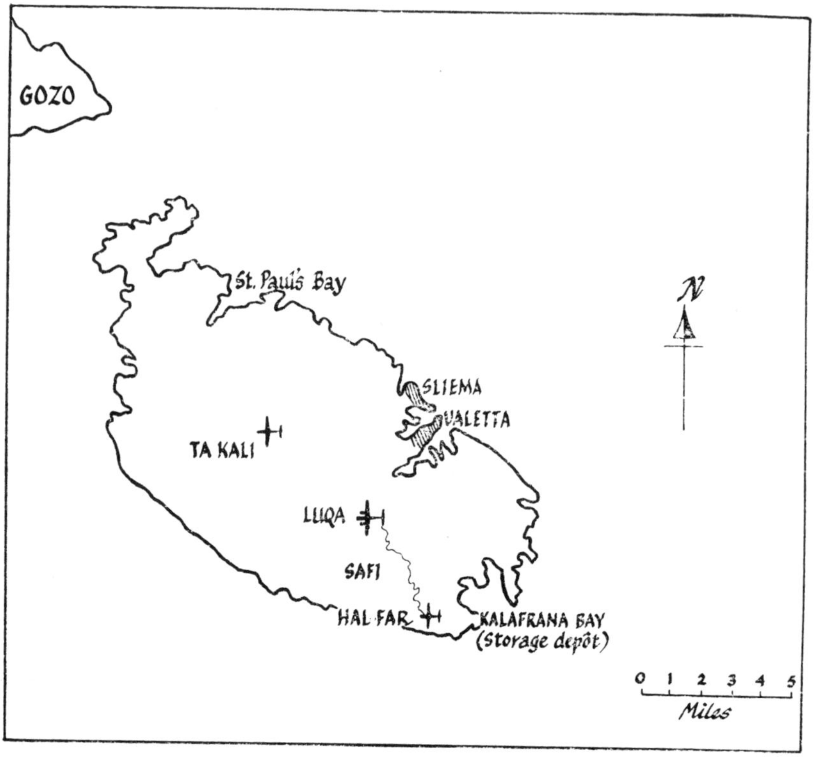

MAIN ISLAND OF MALTA

TAKALI was fighter airfield.
LUQA was bomber, recce transit airfield.
HAL FAR was Fleet Air Arm airfield.
SAFI was used as dispersal area and "graveyard".
These last three were connected together by undulating taxiways of a thousand bends.

launches to be alerted. Every minute was two miles less to have to swim. I let the aircraft drift down on near-idle throttles. This saved fuel. It also gave us our best chance against possible enemy attack. We were most vulnerable from underneath.

"We'll come in," I said, "over the Naval Dockyard. This way the guns of the Navy ships will protect us. Also if we do have to ditch, Grand Harbour is the best place."

My big fear now was that the engines would die from lack of fuel *after* passing Grand Harbour. That two or three miles up a slight rise to Luqa—a distance I had both cycled and walked often enough—now appeared to be enormous. It alone stood between our safe arrival and disaster. I didn't bother about obtaining landing permission, nor about the enemy, nor the wind direction. As soon as the runway nearest Luqa came within range, I closed the throttles and went straight on to it. We rolled to a stop. We were safely down.

My log-book tells me that we were airborne for over thirteen hours that night, and if anyone has ever been longer in the air in a Wellington I shall be surprised.

Days later I learned that we owed our survival to the AOC's secretary Nelly Galea. She was in his outer office when our SOS was first received. She had a boy friend who was the officer i/c of a look-out radar station near Kalafrana Bay. She phoned him. He swung his aerials to the SE, from where we were likely to come.

His powerful set detected one possible unknown blip at the considerable range of eighty miles. It could have been anybody, friend or foe, or even a heavy cloud. He took a chance. "Send him this," he ordered. And they did. I knew this Officer. I had on occasions played tennis with him. Indeed, with both of them. Flying-Officer Bob Povey and secretary Nelly Galea, I hope you will read this. My thanks are long overdue. . . .

Our luckiest moment came when we had been sent to see if we could find a cruiser which was believed to be at the south end of the Straits of Messina awaiting a convoy. This was about the first trip I flew with my new 2nd pilot—Sergeant (as he was then) Norman Lightowler. He was recommended to me by my crew. He was a captain in a Wellington bomber squadron, who, like dozens of others, had had his aircraft destroyed on the ground. I was attracted by the idea of having a pilot who, although a captain, was prepared to fly as a 2nd pilot, rather than twiddle his thumbs indefinitely.

The Italian cruiser and I started playing a cat-and-mouse game at the south end of the straits. She clung to the shore and it took all the skill of my uncannily accurate ASV operators to detect this ship. For the best part of an hour one operator after another thought they had a ship blip, then lost it in the larger land echoes. In the hands of almost anyone other than Terrington, Evans and Haynes the job would have been impossible.

This ship was leaving no wake, nor did she give away her position by gun-fire. Doubtless those on board heard our engines as we tried again and again to satisfy ourselves that we had indeed a target for those at Malta waiting to bomb or torpedo her.

We commenced dropping sticks of flares to see if we could detect anything by their illumination.

On about the second such flare-dropping run—at a time when I had joined the ASV operator on the set, in order to have a look myself—the Italians, at long last, lost patience. They must have got my plane well silhouetted. They opened up with what seemed at least fifty guns, and their colourful ammunition was exploding all around us. "Start avoiding action," I yelled to Lightowler at the controls.

Lightowler at once commenced the classic "rate 1 turn to the left; rate 1 turn to the right" avoiding action of Bomber Command. Perhaps Sergeant B—of Lossiemouth had taught him this gentle ruse? I practically hauled him bodily out of the pilot's seat and put the aircraft into a near-vertical spiral dive. As the fire burst further and further behind and just as I was about to order the W/OP to send out the sighting report, the rear-gunner, Evans, I believe, became screamingly incoherent:

"Crikey, Skipper . . . Cor . . . Yippee! Yeow!"

"Captain to tail. . . ."

"Skipper, you've sunk her. She's all blown up—never seen anything like it. She's blown herself to smithereens. We've sunk a bloody cruiser!"

Certainly all enemy fire had ceased and there now was smoke and fire below. And when we next flew near, the ASV showed us nothing. We didn't sweep low and look as we were almost certain to fly into the steeply rising hills if we did so. But what message was I to send?

It was patently impossible for my parachute flares to have sunk a cruiser. I ignored the enthusiasts on board who were still declaring that we "must have dropped a flare down her funnel!" It was, however, just possible that by her own gunfire the cruiser had destroyed herself through a flash-back penetrating her ammunition hold. I knew about such things, but knew also that in modern ships elaborate precautions were now taken to prevent such disasters.

I reported to Malta as factually as I could, "Cruiser located in such and such position. Enemy has since exploded."

At Luqa they couldn't understand this message, so sent the striking forces anyway.

Not till nearly two days later did I get an explanation from the Navy. They, too, were after this cruiser. One of their gallant submarines—small U-class boats of less than 1,000 tons—had positioned herself at the south end of the straits. The creeping progress of the cruiser gave our submarine a chance to draw within range. But before she could do so, down came my first stick of flares. The submarine captain (Lieutenant Tomlinson or Tomkinson) later told me that he had never been so horror-struck. In the midst of his purposeful stalk, he was suddenly illuminated by million candle-power flares. He felt as if he were on the Palladium stage without his trousers, with every spotlight focused his way. It took iron nerve to stay thus illuminated on the surface. Nothing happened, however, so, when darkness fell again, he moved closer—until once more he had to freeze in his tracks as the next flares drifted down. It was incredible that he wasn't spotted and blown out of the water by the cruiser's guns. However, when the ship opened up at our plane it presented a splendid target. The submarine was soon close enough to fire several torpedoes. Hits were scored and the Italian cruiser went down with appalling suddenness—exploding and disintegrating as it sank.

It was just as well that we hadn't claimed to have "dropped a flare down its funnel".

The important lesson I learned that night was that Sergeant Lightowler was both reliable and imperturbable. He didn't resent my outbursts or show a trace of emotion throughout. I learned also that he was a Yorkshireman. He was of medium height, slim build, with dark eyes and dark close-cropped hair.

With his lean features and slightly high colouring he could at a pinch have passed himself off as a Spaniard. But there was nothing Latin in his nature. The rest of the crew had long learned to live with my quicksilver outbursts of impatience. Sergeant Lightowler henceforth became one of us. I don't suppose for a moment that he was ever officially posted to the SDF. In Malta things like this didn't matter. Administration had lost importance. Apart from the remnants of the original three aircrews our total *official* strength consisted solely of Flying Officer Al Glazer, the ASV expert, and his three staunch radio-mechanics, Corporal Few and LACs Card and Rodgers.

The most furious outburst I ever gave way to in the air occurred during another flare-dropping incident. This task was always difficult to do accurately: when within two or three miles the enemy blips invariably disappeared off the bottom of the screen and became part of the sea echoes. From that moment I was obliged to carry a hypothetical picture of where the ships lay. Then, mentally calculating their course and speed, in relation to our direction and very considerable mph, and bearing in mind the wind factor and the direction from which our attackers were likely to be coming, I endeavoured to bring the aircraft to what, with luck, was the right spot.

"Chiefy", meanwhile, would be standing by the flare chute with another crew member holding a torch for him. The release lanyard would be clipped to the first flare, which would already be in the chute. The rest would be stacked near by.

"Stand-by, stand-by, stand-by—NOW!" I would shout through the intercom. "And another—and another—come on—faster—I want six on this run—get them out faster."

Each flare had to fall below the plane, pull itself clear of the lanyard and trigger itself in doing so. The lanyard then had to be hauled back by "Chiefy" and the process repeated. We needed six flare chutes, but only had one. We speeded up delivery by having two lanyards—each was about fifty feet in length—but it was still necessary to haul in the first line before lifting the next flare—all 25 lb of it—into the chute.

The flares never went out fast enough for me. My aircraft would be covering about two miles per minute, so every fifteen-second delay meant we had moved half a mile further on.

On one such run, after a couple of flares had been released there was an ominous silence from "Chiefy". I knew we had only dropped two flares as I could always see the glow underneath as each flare blossomed out. "Get another one launched," I yelled.

"GET ANOTHER ONE LAUNCHED," I repeated.

This was childish of me, but these were intense and vital moments on the result of which the enemy might or might not escape destruction. Also we would sometimes be under enemy fire at a moment when it was imperative that we flew in a dead straight line.

"Just a minute, sir, I've run into a slight hitch. I'll have to go off the air for a moment or two." When he reported back on the intercom I blasted "Chiefy" so much that for once it drew forth a reply.

"Please remember, sir," said a hurt voice, "that I am doing my best—we've got difficulties at this end—and that I am only an old man!"

This last made me laugh aloud in spite of my extreme impatience.

We now had to run back and do the whole job all over again, bedeviled by the ever-present thought that I was more than likely in the wrong place.

We came home in rather a strained silence. When I handed the machine over to Sergeant Dale—our priceless maintenance chief—he asked the usual, "Everything all right, sir?"

"She'll do," I replied.

"I think," said a mild, almost apologetic voice, "that Sergeant Dale had better have a look at the hole in the roof."

"What hole in the roof?"

"The one that caused the fire, sir."

"The fire? What fire? What hole?"

We climbed back inside, and by the light of torches inspected the damage. Stars could be seen through the roof where a section was missing. There were other signs of fire damage, too. The long casing of an expended flare was still protruding through the metal framework of the fuselage.

I could only stare in astonishment. When I regained my voice I started to ask questions.

"What in God's name has been going on? Were we hit by that flak? Why didn't someone tell me? What the devil is this thing sticking out?"

"Well," continued "Chiefy," "you seemed to have enough on your plate at the time, sir. And I didn't want to worry you. It was all my fault really . . ." He tailed off, leaving me to remember how mad I had been with him.

"Go on," I said quietly, "tell me all about it now."

"Chiefy" Wavell, in order to speed up the flare dropping, had got into the habit of pushing each flare down the chute and then *immediately* whipping back the lanyard. This could then be clipped more rapidly to the next flare. The lanyard, as explained, set off the flare, and the fifty-foot line was designed to provide an adequate safety margin. By whipping it back immediately, this margin was somewhat reduced, but at the speed at which we were flying the plane was not in any great danger. On this occasion the flare had stuck in the chute. Instead of falling clear it had blazed forth inside the chute. Part had gone down and out and part had been shot backwards into the metal geodetic frames making up the roof. And the intensely inflammable magnesium compound of the flare had set fire to almost everything near by.

This was the "slight hitch" to which "Chiefy" had referred. I realised too that he had temporarily gone "off the air" in order to beat out the flames. I looked at this little old man—nearly old enough to be my father—with wonder and amazement. He allowed himself a rare grin.

"It was really rather lucky, sir, that I didn't have my head blown off. I *usually* look down the chute to check that the flare lights up OK." Then more anxiously, "You won't be requiring a report from me, will you, sir? There will be no enquiry, will there?"

Sergeant Dale was grinning, his eyes brighter than usual.

"No, 'Chiefy'," I said, "we'll write this one off."

"Oh, thank you, sir. Thank you very much," he said.

I was glad that it was dark. I think by now I was close to tears.

23: Personalities: Malta at War

IN writing these few pages about Adrian Warburton I do him an injustice. "Warby" deserves a book on his own.* However, it is necessary to describe Warby to some extent in order to understand Hugh Pughe: Air Vice Marshal Hugh Pughe Lloyd, AOC Malta, about whom I will write later.

I do not think that I do Warburton a disservice if I describe him in full. The complexities of this extraordinary character need to be told, for he was not cast in any normal mould.

He joined the RAF shortly before the war on a short-service commission. Early war days found him serving in a Beaufort squadron. This was 22 Squadron but Warburton had failed to convert to the new type. He had also piled up a number of personal and financial problems of such magnitude that his CO arranged for Warburton to navigate a Maryland which was being ferried to Malta as part of a new 141 Flight.

After a few operations as a navigator, an opportunity to fly the Maryland arose. At first Warby, as all now began to call him, had many difficulties but, showing great courage and perserverance, he began to prove himself a remarkable Maryland pilot. A strange affinity between man and the beleaguered island had begun.

141 Flight soon became 69 Squadron. Its duties were to carry out photo reconnaissance of the enemy's ports and airfields. Warby's low level pictures of the Italian battlefleet inside the well-defended Taranto harbour did much to ensure the success of the famous Swordfish attack of November 1940. Within months, the pilot who had been hastily got out of England to avoid legal and other difficulties was being awarded the first of his four DFCs.

*This has now been done; *Warburton's War*, Wm Kimber, 1987, by Tony Spooner.

Unofficially Warby began to carry bombs. The Maryland had no bomb-racks. Accordingly they were delivered by his outstanding WOP/AG, Sgt Paddy Moran who simply kicked them out of his lower turret.

Warburton's lone bombing raids upon heavily defended Sicilian airfields were more or less the prelude to the air battles he fought with the enemy defenders. Success followed success until he and his crew in their reconnaissance plane could claim at least seven enemy aircraft destroyed—more at that time than any *fighter* pilot in the island! This on top of numerous bombing successes. They were shot at and shot up but always managed to return home. On one occasion Warby, whilst still flying, was obviously in some difficulties.

"What are you doing, sir?" asked his radio-officer Paddy Moran.

"I'm extracting a bullet from my heart."

"Did you say your heart, sir?"

"Yes."

"Aren't you supposed to be dead, sir?"

"I suppose so," said Warby, but he had other things on his mind then. The canopy had been shot away and one engine was on fire.

After nearly 150 operations, on all of which he brought back the required photographs, Warby and his crew, P/O Frank Bastard DFM, and Paddy, also with a well deserved DFM, were posted to an OTU in Egypt for an overdue rest. However, Warby instead attached himself to 2 PRU at Heliopolis and began to operate with a Beaufighter which the enterprising CO of the unit had had converted for photo reconnaissance operations. In all, about a ton and a half had been removed. The aircraft was painted dark blue and polished too as to provide it with sufficient speed with which to outrun all enemy aircraft. Within months Warby was back in Malta with Beau T 4715. Although he had returned in order to carry out a secret mission for Air Marshal Tedder, he was soon again working closely with the AOC Air Marshal Hugh Pughe Lloyd. In fact the two had become personal friends and, sensibly, Hughe Pugh (as many referred to him) gave Warby a completely free hand. Again Warby was photographing the enemy's airfields and harbours.

We had been trying to get this information for some time. By next morning Warburton had photographed the lot and they were excellent photographs, too. They were sometimes taken from the "suicide" height of 6,000 feet or less. The following morning he brought back similar photos of all the airfields in Tripolitania. Sometimes he would even cover both enemy areas during the same day! He photographed anything anywhere from any height. He was always unharmed, even when shot up in error by our own Hurricanes. "You should speak to them," he said. "Their shooting was terrible."

He refused to park his aircraft in the dispersal areas. Instead he parked it as near to Ops room as he could. It was never hit by bombs, although Luqa was raided at least once every clear day. He flew hundreds of such missions. He photographed the Italian Fleet in their naval base of Taranto in appalling weather from less than a hundred feet. He navigated himself unerringly all over the Mediterranean—without adequate meteorological services or navigational equipment. He went when they expected him and when they did not. He was often shot up and would be followed home by an armada of enemy fighters. He carried no guns or armour. He refused to fly with regular aircrew. He chose to fly with AC2 Haddon and LAC Shirley, their role on board being to change the camera spools and to count aloud the enemy fighters following him. He liked to take his coat off and to assist in servicing his own engines—a task for which he was not qualified.

He would fly in almost any clothes provided they were *not* the official ones. A thigh-length pair of sheepskin leggings which he had acquired in Crete were characteristic. Above this he would wear Army battledress with air-force stripes (he was now an acting flight-lieutenant). He preferred an Ascot cravat to a tie. He was proud of his ash-blonde hair, so let it grow to near shoulder-length. He had a notoriously grease-stained cap which he used to wear at times—on top of his flying helmet even. Against orders he smoked as he flew. He would take little part in mess life at Luqa, but instead could be found on occasions playing cards with the airmen at the dispersal site in one of the home-made huts there. Yet on one occasion at a time when most of us had run out of buttons, polish and smart uniforms, he turned up in the mess immaculately dressed in order to meet the new group-captain. He was like that—utterly unpredictable.

He lived in a flat in Valetta with a charming cabaret artiste, and he drove himself to work in an old car.

On and on he went, tireless, controversial, cynical, aloof. But in value absolutely beyond price. Although not by nature a normally contented person, I believe that he found himself and happiness—in Malta. And, later, when posted to other Mediterranean bases he found unofficial ways of returning to the island that welcomed him and appreciated him.

Malta, facing an invasion daily, was, thanks to him, able to study every enemy movement. Warby virtually ruled the skies over Southern Italy and North Africa, and not only did he live a charmed life, but his individually-fashioned Beaufighter did likewise. A second DFC followed the first. Then came a DSO, a third DFC, and a second DSO. He earned each medal several times over.

Shirley and Haddon were each given the DFM as well. They were not officially aircrew so were apt to be arrested whenever any keen-eyed RAF policeman spotted these airmen wearing flying medal ribbons. His constant companion was also decorated, officially for her services in HQ.

With the Beau at last damaged, Warby, with his two decorated aircrew "erks" on board returned to Egypt and was soon again operating with 2 PRU. By then this unit had acquired PR Spitfires and Warby at once began a successful love affair with this famous aircraft. Soon, as before, he was back in Malta with a Spit. 69 Squadron were equipped with a number of these and Warby took charge of their Spitfire Flight. In November 1942 over Bizerta, Warby was shot down. However he just managed to crash-land at Bone, a Tunisian airfield captured only the day before by British paratroops which had literally "dropped in".

After a series of amazing adventures, which included persuading the Tunisian Governor, a French Admiral, to throw in his lot with the Allied forces which had just invaded his territory, Warby got to Gibraltar. Here he "borrowed" a transit Spitfire, returned to Bone to pick up his camera magazines (Warby *always* got his pictures) refuelled and rearmed, flew the aircraft back to Malta and shot down a JU 88 almost over the spot where he himself had been shot down five days previously. Meanwhile he had been assumed "missing believed killed". Back from the "dead", Warby delivered the films to the processing department with apologies for "being a little late." In his absence, his promotion to Wing Commander and to CO of 69 Squadron had come through. Later the Spitfire Flight of 69 Squadron was hived off to become 683 Squadron with Warby as its first CO.

By then the Americans had come to Malta and the invasion of Sicily was being planned. Warby and the Americans hit it off wonderfully well. They had never seen an RAF officer like him! He was soon flying their aircraft . . . and in an American Colonel's uniform, too. His fourth DFC was awarded to him by them for the part that he played in preparation for the Sicilian invasion. For the outstanding photographs taken for this, Warby was personally thanked both by General Alexander, GOC, and Air Marshal "Mary" Coningham.

Warburton's final mysterious disappearance into oblivion is no part of this Malta story. Needless to say, he was flying an aircraft (an American one) that didn't belong to him, and he disappeared under circumstances that only those that knew him could begin to understand. Some profess to believe that he is still alive, just as some still cling to the belief that Lawrence of Arabia still lives. With such men, and there was much in common between them, anything is possible—anything other than the ordinary.

Since Warby and I were both freelancing for Hugh Pughe, I knew him better than most. He was supreme. But without Hugh Pughe there could never have been a Warburton. Hugh Pughe is reported to have said, "There was something about his fair-haired good looks that reminded you of Lawrence of Arabia. And like Lawrence he was absolutely unorthodox and a complete individualist. *You had to let him do things in his own way. . . .*" He was certainly quick to spot that this off-beat character could regularly produce the impossible, provided he was not interfered with in any way. If anyone had ordered Warburton to cut his hair, to wear proper uniform, to live in mess or to conform to any other conventional pattern, the RAF would have lost one of its greatest flyers.

Marshal of the RAF Lord Tedder, then AOC-in-C in the Middle East, is reported to have described Adrian Warburton as "the most valuable pilot in the whole RAF". At that time Warby was flying more operational sorties than any one else in the entire RAF. And on every one of these he brought back results that astonished the experts. If necessary, he went in low and photographed at low-level. For as long as he was allowed to go his own way in Malta, the enemy's dispositions in the Central Mediterranean were as clear as an open book.

One pilot—a tallish, slim, blond youth, one who could have been mistaken for a ballet dancer or a fast wing-threequarter—an arrogant, aloof young man with a sneer—a pilot with a log-book containing the record of 350* or more Malta operational sorties, yet only "average" or even "below average" assessments (I once saw it lying about and hastily flicked through its pages)—one pilot did all this. Warby was an iconoclast, an individualist, an extrovert, almost an escapist from his own land. Malta was a place where desperadoes could flourish. Hugh Pughe was a man who appreciated worth. Came the hour, came the place, came the men. Hugh Pughe backed Warby to the hilt and in return this egotistical, controversial character learnt to look upon his AOC as a son looks upon a fond father. For "him" he would dare anything and did so daily.

Hugh Pughe himself was also part showman. In Malta he played the role in much the same manner as did Churchill at home. He was driven around in his pale-blue car with its white-wall tyres. He smoked from a long black cigarette-holder. He had certain almost theatrical gestures—the proud throw of the head, his clipped yet dynamic powers of speech, and the same Churchillian sense of history and drama. He saw Malta for what it was—a bombed and blasted pile of rock that stood in the enemy's way. He determined to see that it took its toll before the enemy seized the place. Like most of us I believed that, in his heart, he was convinced that one day they would attempt to do so. However, this was not spoken of. To make Hugh Pughe mad it was only necessary to enquire innocently, "How goes the defence of the island, sir?"

"*Defence!*" would come the reply like a blast from a cannon. "What *defence?* Malta is on the *offensive*." This was magnificent talk at a time when the board in the ops room showed that the island possessed a bare dozen serviceable aircraft.

But he made good his words. Once, during a rare lull in the bombing, the devoted mechanics proudly produced no less than ten patched-up but serviceable Blenheims. He ordered all ten to carry out a low-level daylight bombing attack on Castle Ventrano—a heavily defended Sicilian airfield crowded with enemy planes. The Blenheim was known to be no match for any enemy fighter. It was virtual

*Warby's Log Books terminate long before his death in April 1944. They do NOT include the many unofficial flights he made as Wellington air gunner; in Liberators of the USAAF; in an officially "written off" Wellington (to collect booze from Egypt) in a bombed up Beaufighter; in a Blenheim etc.

mincemeat for the hundred or so Me-109 fighters then based in Sicily. When the news of the attack leaked out to the Blenheim pilots at Luqa, nearly all silently and purposely sought solace at the bar. The "betting" was that at least half of them would be shot down.

The AOA himself came to Luqa and carried out the briefing. He spoke with such force that the pilots actually ran to their planes, took off, flew in formation, bombed the airfield from tree-top height and all ten planes returned. Hugh Pughe didn't leave it at that either. It so happened that three Wimpeys of a depleted bomber squadron were also available for a night attack. These he despatched to add to the fires at Castle Ventrano. And when they returned, he had another three crews standing by. The same planes were refuelled, rebombed, recrewed and sent out again—and again a third time whilst night and the advantages of darkness still lasted.

But I judge him best by two other incidents.

An enemy convoy had been damaged by Blenheim or Maryland attacks and, fearing further attack, had taken refuge in Sfax, in neutral Tunisia. When he learnt about this, Hugh Pughe mustered a force of attacking planes and attacked the ships where they lay in the heart of Sfax harbour. It is true that enemy ships in Sfax had been attacked once before by Warburton on his own initiative, but this planned attack clearly created an international incident. I kept my fingers crossed for a while, as I feared that politicians might demand the head of my wonderful AOC, but the incident passed off without public comment. I believe that Air Chief Marshal Tedder, AOC-in-C, was disturbed, but Hugh Pughe appeared unruffled. He had won his point, too. For never again whilst I was in Malta, did the enemy seek safety in Tunisian ports. If they had done so and got away with it we would never have been able to inflict the damage that we did by sea and air.

On another occasion Hugh Pughe sent for me. His office underneath the great viaduct joining Valetta to Floriana was a stone hut with a tin roof. On a low step which led to a raised dais similar to a teacher's desk, sat my chief—a huddled figure lost in thought.

I cleared my throat. I was not used to seeing the AOC in this pensive, almost humble posture.

Eventually he crossed the space between us.

"Spooner," he said, "what do you think of the British Empire?" His arm was now around my shoulders.

Few acting flight-lieutenants can have been asked this question by their Air Officer Commanding.

I was still mulling over some kind of suitable reply when he continued. In the next five minutes I was made to see the Empire as I had hitherto only seen it in my dreams; it was in his words, a way of life that would far outlive the significance of its territorial boundaries. I was made to see that its only possible parallel in history was the cultural way of life that the ancient Greeks had handed to their Roman conquerors and, via them, to the world at large. The USA was analysed, admired for its power, and dismissed. The Germans were what they were. The Empire and Churchill and the British-way-of-life rode unsullied through this dark forest like Sir Lancelot on a white charger. The idealist in me was roused. By the time he told me: "Spooner (pause), tonight (Churchillian pause) the fate and the future of the British Empire may well lie in your two hands," I was prepared to dive-bomb my clumsy Goofington down the funnel of the nearest and biggest Italian battleship.

"I am asking you, Spooner, to leave Malta just for this once in broad daylight. But (pause) Spooner (pause) you will be given the protection of every single fighter on this island."

When it transpired that afternoon that of all the fighter aircraft at Takali only two Hurricanes were available as fighter escort I didn't feel let-down or disappointed. With spirits high I took off; kept low; sneaked over the harbour where the friendly guns of *Aurora*, *Penelope*, *Lance* and *Lively* were by arrangement poised to protect me, and headed out to sea without in fact seeing either Hurricane.

I now saw more clearly why those Blenheim pilots went off on their suicide mission and why the normally cynical and bored Warburton would be roused to sudden anger if anyone dared to criticise Hugh Pughe Lloyd.

It is all very strange. Whilst part of me realised that an element of "posing", and an element of melodrama were being deliberately employed by my AOC, yet *all* of me realised that Malta was a place for Men and that the man commanding the RAF was a Man. I felt privileged to serve such a man with or without the Churchillian phrases.

All this is leading up to the point that, whilst it wasn't absolutely necessary to be crazy in Malta, it undoubtedly helped.

No place on earth had been bombed as was Malta. I arrived there when the official number of raids on the island was between 800 and 900. I was there just six months. By then the official tally of air-raids was well over 2,000. By the end of hositilities the total was 3,340.

I have never decided whether I was lucky or unlucky not to be the victim of German bombs. They fell wherever I went, but they never actually harmed me.

As soon as it was established that I worked directly under the AOC and for the Royal Navy, I found that I was virtually free to live where I chose. The first damp billet I found was in a long, single-storey barrack block at Luqa. This was flattened by a bomb whilst I was away on a sortie at night. I retrieved what possessions I could, and for a night or two joined my sergeants, who had temporarily found billets in a poor-house attached to a leper colony at the foot of Luqa hill. The atmosphere of death and the sight of the semi-faceless lepers was not to my taste. We were assured that leprosy was not infectious and that there was no other billet available, but two nights was enough for me. However I managed to find another damp room at Luqa itself, when a Blenheim squadron lost nearly all their pilots and all their planes within a week during a series of daylight attacks on enemy convoys.

Like all the new, rough-hewn stone buildings of Malta, my soft, porous stone sweated and "wept" whenever the humidity was high, which meant during the whole of winter. The snag about this room was that a Bofors gun emplacement was directly outside its one window. The roar and traditional brass ring of this gun made sleep difficult. I had just about learnt to sleep through the sound of Bofors fire when the Germans demolished this building with an experimental rocket bomb. This awakened me, frozen with horror, as it screamed earthwards with a noise such as I had never heard. My skin prickles now as I write about it.

Neither I, nor my dwindling stock of possessions, suffered damage, but I had to move again. My friend Bob Povey, an RAF Radar Officer with whom I occasionally played tennis, then suggested that I moved to the mess at Kalafrana Bay, where he himself lived. This was miles from Luqa but I now had a car so I was able to accept this offer. The comfort here was glorious. There were seasoned walls that didn't sweat; also decent bedding in contrast to the paliasses, the lack of sheets and the rough blankets of Luqa. Carpets and curtains were provided, and there was a shaded portico outside for the long summer evenings to come. A tennis court was actually within view.

The fact that I was an air force officer living in a semi-naval establishment didn't seem to bother anyone. So few people had transport and Kalafrana Bay was virtually out on a limb by itself. This was another advantage, as this station, alhough a supply depôt, was very rarely bombed either by day or night.

When winter gave way to spring I used to slip down to the disused naval torpedo station, climb the neglected wire fence, and in a corner remote from prying eyes, slip off my clothes and swim naked in the clear, cool waters—apparently the only person on a fair and glorious earth—idyllically peaceful, until the sirens announced the next air raid.

Once again the wing where I slept was demolished. I had by now learnt to sleep through virtually every noise, and the first I knew about the raid was when in waking I turned over in bed and sent a shower of broken glass onto the stone floor. I slept under the open windows, the entire frames of which had been blown into the room during the night. But again I lost almost nothing in the way of personal effects. Lucky or unlucky? As far as I know, no other bombs fell upon this Mess.

David Beaty and the other SDF crews were at that time working on a scheme to live in Sliema, the pleasant resort (and submarine base) across the harbour. They had found or rented an abandoned apartment and were busy decorating and equipping it. They kindly asked me to join them. Just before we all moved in, a bomb demolished the building. Meanwhile, I had found another pleasant room at Kalafrana, and later David came to join me there.

Unlike most service personnel I was lucky to make friends with a Maltese, with whom I used to play tennis. It was pleasant and beneficial to get away from service company just for an hour or two. Once when we were crossing the harbour to play tennis at Sliema Club, our dhaissa (pronounced "dicer") was nearly hit by a bomb which fell in the harbour only fifteen to twenty feet away. We were all soaked by the huge splash, but the boat remained upright, and after our tough Maltese dhaissaman had picked himself up, he resumed his traditional standing-up type of one-oar rowing, whilst we, his passengers, set to and bailed.

The bomb that came nearest to me was also connected with tennis.

We were playing at Sliema Club when a big raid on Takali, the fighter airfield, began. Two of our foursome departed, leaving my Maltese friend and I. We watched with the almost sadistic pleasure that we had come to adopt whenever someone else was the target.

"Poor old Takali," we muttered with an ill-concealed gleam, until my friend shouted, "Look, Tony!"

I followed her pointing finger. I saw a Ju-88 in about a 60-degree angle dive pointing itself directly at us. Clearly the pilot had been ordered to attack the Sliema Club in the hope of finding an officer or two there. The situation was one of such inescapable doom that I remained rooted to the spot.

My companion, with quicker wits than I, propelled me a few yards towards the club itself, and together we crouched under the stone staircase that led up to the flat roof.

One enormous bomb, estimated at 2,500 Kg (5,500 lb), hit the very spot where we had been standing a few seconds before. The Sliema Club building collapsed like a card house. We were both old hands at being bombed, and we had automatically tightly covered our nose and mouth with our hands, but even so we could feel the pressure waves from the exploding bomb sucking hard at our lungs. We were huddled together, yet quite unable to see each other for the thick blanket of dust which rose up and enveloped everything. The shattering roar in our ears numbed all thought for a while.

Miraculously we suffered nothing worse than superficial cuts and scratches, although part of our clothes had been ripped by the blast. But we found ourselves trapped in a space not much bigger than a broom closet. We spent the next thirty minutes or so cautiously shifting the big blocks which held us trapped. The stone stairway had saved us, but when at last we freed ourselves we found that the locker rooms had been flattened and we could barely rescue enough of our street clothes to cover ourselves decently.

An inexplicable feature was that when we came to examine the crater—the largest I had ever seen—we found two tennis balls right on the edge of the huge hole more or less exactly where we had dropped them immediately before our dash for cover.

We were still wandering through the streets of Sliema curiously attired, looking in vain for a gharry, when the siren for the next raid sounded. We sought the nearest shelter. This was my only visit to one of the famous deep Maltese caves literally chopped out of the soft, moist rock. The atmosphere inside was frightful. The shelter held hundreds, and an air of numb fear and human sweat matched the dampness of the walls. Outside we could hear the boom of our guns.

We caught each other's eye and silently climbed the long staircase out into the freshness of the fast falling night. There we stood and breathed great gulps of real fresh air. Now, thoroughly chilled by the evening air, we went briskly on foot down one of the narrow step-streets leading to the waterfront. Here we eventually found a dhaissaman to row us back across the harbour to where I had left my car.

The daily life we all lived wasn't natural and the food situation was becoming grim. Malta was being forced to her knees through lack of supplies. We ate goat or shoat (half sheep, half goat), tinned stew, coarse bread, tinned vegetables, so-called margarine (axle-grease?), the local potatoes and fruit in season, oatmeal and whatever else we could obtain or scrounge. Toni's clubs, bars and hotels in Valetta used to serve better meals than the mess. We didn't know how he got hold of the stuff. We just ate it and were thankful. The local brewery kept in business for a time, making a potion that just passed as beer. After the coal shortage closed even this supply, a variety of strange spirits appeared. We didn't care. We drank whatever anyone offered us and some really wild nights resulted—especially at the upstairs bar where RAF and RN officers nightly collected and repulsed all attempts by the Army officers to join us.

I don't know how this childish inter-service feud began. It created interest and helped to bind the RAF and RN closer together, so no real harm was done, although one Army officer was once dropped out of the club's first floor window. Had the island been invaded, as was expected, all three services would have fought shoulder to shoulder. As it was, only the RAF, RN and AA brigades had any fighting to do. Later, after General Beak arrived as GOC, the Army served us well at Luqa and even serviced some planes for us as well as keeping the airfields operational. An Army officer called Gammige was employed as one of our RAF Intelligence Officers (God only knows how he came to be at Luqa!) and we would bring him into the bar with an appropriate "fighter escort" and cries of, "He's one of ours. Don't throw him out, chaps!"

Off duty we played some crazy pranks. Once we "ate" a senior officer's hat! The gold braid on the peak was commonly referred to as "scrambled eggs", and all it took to start this nonsense was for some ass to exclaim, "I haven't had scrambled eggs for months", and within minutes a crowd of grown men had solemnly munched up every indigestible scrap of this emblem of senior rank. At other times, quite angry wrestling matches took place. I suppose we were all pent up. Some brave officers volunteered for Bomb Disposal duties after nearly all the official experts had been blown to bits on this most hazardous of jobs. This was vital, as the enemy dropped thousands of delay-bombs as well as various novel ones.

Warburton and I and a few others were the lucky ones in that we had regular jobs to do. Many pilots had no planes to fly and virtually nothing to do for months on end, other than be bombed night and day, eat the uninspiring food, drink the semi-poisonous drinks and get themselves steamed up. There were virtually no English women on the island, which had approximately 26,000 British and Allied men in uniform! There must have been several hundred aircrew, as once a pilot arrived on the island there was almost no way for him to get off it. The row upon row of damaged planes told the story. These planes had all arrived on the island in the hands of aircrew. It was still possible to fly *into* Malta but almost impossible to leave.

No wonder that some liaisons with local girls developed, and that an occasional man deserted to go and live with his girl friend or to start up a dubious business in the back streets of Valetta. The military police did not chase deserters too hard. Each one absent was one fewer on the official ration strength! Also, deserters obviously could not run far as there was no place to run to, and it was generally believed that when the invasion came those "over the hill" would return to the fold. This "return" did indeed happen when a report of "a large enemy convoy approaching" was erroneously received. The church bells rang their warning. The Army took up their defence positions. We and the Navy were brought to full alert and the deserters gave themselves up. However, it all turned out to be a false alarm.

The authorities positively forbade officers to marry Maltese girls, and made it as difficult as possible for the troops to do so. They also put the "Gut"—the street of the local prostitutes—out of bounds.

Officers were also banned from other back streets. But I gathered, from listening to the talk of others, that there were ways and means of circumventing these prohibitions.

One of the half a dozen English girls still on the island was in such demand that she was able to date officers *by the hour.* And even then she would not condescend to date anyone of lower rank than Army captain! She could be seen in the Union Club of Valetta having tea with this one—then a sherry with that one—then dinner with a third and coffee with another.

At Luqa most of us simply forgot that there were such things as girls. Yet there was no homosexuality either. In the great flapping tent which served as our mess after the original one had been destroyed, we played much bridge, drank profusely whenever it was available, organised ridiculous pranks and let off steam by occasional fist fights. We naturally divided into two groups. Those who took to the shelters and those who didn't. Bronco and Harpic—the two pups I had brought with me—joined the former. Whenever the siren wailed these two long-tailed, stumpy-legged mongrels would be first down the shelter steps.

Shrapnel from our own AA shells was the biggest danger to those of us who didn't take shelter. It would pour down like rain at times, so we took to wearing Army tin hats. In a slit trench we reckoned to be safe against anything other than a direct hit. Also from a slit trench we could enjoy grandstand views of the raids. Once you got accustomed to it, dive-bombing by Ju-87 and Ju-88 wasn't at all bad. At first it was absolutely terrifying and exceptionally noisy, but we soon learned that if the dive-bomber wasn't actually diving at you there was little real danger, and ninety-nine times out of a hundred the bombers could be seen diving at other targets. Provided you kept your hands tight over mouth and nose as the bombs near you exploded, you were unlikely to be hurt even by bombs falling comparatively close. The tin-helmet kept the chance of injury by shrapnel or flying rock to a minimum. The slit trench was also a protection against being bowled over—especially if it had been cut to a zig-zag shape. The ground was nearly all rock, and bombs mainly made smallish craters, although flying rock and rubble rose crazily into the air.

Later, when our gunners ran short of AA ammunition, it was humiliating to be machine-gunned by Me-109 fighters but this didn't seem to cause many casualties either. Until the German fighters started this indignity, a group of us, when feeling particularly crazy, would rush out to the runway, pitch stumps and pretend to play cricket with the Germans overhead. We hoped that if we were photographed they would be puzzled; and if they understood what we were doing, they would realise that our morale had not been in any way destroyed.

High-level bombing, although it seldom hit anything of military value, was more annoying. From the ground you were never quite sure when the planes were going to unload their bombs. Nor could you judge where the bombs were likely to fall. The surprising fact was that by and large the enemy continued to waste many of their bombs upon the lines of already wrecked aircraft, which we had towed out to our satellite airfield at Saafi about two miles from where we operated our few serviceable planes. We protected these latter as best we could by building fourteen-feet-high anti-blast pens around them. A few of these were built out of rock but mostly the airmen, much aided by the Army, built these pens block by block, using empty four-gallon petrol tins filled with earth, rubbish, loose stones, etc. We had millions of these tins and we built some really elaborate pens out of them. They shielded aircraft well, and kept the men busy. Captain Agnew sent a naval detachment up to Luqa. They came to build 90 feet by 90 feet pens round our two remaining Wimpeys. They departed when a good job had been done. Our planes were *their* planes. We felt greatly honoured.

Digging our own SDF slit trench kept my crews busy and kept them together. My boisterous sergeants didn't hesitate to throw out others who sought cover in the trench that they had hewn out of rock with their own hands. We were literally a fighting-proud unit, as was demonstrated on Christmas Eve when the officers' mess held open house to the sergeants. The evening turned into a wild party. The gentle and normally polite Sergeant Terrington collared the squadron-leader of 69 Squadron by the head and was repeating insistently, "The SDF is the best unit on the island?" and whenever the squadron-leader begged to differ in no uncertain terms, "Terry" punched his nose. I admired my sergeant's loyal feelings but on this occasion hastened to the rescue of my fellow officer before he put Terrington under arrest—Christmas Eve or not!

Later that evening—a pouring wet one mercifully free from

raids—I drove over to Hal Far and joined my FAA friends from the Swordfish and Albacore squadrons. Later I was "put to bed" in splendid quarters. I complimented my hosts on their grand style of living. Not until rudely awoken later did I realize that I was the victim of a prank, and that I had been put into the bed of the CO of this FAA station. I was even wearing his red silk pyjamas which I had been so kindly "lent"!

Wild parties broke out all over the island that night. It was lucky that the weather was too bad for any kind of flying on either side, as I reckon that the Germans could have captured the island with ease—with a handful of sober men!

My Plymouth car was a great joy to me. It was also the envy of others, as apart from the AOC's sky-blue Lincoln it was the best of the RAF cars. Certainly it was much superior to that used by my Luqa Station Commander. Yet I can't remember how I came to acquire it! Doubtless Sergeant Dale assisted me.

Sergeant Dale was the man who looked after our planes on the ground. He had originally belonged to a Wimpey squadron which had long since departed. He adopted us, and the SDF found itself a fairy godfather. He was a huge man, with a ramrod straight back and a splendid handle-bar moustache. His large brown eyes knew how to twinkle and I never once saw him throw his weight about. He never had to. He had been in the RAF, man and boy, for many years, and he not only knew the King's Rules and Regulations but he also knew how to get things done in true Malta Style.

None of us on the flying side, knew any of the King's Rules and Regulations as we had neither adjutant, experience of our own, nor orderly-room corporal to tell us. In the nicest way Sergeant Dale virtually took over all essential administration matters. He never bothered to tell us the details and we seldom asked. He was also a tireless worker, a fine engineer and a leader in every sense. If it was humanly possible to get a Wimpey repaired, he did so, and, by and large, we managed to keep at least one and sometimes two aircraft serviceable.

He himself had acquired a light van. He used to pick us up at Ops Room in it, and he used to meet us on our return and drive us back to Ops after each sortie. I can't remember his ever being ill or taking a day off. I never knew or enquired how many men he had on his strength, or where they came from. He was never even an official part of our unit. Officially he belonged to a bomber squadron. As I now recall it, he tactfully asked me one day if I could drive a car. And then indicated that he knew of one that no other CO claimed. Thereafter I drove a splendid Plymouth and Sergeant Dale kept it full of petrol for me. Hugh Pughe was delighted that I could now always get to his office in Valetta at short notice. In fact, everyone was happy except for those officers senior to me who mostly had no cars at all or who, at best, drove broken-down crocks inferior in size and style and vintage.

Sergeant Dale became so much part of our unit that he once came on a night sortie with us. It was his idea, and he so seldom asked me for anything that I readily agreed. We ran into the famous Tripoli barrage that night and that was enough for him. This display of AA fire was gloriously colourful, though not, in this case, effective.

When reduced to one aircraft, Hugh Pughe was kind enough to give me a carte blanche verbal order to seize any plane that I thought might be of use to us. These planes would refuel in Malta *en route* from Gibraltar to Egypt. I seriously thought of commandeering an ASV-equipped Hudson one night, and on more than one occasion did grab an ASV-equipped Wellington belonging to my old Squadron 221. This squadron was being moved to Egypt, and their planes were coming through our island one at a time. I dare not purloin aircraft from the new squadron CO, but took several after that—until my old friend Eric Starling arrived one night.

He was now a squadron-leader and I let him keep his, too—but not before we had spent a memorable night in Toni's bar. We were so late that we couldn't find a gharry to take us home. Usually these ancient horse-drawn cabs would wait for us until the bars closed. However, Toni looked after us in his renowned black-market hotel, about which I had heard so much but had never before visited. The food, bedding and comfort provided was far beyond normal Luqa standard. We were even offered company for the night, but all we wanted was sleep.

Eric probably carried away several false impressions of how we lived in Malta. However, my clearest recollection of him was on the morning when he arrived. He was roused by an air-raid warning, and was standing near the mess at Luqa wearing his pyjamas and a borrowed tin hat, sucking his pipe and watching an aerial dog-fight in which a Ju-88 went down trailing smoke. He seemed utterly unconcerned and at ease. It was a pity that he couldn't have stayed and joined us.

24: Farewell to Malta

JANUARY was a busy month for me. We didn't assist in many sinkings, as by now the enemy seldom dared to run the gauntlet, but I spent ten or eleven whole nights in the air. So few planes were now serviceable that my log-book tells me that I actually flew more than ten per cent of the total hours flown by the entire Malta air force. However, shortly after this my health began to deteriorate. Whitlows, boils and carbuncles appeared, and I developed some kind of dermatitis. A long-lost stammer reappeared, too. The MO was a "gentian violet" enthusiast, and I soon began to resemble a piebald horse with splotches of indelible violet all over me. I had a minor operation to relieve the whitlows on my hands, and I remember an alarming cycle ride home in the dark that same evening. I was completely "drunk" with pentathol, and had both hands tied up, but I had been discharged.

"Have you got transport?" enquired the busy MO.

I started to tell him that if he meant had I got a car the answer was "Yes, the finest in the island, but not with me", when he cut me off and signed the discharge. I was singing happily when I set off, but as the drug wore off and as I kept falling off my machine into ditches in the dark, my happiness soon evaporated. It was pouring with rain and I had about eight miles to travel over unfamiliar roads.

Apart from occasional bouts of food poisoning (Malta Dog) I had, till then, kept fit. Malta Dog was a curse, and I once flew almost a whole nine-hour trip sitting on the Elsan portable toilet directing the flight from this throne. Malta in winter is perpetually damp, and I now possessed little beyond one change of clothing. Also, we had no coal or fuel, so could never get warm or dry. We had long ago run out of soap, toothpaste, shoe-cleaning and button-cleaning materials, razorblades and all normal toilet articles, and we must have been more than slightly unhygenic. My Maltese friend had scoured the few remaining shops in town and had brought me, in great triumph, one square of dog soap. It was the kind you wash dogs with in order to rid them of fleas. It smelt strongly of disinfectant. I welcomed it as if it had been the rarest of French concoctions. I washed with it, used it as shave cream and cleaned my teeth with it. I hid it from the others lest they should steal it. I made it last over a month, savouring every gramme.

During the height of my gentian violet phase I was summoned one evening to the AOC. Hugh Pughe had a job for me that night. I was deadly tired, sniffling with a head cold, and must have looked "all in". He paused in his briefing.

"Spooner, you're not well."

"I'm all right, sir."

He stood me under the light, examined the splotches on my hands and face, and then with less abruptness than usual, "Spooner, I'm not going to ask you to go tonight. Who else would you recommend?"

He waved aside my protests. After we had finished telephoning to David Beaty he had me sit down and fished out a strong drink from some hidden place. Unlike the Navy he was not normally a great man for "gin-before-business"!

I told him what the doctors were doing for me. In his usual manner he came to a sudden, definite decision.

"I know what's the matter with you. Been working too hard. Not enough sleep. Too much tinned food. Run-down. Scores of chaps like you. All this damned bombing. What you want is rest and good food. Do you know where St Paul's Bay is?"

I had vaguely heard of the place. It was somewhere in the north of the island, towards Gozo. I nodded.

"Spooner, you're going to St Paul's Bay right now: tonight, if possible. And you're going to stay there until you feel absolutely fit. There is a Rest Camp there. I'll see that you get fresh food—lots of fruit, vegetables and fresh meat—none of that tinned stuff. And Spooner, see that you walk at least ten miles a day. Not at first, but after you've shaken off that cold. Bed at first for you. Can you do all this?"

It was more of an order than a question, and by now the sense of relief that I wasn't going to have to fly once again, all that night, had taken over. Until officially "stood down", I hadn't realised how desperately weary I really was, weary in limb with my damned cold, weary in spirit too. All I could do was to nod weakly.

Later my mind came more alive, and I pointed out that I couldn't go right away as I had to hand over the car (and with it the authority of the unit) to David. But I promised to get myself to St Paul's Rest Camp by the next day.

"Stay there as long as you want to. We want you fit. Must get you fit, eh?" were Hugh Pughe's last words before I departed into the night. I felt glad that I would be getting a rest and that I could at long last have a chance to shake off my cold and, I hoped, the boils and carbuncles too. But I also felt that I had to some extent let down the man whom I most respected and admired, and to whom I owed all that I had become in Malta.

I stayed at St Paul's Bay nearly a month. Towards March the weather began to improve and it was as peaceful a place as any on the island. The food was all that Hugh Pughe had promised. It was fresh and simple. No enemy plane ever raided us and we were sufficiently far away not to be bothered by the noise of bombs, guns or mines. In Valetta, the town would be rocked about once an hour by an exploding depth charge dropped by our own Navy in the harbour in order to scare away any attacks on our ships that the Italians might attempt with their ingenious one-man submarines.

For the first four or five days I slept nearly all day and night. I had had no idea that I was so utterly exhausted. Then I began the prescribed walks, rain or shine. Sometimes I did twenty miles a day, never less than ten. I walked all over the northern parts of the island. I was constantly challenged by Army defence posts and learnt to say "Friend"! very quickly and dutifully.

I studied the ancient Phoenician remains, and the even older cart ruts worn in the stone. I visited several of the huge Catholic churches, as large as cathedrals, which dominated every village, and I paid several visits to the cathedral at Mosta to stand in admiration under that vast dome—the second or third largest unsupported dome in the world. I stood alongside devout Maltese women dressed in traditional black. I could speak no word of their language nor they of mine. In fact I barely spoke to anyone at all that month.

Some of the other camp inhabitants, and we were only a dozen or so, were bomb-shock cases of sorts. They had found a good safe billet at St Paul's Bay and had no wish ever to return to the crazy maelstrom outside if they could help it. I didn't agree with them but I didn't blame them either. They had precious little to return to other than raids, routine, poor food, danger and discomfort. A rare strip of fertile land crosses the island at St Paul's Bay and this supplied the camp with ample fresh food. I used to watch the busy locals extracting full value out of every square yard of their precious productive land. Malta had always been deficient in soil. In semi-pre-historic days, when Malta was a trading centre for a seafaring race of Phoenician origins, ships landing at Malta were obliged to bring in top soil as harbour dues. Today the characteristic stone walls all over the island are there to prevent the precious soil from blowing into the sea. Here they rubbed it between their fingers with feeling.

I also explored the beaches and the various defence lines. Some of these were new, others were a relic from former days of siege. As I explored I wished I possessed a good library of the history of this interesting and ancient island. I read all that I could but I was left with many gaps.

I shunned the friendly overtures of my colleagues at the rest camp. I was still feeling that I had failed Hugh Pughe. I made progress only very slowly. The heaviness of mind stayed with me even after the physical improvement began. I kept thinking about Dennis Reason. I thought with shame of how I had sat down three or four times to write to his parents and of how in the end I hadn't done so and now knew that I never would do so.

This was odd, although in part it fitted in with the attitude I had adopted towards my own parents. Not once did I write to them, nor to my brother, during my stay in Malta. I wrote frequently to my wife and to no one else at all. I began to suspect that subconsciously I had gone to Malta expecting never to return. Certainly I could see no way of ever leaving the island. Apart from the fast minelayers, the *Welshman, Manxman* and the gallant *Breconshire* and the wonderful submarines, no ship now ran the blockade to Malta. Few convoys were able to force a passage to Malta. In one, HMS *Nelson* had been damaged by aerial torpedoes, and one of her few casualties had been a friend who had lived next door but one to me at Littlehampton. On some attempts our naval losses had been terrible. *Ark Royal* had been sunk, as had the *Eagle* and the battleship *Barham.*

Then one night it came to me why my spirits continued to remain so low, and why it was that I so often thought of Reason in spite of the fact our relationship had never been anything closer than crew-mates. Dennis Reason, I now realised, had represented England. He had been the uncomplicated, simple, straightforward young man (I had just turned twenty-five but felt about middle-aged myself by now) who typified all that was best in the England I loved. He represented the backbone of the spirit with which Hugh Pughe had so fired me that night when "the fate of the British Empire lay in my hands". I realised at the same time that there could be little point in winning the war if all that was soundest and fairest in our land—all the Reasons in fact—were to be killed in doing so. If only the malingerers and the Smart Alecks were to survive what worth was there in ultimate victory? It would be a Pyrrhic victory indeed. I eventually went to sleep leaving unanswered the riddle "what Hope lies in our future if in winning this war, all our young men, our Reasons, lie dead, unburied and forgotten? Who then would inherit the spoils?"

I thought of Alice Miller, the American poet, who wrote in her "White Cliffs of Dover" thus:

> "I see here much to forget, much to forgive,
> But, in a world with England dead, I do not wish to live."

I then began to sleep better. Possibly having discovered the cause of my inner ailment, it went away by itself just because it was now no longer unknown.

Shortly after this I seemed to recover my spirits. I think that the arrival on the island of its first Spitfires had something to do with it. January and February 1942 had been terrible months for Malta. The Germans had moved another entire air army into Sicily, and, under Kesselring, Malta was attacked daily by hundreds of enemy aircraft. Many of these were first-rate machines such as the Ju-88 bombers and the Me-109 F fighters. They were well manned, too, by German crews of experience and determination. All that we could destroy during these two months were ten in the air and another dozen or so by gunfire. For our part we had lost about seventy aircraft on the ground alone.

The weather in the main was appalling. Both Hal Far and,

especially, Takali became flooded, and for a time every aircraft in the island was kept at Luqa. Here, too, the rain affected us. Our long, tortuous taxi-tracks, which went up hill, down dale and around sharp bends to our wide-flung dispersal areas, became abominably slippery, turning into quagmires and being washed away in places. The main runway itself was also in a deplorable state. It had to be patched daily as up to 200 craters were made by the enemy on some days. At best it was a dangerous runway, being steeply downhill with a quarry at one end and with a gully at the other. One Wellington pitched into this gully after landing at night with a gunner still inside the front turret. All that remained of him had to be sprayed out with a hose. It shocked us all, and my gunners rightly avoided the front turret both for take-off and landing after this.

Luqa lacked all modern aids. It had no tractors, no hydraulic drills, no power tools, no refuelling bowsers, no hangars. Luqa had far too few mechanical rollers and cranes, and the men had no proper shelter from the rain. Aircraft were refuelled by hand from four-gallon petrol tins. We had no spares and few tools. Yet Sergeant Dale and the men he had collected were gaily contemplating changing the wings from one damaged aircraft to another and even mating the remains of one of our Wellingtons with those of a damaged Hudson!

The shortage of AA ammunition left the airfield gunners sitting idly by whilst enemy fighters held mock dog-fights with each other over our very runways.

The food situation is best summed up by the remark in the mess suggestion book: "Suggested that the standard meal of hard bread, axle grease (for butter) and glutinous crystallised substance posing as jam be changed to one consisting of hard toast, axle grease (for butter) and glutinous crystallised substance posing as jam."

Thus it was a tremendous boost to us all when the aircraft carriers of the U.S. Navy and Britain advanced sufficiently far east from Gibraltar for some forty Spitfires to fly off their decks to Malta. The Spitfires could at least match the Me-109 F, which was obviously so much faster than our ancient but honourable Hurricanes, and the toll of enemy planes destroyed mounted again.

Two ships really kept us alive during these miserable months. Two ships, plus an occasional flying-boat (one brought me several hundred flares), and some gallant submarines, enrolled to act as freight carriers.

The two ships were the *Welshman* and the *Breconshire*. The first was a fast forty-knot minelayer which, carrying deck cargo, could reach Malta from Gibraltar in a day and a half: and the latter was a Navy freighter-cum-tanker which bravely brought us aviation spirit, fuel oil for the Navy and other vital spares. She travelled at a bare seventeen knots and made several memorable solo runs to us from ports in Egypt.

In February a convoy destined for us was beaten back. This was a terrible blow, for unless we could get supplies we clearly had "had it". A surrender date could even be calculated. For by late summer we would have been starved into submission.

Nor were we inflicting much damage on enemy ships, which now passed beyond Swordfish range. Force K was severely damaged and never went to sea again as such. Bomb damage was added to that which the mines had first inflicted. HMS *Penelope* became HMS *Pepperpot.* The extra warships of Force H, or what was left of them, limped back whence they had come. Even our consistently successful submarines were now not inflicting damage as in the past. Nearly all the enemy's Tripoli (or Benghazi) convoys were reaching their destinations now that we had no surface naval units to oppose them.

Back at Luqa I established contact with a Wimpey squadron which was based in Egypt, and together we worked out ways of attacking ships by night with Wellingtons. They were equipping themselves to drop torpedoes. We knew how and where to find ships. Together we worked out a scheme. Our role in this joint enterprise would be to find the enemy. We would then link up with a torpedo-carrying plane and together the two Wimpeys would return to the enemy so that the torpedo-carrier could attack. I wished that I could have combined both ASV and torpedoes on our planes, as we were confident of success had this been possible. But in Malta we lacked the facilities to modify our aircraft.

As it was we carried out one splendid operation during a night with a good moon. The rendezvous over the Ionian sea was effected by the use of flares and navigation lights, and the two planes linked up and returned to the enemy ships flying in close formation. We had forgotten one thing however. We hadn't looked at our almanacks. By the time we returned to the enemy a total eclipse of the moon was in progress, and although taken to within three miles of the target the torpedo-carrying Wellington failed to find it in such dark conditions. Before we could try again it was recalled to its base in Egypt.

The last week in March 1942 will remain in the memory of all who were in Malta at the time. Admiral Vian, from Alexandria, made a most determined effort to force a small convoy through to us. Our good friend the *Breconshire* was joined by three merchantmen, the *Clan Campbell,* the *Talabot* and the *Pampas.* In the words of Vice Admiral Weichold, the German Admiral, the action which followed surpassed everything that the Royal Navy achieved in those waters.

Admiral Vian, with five light cruisers and six destroyers, and embarrassingly encumbered by a slow convoy, fought off and defeated an Italian force containing a battleship, six heavy cruisers and a large number of destroyers. This force was assisted by huge Luftwaffe formations based in Crete, Greece, Italy, Libya and Sicily. Admiral Vian's action in advancing his destroyers (including our great friend Commander Hussey in the *Lively*) in their own smoke screen and using these little ships to torpedo the Italian capital ships is now Naval history.

However, as the convoy neared Malta the air attacks upon it continued. The *Clan Campbell* was sunk and the *Breconshire*—under Captain Hutchinson, RN—our good saviour of the past, was badly hit when within sight of the island. Eventually she was towed into Marsaxlokk Bay where she burnt and sank. But men at once went to work on her as she lay on her side, and part of her invaluable cargo, including some of her oil, was salvaged.

But the *Pampas* and *Talabot* (a Norwegian ship) arrived safely in Valetta. The island said grateful prayers for Admiral Vian.

Every gun that could be moved had been assembled around the harbour, and we waited for the avalanche of bombs which we were sure would now fall upon us. The enemy knew the value of those cargoes, and they brought up several squadrons of Ju-87 vertical dive-bombers to add to their already huge air force.

Really bad flying weather gave us a wonderful break, and for the next two days hardly any Axis planes were able to attack Malta. Every man on the island had his coat off and was standing by to unload the two ships, but for reasons which were never understood the order to get on with this essential job regardless of dock labour, air-raid warnings, or of recognised methods or procedures, was never given. It was a blunder of the first magnitude. Some RAF gangs took the initiative into their own hands, and regardless of what else was taking place, or not taking place, they unloaded engines and spare parts vital to their own continuation as a fighting force.

On Monday the low cloud cleared away and down came the Ju-88 and Ju-87 aircraft on the biggest raids that Malta had seen. More bombs fell around the harbour on that day than had been dropped by the Luftwaffe on their ignominious Coventry raid.

I was driving into town to see Hugh Pughe. An early raid took place as I was driving into town to see HP and I stopped to watch. In his office he bombarded me with questions. What had I seen? Were either of our precious prizes damaged? I told him that smoke was coming from the *Talabot* but that she was still upright.

"Let's go and see for ourselves," said my chief.

His office was on the floor of this huge ancient Ditch—a man-made canyon with sheer hundred-feet-high sides. Unknown to me there were some iron rungs let into these vertical walls. Hugh Pughe swiftly climbed them. I have always disliked heights (except when in aeroplanes) and with difficulty I followed him. On top was a small grass plateau no wider than a living-room. Beneath us lay the harbour and the *Talabot* with smoke ominously belching from her side. Were the fire-fighters winning or losing the grim struggle aboard her?

Our speculation was cut short by the next raid which announced itself by a bomb landing uncomfortably close. Every one of the hundreds of guns massed around the harbour, including those from Force K, opened up at the attackers. We glanced up and the sky over our heads was full of Ju-87s, ack-ack bursts and a few fighters (since we only had a handful left), which regardless of our own gunfire were pursuing the German planes relentlessly.

Some thirty or more Ju-87 dive-bombers came hurtling earthwards, and their bombs whistled a few feet over our heads before exploding in the harbour below us. Pieces of shrapnel from our barrage pattered down all round us. Luckily I had grabbed my tin hat before scaling the canyon's side. I tried to hold it over the two of us. We were crazily exposed and we knew it. Only sheer luck could save us from shrapnel wounds.

After the Ju-87s came an even bigger force of about fifty Ju-88s. They dived at a lesser angle—about 40 degrees to the Ju-87s 80

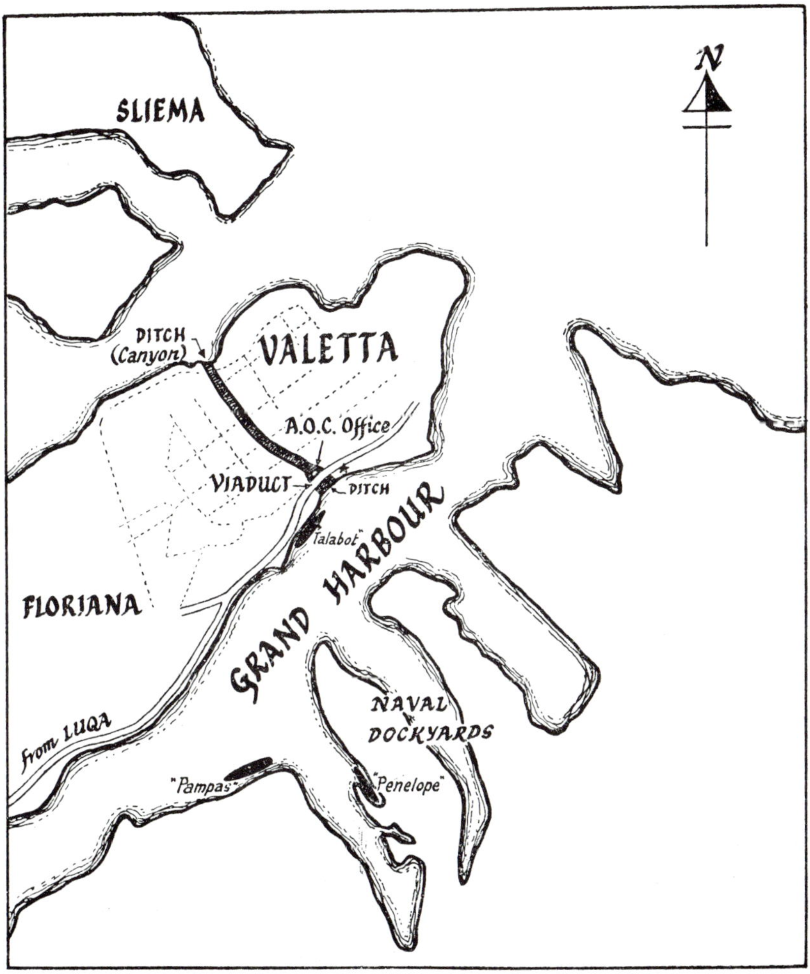

GRAND HARBOUR—VALETTA

The A.O.C.'s office was under the viaduct spanning the Ditch. The ★ is the narrow ledge from which the attacks on the *Talabot* and *Pampas* were observed.

degrees—but they carried much bigger bomb loads. These too all went screaming over our heads towards the smoking *Talabot*, the damaged cruisers at their berths and at the already hit and sinking *Pampas*.

Several bits of hot shrapnel fell within inches of us, but we escaped unharmed, possibly thanks to our finding a bomb crater and huddling together in it.

We saw enough to realise that *Pampas* and *Talabot* were unlikely to last the day, before sadly returning the way we had come.

Hugh Pughe went down hand-over-hand as sure-footed and nimble as any steeplejack. I thought I was never going to make it at all. My feet were trembling and as I felt slowly downwards each foot would beat an uncontrollable tattoo on the rung beneath, until my full weight on it could still its tremulations. Also my hands tended to clench too tightly on the rungs above, and I almost had to force them to let go finger by finger. It took me minutes to get down to where my chief was silently watching.

I left the island shortly afterwards. Some relief crews, also ex-221 Squadron, arrived to operate what was left of our SDF, and one day Hugh Pughe told me that two crews could go home that same night—"Yours and Beaty's" he suggested. But first he was kind enough to award the DFC to my little "Chiefy"—now a Warrant Officer—and to ask me to name one of my three gunners to receive the DFM. It was unfair to have to single one from three such splendid WOP/AGs. Terrington had flown more trips with me than either Evans or Haynes, so he was awarded the decoration. Yet the other two appeared to be as delighted with the two awards as if they had received them in person.

David Beaty and most of his crew joined us that night when my crew and I seized a transit Wimpey (on the AOC's authority) filled it up in the middle of the night and flew it to an airfield in the Canal Zone, a thousand miles to the east. We didn't tell the incoming Bomber Command crew. They were most impressed by being met in person by a flight-lieutenant in his car and being so promptly escorted, with all their gear, to near-by sleeping quarters. They obviously had a rude awakening coming to them next day.

As a typical gesture Hugh Pughe lent me his famous car and his equally famous diminutive Maltese driver, Sergeant Aquilina, so that I could say goodbye to my dear friend in Sliema before departing in the night. I think I first knew I was going to Egypt at about 6 pm, yet I was over Egypt with the dawn!

It all happened so suddenly that not until the Nile delta came into view with the first light did I truly realize that against every expectation of my own I had somehow physically separated myself from the island where, ages ago, I had elected to do or die.

"Ages ago?" I counted up the months. Then in disbelief counted them again.

I had been in Malta almost exactly six months—a bare, brief six months. Yet it was impossible to imagine what life had been like before, or what it would now hold in store. I felt as if I had returned to another era or another century as I gazed in wonder at the neat lines of trucks and tents, the hangars, the smart refuelling bowsers and the unruffled air of orderliness around me as I climbed out of my borrowed Wimpey into the strong early sunshine of RAF Station El Fayid—Egypt. The station was not damaged. Paint was fresh, buttons shone, boots were polished. The men were not hollow-eyed.

Physically separated—yes. But the mental detachment had yet to come. I'm not sure it ever did. At this time I am very much involved as Editor and Public Relations Officer of the George Cross Island Association and continually hear new stories from both airmen and Maltese of the events of those days.

Malta, GC: it is sometimes asked why the tiny island of Malta was awarded the George Cross, which is just as rarely awarded as the VC. These awards are made to individuals. Malta is the only place to have been so honoured.

The idea came from the King himself, George VI. He knew just what the island, its people and the Service personnel who served there had gone through between 1940 and 1942. Their experience was unique and deserving of a special mark of recognition.

Even today, few people realise that more bombs fell on Malta than fell upon London; or that more bombs fell upon Malta during the one month of April 1942 than fell upon the whole of the UK during any one year of the war. Yet Malta is smaller in area than the Isle of Wight. Moreover, 90 per cent of the bombs fell upon the three principal airfields and the harbour areas.

For Malta, the war began in June 1940. The Italian dictator, Benito

Mussolini, thinking that Britain was defeated, threw in his lot with Adolf Hitler and on 10th June declared war against Britain.

He foresaw rich pickings, not least the island group known as Malta. It lay only sixty miles from the tip of Sicily and, after the fall of France, was almost 1,000 miles from the nearest British bases of Gibraltar and Alexandria at either end of the Mediterranean. In addition, it was almost totally undefended.

A tiny force of three Sea Gladiator biplanes, flown by RAF administration and other pilots who happened to be on the island on 10th June 1940—and aptly named Faith, Hope and Charity—were able to hold the huge Italian air force at bay long enough to convince the harried UK Government that Malta just might be able to hold out.

A few Hurricanes soon arrived and torpedo-carrying Swordfish of the Fleet Air Arm arrived within a week. They began to attack Sicily and the shipping lanes to North Africa, where Mussolini had a huge army with which he hoped to conquer Egypt. The Malta-based Hurricanes proved more than a match for the numerically superior Italian Air Force.

Blenheim bombers arrived to attack the enemy supply ships by day and the Swordfish learned new techniques to be able to attack them by night. Wellington bombers arrived to bomb Tripoli nightly.

Having first advanced, the Italian army was defeated by General Wavell and the retention of the Italian colonies of Tripolitania and Libya was threatened. Hitler came to the rescue of his fellow dictator by sending the brilliant General Rommel and the Afrika Korps to bolster the faltering Italian armies. Rommel took charge and restored order on land.

However, during October and November 1941, the combination of RAF and FAA planes, acting in close co-operation with surface Naval forces, such as the well-known Force K, and with the Royal Navy's submarines, all operating from Malta, sank almost every ship destined for North Africa. The Axis were faced with the choice of abandoning Rommel and the German and Italian armies in North Africa, or gaining control of Malta.

But the German paratroop losses incurred in seizing Crete and the various defeats the Italian Navy had suffered in the sea battles of the Mediterranean in 1940-41 weighed heavily in the minds of Hitler and Goering. Instead of an invasion of Malta, Hitler decided to move one third of his total air strength from Russia (where they were temporarily stalled by the Russian winter) and bring them to airfields in Sicily, with the intention of reducing Malta to rubble.

So began Malta's intensified Blitz. Up to that point, although the island had already had to withstand over 800 air raids, it had not been too seriously threatened. The Luftwaffe had blasted it heavily during the early months of 1941 but, after the invasion of Russia, the job had largely been handed back to the Regia Aeronautica, which failed to show quite the determination of the Luftwaffe. By December 1941, the German blitzkreig had begun in earnest.

January 1942 was bad, February worse and by March the bombing had reached an unprecedented height. By then, the island had almost been brought to a standstill.

A few Spitfires began to be flown in from aircraft carriers which were able to advance within range, but these planes were not in a state of combat-readiness and in many cases were in the hands of inexperienced pilots. Against the battle-hardened ace pilots of the Luftwaffe with their Me-109s, and under a constant rain of bombs, they were all soon lost.

The lack of food on the island now assumed grave proportions. Of the twenty-one ships which had been sent to relieve the shortages during the Spring of 1942, only two arrived to discharge their cargo. The others were sunk *en route,* had to turn back, or were sunk soon after arrival.

By then, the population had learned to live like troglodytes. Malta is composed of soft limestone rock and caves are easily dug. Here, those locals not engaged in the island's defence were living. The Services battled on as best they could. Rations were down to about one third of normal. With raids now almost non-stop, the men had to keep working throughout alerts.

The tonnage of bombs dropped during April, nearly eight thousand, was about four times that dropped during March. A further forty-five Spitfires arrived, only to be written off almost immediately on the ground or in the air.

Malta was tottering.

It was almost out of anti-aircraft ammunition, out of petrol (which had been brought in strapped to the sides of submarines), out of food, out of planes and almost out of hope. Me-109s played with each other at low level over the RAF airfields. What little anti-aircraft ammunition there was left was reserved for the bombers. Axis supply ships now sailed unopposed to Rommel and his Afrika Korps. The Royal Navy even had to withdraw its submarines.

Rommel was able to mount a successful campaign against the 8th Army in the desert. Tobruk fell; Rommel reached a small railway station called El Alamein, only sixty miles from Alexandria.

It was on 15th April 1942, at the height of the Malta Blitz, that King George VI decided to award the George Cross to the island of Malta.

Malta, long-neglected, where the RAF had only remained operational by "shanghai-ing" planes landing to re-fuel *en route* to the Middle East, was now seen as essential. The Allies decided to make one more desperate attempt to relieve Malta.

On 9th May, sixty-four Spitfires were flown off the decks of the carriers HMS *Eagle* and USS *Wasp*. This time, they had been prepared for immediate action, and the reception of each at one of Malta's three airfields had been planned in minute detail. Within nine minutes of landing, they were re-fuelled, re-armed, had their overload tanks removed and were taxi-ing out in the hands of fresh, experienced pilots. The Luftwaffe were in for a surprise.

By 10th May, the air battle for Malta had been won. Up to sixty-three enemy planes were lost that day. Even Rome Radio, notoriously inaccurate, admitted to the loss of forty-eight. Air superiority over the island had been regained, never again to be lost.

Within weeks, the RAF and FAA torpedo-bombers had returned. The submarines came back. Rommel's supply lines were severed once again. Then came many more Spitfires, and "Screwball" Beurling's remarkable shooting epic (twenty-seven shot down within a few weeks).

Thereafter, Malta never looked back and the 8th Army's success at El Alamein was the result.

A heavy price had been paid: 3,340 air raids; thousands of Maltese killed; 29,674 private dwellings damaged or destroyed; 111 churches hit; hundreds of aircraft destroyed on the ground but about 1,300 of the enemy shot down by the planes and gunners of Malta, with the fighters claiming over 1,000 of them.

In Valetta today, there is a Memorial to the 2,301 airmen who have no known grave but who were lost whilst serving in Malta and other Mediterranean theatres of war. The inscription on it reads:

PROPOSITI INSULA TENAX TENACES VIROS
COMMERORAT

which can be translated as "An island resolute of purpose remembers resolute men".

King George VI did well to award the George Cross to the island of Malta and its resolute people.

Malta GC will never be forgotten by those who were there.

25: U-Boat Hunting Again

I SUPPOSE that by normal standards the two and half years of war which followed were both exacting and varied. A long sea journey home by way of South Africa was followed by a period of instructing back in Limavady, and by a happy chance alongside both Eric and Blisso again.

Blisso was his usual self. On one occasion he lectured his crew about the evils of drinking before flying! Before dismissing them he commenced to stamp his feet upon unseen objects. "Damned blackbeetles," he explained. When I left Limavady he was composing a piano concerto entitled "The Passage of a Meteorological Polar Front". He almost wore out the Mess piano playing this.

I then became involved in the very project that I had so strongly desired in Malta—that of using the ASV-equipped Wellington as a night torpedo bomber. This was fitted with two torpedoes. Later our unit re-circuited the ASV so that it could be read in yards. This enabled accurate attacks to be made at night. The corporal working with me on this project was rightly decorated for this ingenuity.

At that time I was CO of a training squadron based at an airfield crudely carved out from the championship golf links at Turnberry, and I had the good fortune to find my old friend Bibby of the Fleet Air Arm in a similar appointment teaching Naval pilots to drop their torpedoes at night from nearby Mackrahanish. Together we teamed up to let our pupils carry out torpedo attacks on target ships entering the Clyde. In this manner we once "attacked" the *Nelson* (happily repaired) with no fewer than seventy-eight torpedo bombers simultaneously. How we all avoided each other after this "attack" I shall never know, as we came pouring in from all points of the compass in one fell swoop and none of us "dropped" our "tin-fish" above 180 feet!

We could have slaughtered any Navy on earth with our mixed force of Wellingtons, Hampdens, Beauforts, Beaufighters, Barracudas, Albacores and faithful old Swordfish.

Later when the four-engined B-24 Liberator aircraft joined Coastal Command in large numbers, I was appointed a flight-commander of one of Coastal Command's long-range squadrons. For the third time I was promoted squadron-leader. Firstly at Thorney Island near Southampton, then at Beaulieu in the heart of the lovely New Forest, and ultimately at St Eval where I served 53 Squadron in this capacity.

I was sad at leaving Turnberry. It was an efficient station with splendid officers and excellent training facilities. I was also sad at having to part, at last, with my old friend Norman Lightowler. This quietly-spoken former sergeant had accompanied me from Malta to Egypt, to South Africa, Northern Ireland and thence to Turnberry. He had deservedly been commissioned and had been my right-hand man for the best part of a year. His support and help had enabled me to spend much time away from my unit on missions of interest and exploration, and I had found that personal visits to the Navy, FAA, other training units, Group HQ, etc, were invaluable when working out our new Fishington techniques. (A Wellington with ASV was a "Goofington". With the torpedoes added it became a "Fishington".)

Pilot-Officer Lightowler went off to take command of a Halifax aircraft with another Coastal Command squadron.

But my good luck continued, and upon joining 53 Squadron I was allowed to pick my own crew. There were a half-dozen recently trained crews together in a room with six of us second or third tour captains. We had a bare five minutes to decide. I spied a tall officer co-pilot with twinkling eyes and a humorous handlebar moustache.

"What kind of crew have you got? "I enquired.

"Largely composed of rather fierce New Zealanders," he replied.

This was good enough for me. Aussies and New Zealanders had long been favourites of mine, and during my instructing periods at Limavady and Turnberry I had had several of them pass through my hands with distinction.

Jeff Wilkinson or "Wilkie" was my new 2nd pilot. He proved to be as reliable, loyal and resourceful as Reason and Lightowler in the past. No pilot can be blessed in a more practical manner than to be given a superlative 2nd pilot, or co-pilot (as he had now more accurately come to be called).

This time my *ab initio* crew had been properly trained, and had worked together as a team for many months at the beautiful Nassau training airfield in the Bahamas.

The WOP/AGs—and I now had five of them—knew how to work their guns and how to operate their radar and wireless. The navigator had had previous operational experience and had come from a Halifax squadron. Wilkie was thoroughly efficient himself, and had been leading his team as their training captain. I even carried a flight engineer as part of my ten- or eleven-man crew.

But the greatest joy of all was to be given really effective radar. No longer were we to battle with the limited ASV Mark II. Now we had a circular screen which depicted the area around as a map orientated about our aircraft as the centre. Equally gratifying was to find that the Liberator could fly with one or possibly two engines inoperative. The aircraft was also fitted with anti-ice devices and a radio altimeter, and the radar was powerful enough to spy out the Atlantic U-boats that once more were our prime objectives.

On an early sortie we were jumped upon by four or five Me-110 fighters—aircraft with such a tremendous speed advantage over us that they could circle us from underneath, and pull sharply up to fire at our undersides where we were least protected and least able to fire back.

I climbed and prayed. I literally shoved the throttles through the quadrant as we overboosted our turbo-supercharged engines in a desperate attempt to reach the safety of cloud cover.

The Germans made a nasty mess of our Liberator. Two engines were hit and damaged; Tommy Thompson, an ex-New Zealand coal-miner, was hit in the foot as he fired his guns, and our star gunner, the Maori, or part Maori, Heays was fatally felled by a 20 mm cannon shell exploding in his back as he manned one of our 0.5 inch side guns. We eased his pain with morphine injections and wrapped him in the silk of an opened parachute. It was all we could do. He was still just alive when we landed back at St Eval. The aircraft barely survived too, and I shall never forget the horror I experienced when, after coming to a stop alongside the waiting ambulances on the runway, I first observed that the main undercarriage drag link had been completely holed by another 20 mm cannon shell.

The whole experience was a nightmare. The crew were only on their second or third trip, but their behaviour and training stood them in good stead after recovering from the initial shock of being "jumped" by a surprise attack. At least one of the attacking twin-engined fighters was badly hit and went down with smoke pouring from it. Flying-Officer Niven, an experienced gunner who was with us that day, was confident that the Me-110 had crashed into the sea. The others called off their attack to aid their companion. Certainly we were glad of the respite. One more pass at us and they must surely have finished us as we were rapidly becoming a lame, limping target. It is reasonable to suppose that they regarded us as finished already.

I was half scared out of my wits by it all but luckily remembered the need to go flying again at once. This restores confidence and prevents brooding. The squadron sent me another aircraft that same day, and I flew this back to our base at Thorney Island that very afternoon.

As a crew we flew as much or more than any other in the squadron in spite of the administration duties which I had now acquired. There were two squadron-leaders to each squadron, and after the first of my co-flight commanders, Squadron Leader Ken Aldrich (a tireless worker who carried most of our twin burden) was killed, George Crawford took his place. He and I had been together in the RAFVR at lectures before the war. Such days now seemed far away in the past.

George and I hit it off well and worked happily together under a wing-commander who largely left the operational duties of the squadron to us. He seldom flew, but concentrated upon the ever-mounting paper work. He was my second CO in that squadron. The first was a brilliant pilot—a man of resource, ingenuity and skill, a fair-minded near-genius who perhaps should have been a test pilot rather than a squadron commander. He, too, came to grief in the grey, swirling waters of the Atlantic, and although he survived, all his crew were lost.

My turn almost came on the same night my CO crashed. I was way out in mid-Atlantic, a thousand miles from Europe, one of our engines "ran-away" and the windmilling propeller could not be dislodged from the fully-fine, or maximum drag, position. Normally the Liberator made light of flying upon three engines, but this extra drag burdened and slowed her horribly. Also it meant that we had to gobble fuel at a greedy rate in order to stay aloft at all.

The navigator threw his hand in. It was a genuine case of shattered nerves. He had been on operations too long and had become convinced that we couldn't possibly reach friendly territory. This added to our already grave situation. The three remaining New Zealanders and my excellent Senior WOP/AG (an Englishman) Tommy Barnes responded nobly to my command to "lighten the aircraft".

The Leigh light and its batteries were jettisoned. Four Browning .303 machine-guns with 10,000 rounds of ammunition went overboard, followed by our two sideways-firing American 0.5 inch guns together with their heavy-calibre shells. Other 0.5 inch guns were removed from the upper gun turret and another two from the front gun turret. After that my "All Black" troops roared round the plane wielding axes! Even our parachutes went overboard, and a gallant attempt was made to chop away the huge retractable "dustbin" containing the radar gear and which must have weighed about a ton.

I was doing my damndest to reach Gibraltar, but when still over a hundred miles away the sight-glass petrol gauges were all showing zero. I left Tommy Barnes on the one remaining radio set (the New Zealanders had taken the others) in order that he could transmit our final SOS ditching position. I sent the rest of the crew to their ditching stations amidships.

When seventy miles from Gibraltar we passed *over* the Air Sea Rescue launch being sent to pick us up! We saw it turn round and follow us. I wondered whether to abandon the struggle and "ditch" alongside it. But with no fuel reserves aboard, and precious little else either, she was now flying as easily as a soaring seagull, and by a near miracle we were able to half-fly, half-glide the machine straight down on to the famous runway protruding out of Gibraltar's rock.

We had been aloft fifteen and three-quarter hours—the last nine and a half with one propeller windmilling in fully fine pitch!

Soon after this I was being "put to bed" by colleagues who forestalled my attempts to drink Gibraltar dry.

I awoke with a horrible head to find that other losses that night had left my crew and I in almost entire charge of the squadron. Nearly every senior officer and section leader had taken their last flight that night when bad luck and bad weather had decimated the squadron.

Our own aircraft was a wreck but we borrowed another pilot's Liberator and I flew back home as soon as I could.

George Crawford spent his first three days on this squadron representing us at various funeral services up and down the country.

George was the wealthy heir to a family firm. He joined this at an early age. By the time war broke out he was already general manager or some such title, although he was only about twenty-four. He was a fine pilot, a tireless worker and a natural leader. We worked in such proximity that on occasions we used to bare our souls to each other.

In this mood George once told me, "This war has taught me something I shall never forget. It has taught me that I can think straight and that I can manage other people. I started as you did, as a sergeant-pilot. In the RAF I had no family firm behind me. Now, less than four years later, I am a squadron-leader with both DFC and AFC. This has given me the confidence that I never otherwise could have acquired. When I get back to the firm after the war I need never again feel that I owe my position entirely to family connections. That firm had better look out, as I am coming back to it brim full of new ideas, and this time I will not let any of the 'old hands' talk me out of them."

Not boastful. Just true.

The tragedy was that within six weeks or so he, too, was lost over the Atlantic. In coastal squadrons the finest always tended to get killed. They pressed home their attacks harder. However, in spite of our heavy losses, it was the U-boats which suffered worst. Allied shipping losses began to fall dramatically and German U-boat losses mounted monthly. At long last the Battle of the Atlantic was being won—by the same RAF-RN team that I had seen work so well in Malta.

It was a tactical struggle of such profound interest that I could hardly tear myself away from the Intelligence Office where I read and re-read every file on U-boats, frigates, corvettes, convoy strategy and other squadron activities.

Sometimes the U-boats fought back on the surface. At one time they even tried to cross the Bay of Biscay in formations of three, each armed with up to ten Oerlikon guns. We then attacked them in groups. At other times they dived whenever sighted. Finally they resorted to lying submerged during most of the daylight hours. Our constant air patrols had dictated this. We then resorted to the use of searchlights—the Leigh light, called after its inventor Wing Commander Leigh, and a project on which Blisso had worked.

This two million-candlepower beam was torched by no less than

600-lb weight in dry batteries. The fact that it was attached to the plane far out under the starboard wing was a mixed blessing. Here it didn't blind us, but our already overloaded Liberators were made lopsided and we used to stagger off with almost full aileron trim applied in order to keep the wings level. Extra wing-tip fuel tanks, extra depth-charges, increased fire power in the shape of rocket carriers, additional armour plate, were gradually piled on until our once easy-flying aircraft was barely capable of leaving the ground. It was for this reason the squadron departed from Thorney Island for the slightly longer runways at nearby Beaulieu, and St Eval.

The squadron usually kept a half-flight at Ballykelly in Northem Ireland. Here the main runway had been extended across the railway lines. The Flying Control Officer in the tower had over-riding control over the railway signals via a switch. Inevitably someone obtained a red tie, a porter's hat, a flag and a whistle. These would be solemnly used whenever changing the railway signals!

The sense of anti-climax which was so hard to shed after those six frenzied months in Malta began to wear off. The stalk and chase after an enemy U-boat over the sea at night was at least the equivalent of those long night-shadowing missions of the enemy ships attempting to slip past Malta.

We had reason to suspect that U-boats were equipped with radar detectors. Thus, if a surprise attack was to be made, we needed to approach with a blend of cunning and caution. At night any other than a surprise attack was pointless, as all a tough U-boat needed to do to avoid being damaged was to slip beneath the waves. When submerged deeper than fifty feet or so he was inviolate against the shallow hydrostatic fuse settings that we were obliged to use for our attacks.

Thus it was that as soon as I heard the glad cry, "Captain from Radar, I think I've got a blip 12 miles away 30 degrees to port," the WOP/AG operating the radar set would follow pre-determined drills and would stop the scanner, leaving the pulses streaming forth aft. This meant that we were in no position to further detect targets ahead of us.

Thus the Germans could not detect our radar: but neither could we now use this to locate them.

My Malta experience, plus the months spent at Turnberry on the TB Wellingtons making training night attacks at low level, now stood me in good stead. If there was either a moon or a lighter part of the sky, my immediate next move would be mentally to memorise the enemy's whereabouts whilst guiding my plane toward the darkest part of the sky. (*See sketch.*) After a few minutes I would again ask the radar operator for a "sighting" with the words, "Captain to Radar. Once round."

This meant that he was to allow the scanner one complete orbit of the screen so that any target within range could be noted.

"No blip, Skipper," warned me that I had steered too far away and that I must now edge back towards where I imagined the target to be.

The next order of "once round" would, I prayed, reveal that we were still on the scent. After that my job was to keep working the enemy into the moonpath whilst using my radar to an absolute minimum. I had to be careful at all times to keep the tell-tale stream of pulses away from him.

On the final run-in I would have to consider the side-effect or "drifts" that the wind would be causing to my flight path. I also had to bear in mind that the enemy was also moving at up to 18 knots in some direction unknown to me. Some vague sense of our relative closing bearings would, with luck, be gained, but that was about all. It paid to double all corrections when on the final run in—if told that they were 5 degrees port it paid to alter course 10 degrees port. This way the target could be bracketed down, and some of the small but unknown speed factors preventing a steady run-in on a constant heading could be gauged. From about five miles onwards we would leave the radar on continuously. Our speed was about two and a half to three miles a minute, and it was my intention to switch on the Leigh light at two miles, so fear of "giving the game away" was no longer serious.

The Leigh light was *supposed* to be switched on at one mile or even at three-quarters of a mile, but experience had taught us that the chances of its beam immediately picking up the target and so blinding their gunners was so remote that in practice this admirable theory fell down. By a stroke of luck the first time that we located a U-boat at night, Warrant-Officer Ware, poor Heays's replacement, was on the set and he misread the short-range mileage marks on the face of the screen, with the result that we switched on at two miles range instead of one mile as per "the book". We saw nothing except high rolling seas—the same seas that had caused this careful operator to misread the range. Big Flying-Officer Wells, the splendid ex-master mariner who had

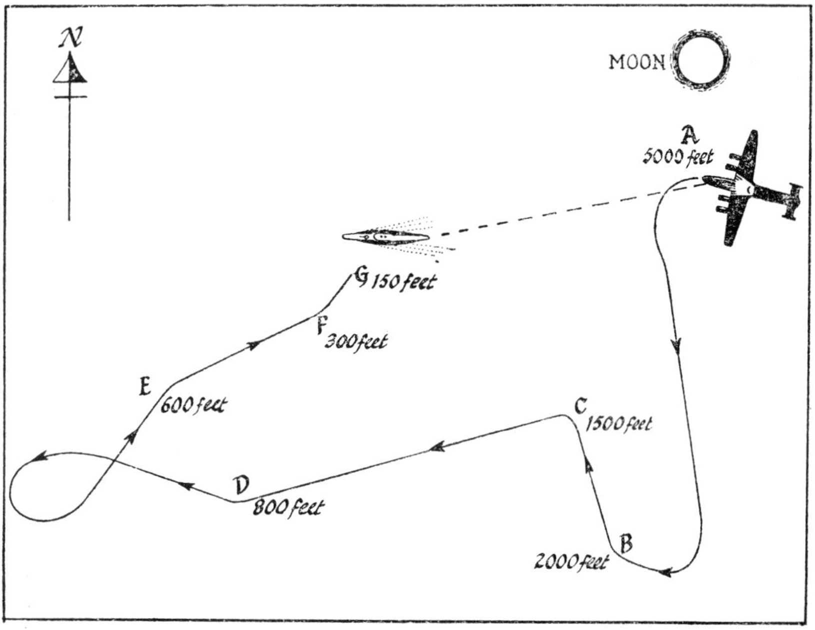

U-BOAT STALK AT NIGHT USING LEIGH-LIGHT AND MINIMUM RADAR

A. "Radar to Skipper. I've got a target 12 miles to port—angle 30 degrees." (Aircraft flies away from the moon for 4 minutes.)
B. "Captain to radar: Once round." "Sorry, Skipper, nothing on the screen." (Aircraft flies towards target for 1 minute.)
C. "Once round again." "25 degrees to port—distance 10 miles." (Aircraft is turned to a course so that target is placed near moon-path.)
D. "Once round again." "110 degrees to starboard now—distance 12 miles. Target rather weak; if we get further away we might lose it." (Aircraft is flown away from moon and then turned direct into moon. Aircraft is turned the long-way-round to avoid getting too close. Turns have radii of one mile or more.)
E. "Once round again." "Slightly to starboard—9 miles."
F. "Once round again." "Slightly to port—5 miles." "O.K., leave the radar on continuously now." "Will do, Sir." "And call distances at every half-mile."
G. "Radar to Captain—range 2½ miles dead ahead still." "Captain to Navigator—Leigh light on NOW. Bomb doors open and, Wilkie, keep calling my height. *Shout* whenever we approach 100 feet or lower."

this, using tracer and incendiary shells, giving away his position unmistakably. We then steered down his line of fire confident that we were still outside lethal range. The firing then ceased as their gunners fumbled furiously to replace the used ammunition drums with fresh ones. By then we had two million-candlepower shining right into their eyes and it was no wonder that nothing very dangerous ever came our way during this vital stage of the attack. We were never hit once.

I deliberately refer to "target "rather than "enemy", for the sad fact was that for every U-boat illuminated—and we tracked down and illuminated more than any other crew in Coastal Command—we detected about two or three lone but friendly ships. Everything from small armed trawlers to the French battleship *Richelieu* and the huge liner *Andes*. This latter was hunted down in a blinding rain-storm, and by the time its huge bulk loomed up we were nearly into it. In this case we had first illuminated its frothy white wake and had turned towards the source of this. There were probably thousands of troops aboard. If any reader of this book remembers a large aircraft beaming a searchlight spiralling crazily and desperately upwards between her very masts on the night of 22nd February 1944, this was us.

Neither Wilkie nor I ever thought that we could avoid hitting her funnel, which at that point-blank range seemed as large and formidable as a gasholder. But most of our friendly chases after friendly ships turned out to be destroyers, corvettes, frigates, etc, that had decided to detach themselves from their escort groups in order to follow up possible contacts detected on their underwater asdic device. Others were fast ships, such as the *Andes*, braving it across the Atlantic without escort.

We became a highly decorated crew. Wilkinson won the DFC, as did Wells. In the end all the New Zealanders, Mills, Bailey and Tommy Thompson, and Tommy Barnes too were awarded the DFM, and I made a second visit to Buckingham Palace to receive the DSO. from the hands of a gallantly overworked and desperately tired-looking King George VI. The change in his appearance between my two Palace visits was marked, but his mind was obviously very alert and technically interested in the RAF, judging by the keen and intelligent questions he asked me in a voice that was slow but completely devoid of any speech hesitation.

Traces of the symptoms which had laid me low at Malta now began to reappear. I think also I had begun to realise that I had but one speed—flat out—but that after a year or so of this I tended to "run out of gas".

Others, like Terry Bullock (DSO and bar, DFC and bar), the greatest of all Coastal Command U-boat hunters, could keep going for ever. Terry scorned all offers of further promotion, squadron or flight appointments, and just flew and flew. He became a roving lone wolf, attached to no particular squadron, but acting directly under his AOC. His Liberator loaded with rockets turned up wherever the need was greatest. He would have made a wonderful Malta pilot. He abhorred red tape, paper work and similar "nonsense" as he dubbed most administration matters. His biography *Coastal Ace* was written by me and published by William Kimber in 1986.

Mick Ensor was another successful U-boat hunter and also had the DSO and bar and DFC and bar. I knew him better than I did Terry, as he and I were "rival" squadron leaders after 53 Squadron moved to St Eval. We belonged to different Liberator squadrons. He could only have been about twenty-three at the time, but had found time to write a lot of sense about U-boat tactics as well as do more than his fair share of the actual killing.

That we were a happy crew was due to several factors. Good-tempered, conscientious Wilkie virtually commanded the crew on the ground as I was increasingly tied up in the office struggling to cope with administrative matters for which I had neither inclination nor training. George and I, however, made a point of one of us always being available. Fred Bailey was a cheerful, brash, friendly New Zealander who did a lot to keep us all in good temper and high spirits. The traditional eggs-and-bacon crew meal prior to departure was almost a riot, with Fred chivvying the WAAF waitresses and even on occasion cooking the eggs. Shrieks and giggles rose from the kitchen.

Everyone loved Fred. He was a splendidly balanced and loyal character. Young Tommy Barnes had struggled to educate himself and had succeeded well. I was delighted, after an argument with the CO, to have been able to get him commissioned. Later he joined BEA and became a radio officer instructor for them. No detail was allowed to get the better of him technically, and he was razor-quick on the uptake. He was a great man to have on the radio during an attack when things were happening fast.

Poor Wilkie saw little of the attacks as I forced him to watch continuously but one thing—the radio altimeter which we now thankfully carried. Our biggest danger during such low-level twisting attacks was that of putting a wing-tip into the sea. (I suspect that we lost many aircraft in this way.) Our aircraft had a span of over a hundred feet: yet we liked to attack from about a hundred feet up. The huge Atlantic rollers several times cut this latter to very close limits, and at night it is all too easy to fly into the sea. Warrant-Officer Ware was as steady and quiet as they come. He was a church bell-ringer in his spare time. He was a devout man, probably from farming stock. His rich and imperturbable manner and voice were a godsend, as we were using a semi-blind landing device called BABS. During such landings one radar operator aboard literally held all our lives in his hands as he "talked down" his own skipper from patterns and traces on our radar screen. We used BABS. for every landing so that by the time it became necessary to land in fog or in other foul weather this hazardous manoeuvre had become standard.

"Dizzy" Moore was a second quick-witted navigator, and a young Sergeant Hinchcliffe carried out our few in-flight engineering requirements with keenness. The young, quick, red-haired Mills and the sullen-looking ex-miner Tommy, still with a limp from the foot wound he had collected over the Bay of Biscay, completed the crew. I could never make contact with this "strong, silent" man, but Mills and Bailey assured me that he was "all right when you got to know him."

Such an aircrew was ten intelligent, keen, healthy young individuals—the pick of their country—welded together into a determined, loyal, proud, fighting unit. Anyone who commanded or was a part of an RAF aircrew during war-time tasted one of the sweetest fruits of life. How tragic that so many men had to die so soon after thus learning to live.

26: D-Day and Hellfire Corner

AFTER over a thousand hours on operations I was "rested" at the first signs of physical strain. The rest cure provided was to be appointed Coastal Command Liaison Officer—a new appointment—attached to the staff of the Vice-Admiral Commanding, Dover (VAD).

Here I lived with the Navy in their mess. I was part of the Admiral's staff, and I was there to ensure that good RAF-RN co-operation took place on and after D-Day.

My *short* title was CCLO to VAD!

My AOC-in-C, Sholto Douglas, then Air Chief Marshal (later Lord Douglas of Kirtleside and chief of BEA), briefed me in person: "You are to serve the Navy. I can't tell you anything about it as there is a security ban, and the Navy are red-hot on security. All I can tell you is that there is going to be an invasion of Europe."

This came as no surprise. The newspapers (and the Russians) had been awaiting such an invasion for more than a year. If I was to serve the Navy now, it needed no second guess to wonder why. Now at last I learnt that the much-forecast invasion was to take place and that I would have a part to play in it—in co-operation with my beloved Navy. This was more than I deserved. Whilst with 53 Squadron I had visited destroyers, frigates and corvettes, been down in several of our submarines and had generally kept contact with the Senior Service. And I had been one of the first RAF crews to attend their great sea-air anti-U-boat school at Eglington and Londonderry.

I had always seen eye to eye with the Navy; more so, indeed, than with my own service, the RAF. To this latter I was an ex-civilian pilot insufficiently versed in their long-standing traditions. In their eyes I was too ignorant of their administrative organisation. But when had I been given a chance to study it? I had been flying their aeroplanes ever since the hour that war began.

Admiral Pridham-Whipple (VAD) reminded me of Captain Agnew. He was tall, dignified and erect. There was something of the traditional Spanish grandee about his appearance. A monocle would not have been out of place on such a distinguished-looking figure. He spoke very quietly and not very often.

"You know about the invasion?"

"No, sir." I wasn't going to let my AOC-in-C down. I thought it best to forget even his final remark.

"Well then, Spooner, the first thing you had better do is to sit down and read all about it!"

So I was duly sworn on to various "BIGOT" and "NEPTUNE" lists, enrolled on the "OVERLORD" planning staff and henceforth spent much time with their Intelligence Officer. I also spent useful hours with the equally informed Hydrographer Officer. He turned out to be the brother of the same Squadron-Leader Lowery who sportingly had taken Reason's place as my second pilot on at least two occasions in Malta.

Once again the job was largely night work. This took place in the tunnels of Dover Castle, where an efficient Combined Operations centre had been concealed. Army, Navy and Air Force worked as one. But as in Malta, it was largely an RAF-RN operation.

Much happened during these months. We prepared Dover. I consider the master-stroke was when we supplied almost every householder in Dover with an ample supply of bedding plus such wartime rarities as tinned milk, dried egg powder, sugar, etc. This last really convinced the citizens that they had a vital role to play. We "alerted" the enemy for the phoney invasion across the Straits of Dover. This fake was a success. Their action in keeping no less than thirty divisions of troops in the Pas de Calais area for six weeks after the real invasion had started was a triumph beyond our wildest hopes.

Those who thought this out and who saw it through deserved the praise of all free men. Thirty divisions is a colossal force to keep out of the way at a time when the fate of the civilized world and the greatest invasion in all history hung in the balance less than 100 miles to their west.

Another task that befell us at Dover was to assist the passage through the straits of the huge D-Day convoys. These sailed from the Thames Estuary on D-Day plus one. They passed without loss well within range of the German guns massed opposite. The smokescreen with which we covered the area from ship, motor torpedo boats, RAF and FAA planes practically blotted out SE England.

I had two assistants with me and we spent many hours following the fortunes of the nightly little-ship war going on between the Germans' powerful E-boats, our MTBs and our RAF Beaufighters. We would spend the night dashing between Naval Ops room, where we had a desk, and the Fighter Control centre "Swingate" situated in the adjoining cavern.

The unequal gun-fire duels was another permanent feature of the months I spent underground in that famous Castle keep. Our fourteen-inch guns were few in number and ancient. They were relics of World War I. Their range, even using supercharge, was barely sufficient to cross the Channel. They were an obsolete Coastal Defence weapon, perched atop the cliffs in the open. The enemy's guns were numerous. They were housed in caves or kept in rail tunnels. They were large and modern, and their range was so colossal that on one occasion they shelled Chatham—nearly forty miles behind Dover!

The "doodle-bugs" also began whilst I was there, and of the 10,000 or so flying bombs launched by the enemy from across the Channel, practically the whole lot came over our heads. I must have seen hundreds destroyed.

To save London from ruthless destruction, our fighting services put up a tremendous effort against these flying bombs. I often wonder if the citizens of London realised how much was put into the effort to destroy these flying bombs before they could reach the capital itself. And this at a time when the invasion demanded maximum effort elsewhere.

On clear nights we could actually see these flaming bomb-planes rising up from their launching sites, which had been systematically attacked for several months prior to their exact purpose being known. However, many sites still lay hidden in the woods. Over the Channel our Mustang and Mosquito fighters would do their damndest to fasten on to these fast ram-jet powered moving targets. Pilots overboosted and burst their piston engines by the score. When about three miles from the coast the Mustangs and Mosquitos abandoned their chase and the remaining doodle-bugs would then be attacked by the greatest concentration of AA fire ever assembled. The guns stood almost side by side along Dungeness. The proximity fuse invention released for this campaign made this barrage doubly effective. These guns were British and American (Navy and Army), and they almost covered the sky with shell bursts, and the few flying bombs that survived were by then often off-course or malfunctioning in other ways.

After crossing the coast the sky was clear for the fastest planes we had. These were the Tempests, Typhoons and Spitfire XXIIs. These fighters, plus a few jet Meteors advanced from the secret list for this purpose, were specially prepared for high-speed at low altitudes, and they shot down the pilotless invaders in their hundreds. And when the guns of their fighters were empty the pilots would ram their prey or make attempts to tip them over with their wings. All this at less than 4,000 feet—a height when bail-out by parachute was of doubtful safety.

Nearing London itself stood a barrage of balloons trailing explosive cables. Practically every balloon in the country was marshalled for this purpose. And behind these were the AA guns of London itself. Thanks to this tremendous effort and the tireless devotion of all, a situation which at first looked as if it might destroy London was avoided. And in the end some ninety-nine out of every hundred of Hitler's secret weapon were being destroyed before arrival at their objective. The population was spared the over-frequent recurrence of that fateful moment when the engine would abruptly cease its phut-phut. Then the ingenious weapon would plummet earthwards and explode with a tremendous blast—bringing down as many as thirty or forty houses at a time. No one who ever experienced it will ever forget that awesome hush as the noisy jet engine ceased abruptly. But for all its novelty Hitler's secret weapon No. 1 was defeated.

However in Naval Intelligence we were more worried by reports coming in about a "W-boat". This was an enemy underwater craft that could travel at twenty-five or more knots below the surface and which never (or seldom) needed to leave its underwater protection. Some naval experts said that such an underwater speed was impossible. Few of us could imagine any defence against such a weapon. But we worked out a dozen possible reprisals.

In the end the W-boat never appeared. The Germans were indeed prefabricating smaller U-boats and they did perfect the Snorkel which enabled U-boat engines to breathe whilst still submerged, but the fast W-boat threat never existed.

Lastly came the awful shelling when the Germans at last realised, far too late, that they had been fooled by our fake invasion preparations. They seemed then to mark down Dover for "special attention".

A few weeks later the huge German Army in the Pas de Calais area was by-passed, cut off and trapped. Nor did these troops try too hard to fight their way out. Either the will to fight was lacking or they believed that Hitler would eventually turn back the sweeping Allied tide and come to their rescue. He had issued another of his absurd "Don't retreat a single yard" messages. So a vast enemy Army sat there whilst the tide of battle raced into the Low Countries behind them.

When it finally dawned on them that they were never going to be rescued, they turned their attention to Dover and the other Cinque Ports. They still had their splendid batteries of well-protected long-range guns, and an almost inexhaustible supply of ammunition.

For six weeks they fired the lot at Folkestone, Deal and especially at Dover. Longer shots at Tunbridge Wells, Maidstone, etc, shortened the life of irreplaceable gun barrels, so they elected to plaster the easier targets across the water. Here, too, they could partially observe results.

I had been through over 1,300 air raids in Malta—many of them dive-bombing attacks. I had seen thousands of doodlebugs in flight and had heard scores of them stop, dive and explode near by. I had been virtually blown out of bed by one whilst on leave in my aunt's house in SE London. I had been on board *Aurora* with her guns firing. I was accustomed to AA fire, gunfire and the sound of exploding bombs, but I never got used to being shelled by those merciless long-range German guns.

The shells came over with no warning whatsoever. The alert was in permanent force, and the first that those in the area knew about the arrival of each shell was the tremendous roar it emitted as it exploded. (I believe that V2 rockets, which never came our way, arrived in a similar sudden fashion.) Being largely solid, in order to withstand the tremendous gun barrel pressure, the shells didn't do much damage. One house at a time was all that such shells could demolish. The pressure of our work at naval HQ was now lightened and I had moved my wife into the area as soon as the return of civilians was permitted.

We had rented a house in the town. But the shells still arrived at irregular intervals every hour or so. Some days were "hotter" than others. Weather didn't affect the situation. They kept it up at night, too. Dover was never the target for a steady barrage or for salvoes of shells. Instead they came over one at a time day and night for about six weeks. I don't know how many rounds they fired our way but they arrived with such an ear-splitting roar that we reckoned we heard the lot. Sleep was really difficult. I, who had learnt to sleep with a Bofors gun firing under my open window, couldn't outsleep these final bursts of Hitler's crumbling Empire.

All in all it was a strange "rest period" for one who had been told that he was exhibiting signs of operational stress! Life with the squadron would have been peaceful by contrast. I did get occasional news of the squadron. Alas it was usually sad news. In this way I learnt that George Crawford, Carmichaels (who had taken over from me) and others had gone for evermore. Wilkie had taken over my crew as I had previously, and secretly, planned. Normally a second pilot had to return to an OTU for another full course before being appointed a captain. This was another example of how thoroughly we now trained our aircrews.

As so often was the case, I compared these training methods, as I did almost everything else, with those at Malta. Poor Mac's training was merely to act as co-pilot once or twice, and, after an all-night trip, to carry out the final landing. And when the doodlebugs flew over I would think of the swooping Ju-88s diving at our two precious merchantmen in Grand Harbour. I mentally compared the tremendous Dungeness barrage with our pathetically weak all-out efforts at Luqa and Valetta. The ear-splitting noise of the German long-range shells reminded me of one time when I had stood on the *Aurora* during an air-raid and helped to work one of their pom-pom guns whilst their heavier three-inch weapons fired directly behind me.

By most standards I was having a hectic war. Nonetheless only when actually under fire or when personally stalking the enemy over the sea or following his destruction on the huge plots displayed on the walls of our underground Ops rooms did I come truly alive. Then and then only was I rid of the feeling that for me Malta had been the only real war—and that ever since then I had been engaged upon a giant mopping-up operation.

To have been under siege in Malta was to have been made aware that there was a positive quality about living. Not to have been invaded during the night was to wake up feeling triumphant. To be able to hit back was glorious. To have been with the ill-dressed, ever-cheerful airmen, sergeants and officers at Luqa was to have shared moments with the gods.

27: Victory

THE shape of the world was changing fast. Roosevelt, the great American President, was suddenly dead. Whilst he was President we instinctively felt that the might of the USA would remain purposeful and honest. Now this great man was dead, would gangster rule again prevail in the world? None of us knew. We only knew that Anglo-American relations would never be the same again. We had lost our greatest friend and the whole nation was sad.

Then came the atom bomb. Here was power beyond the wildest dreams of man. In the triumph of our having invented the ultimate weapon, a kind of chill ran through us all. We were aghast at our own achievements. We had opened a new and dreadful door. What lay beyond?

The Beveridge Report was all the talk at home. This great programme to implement "Freedom from fear, freedom from want—from hunger and disease" was unfurled like a flag and, like crusaders, we raised our tired spirits and gave a cheer. But did Beveridge and the atom bomb match up? The horrific force of the one denied the lofty idealism of the other.

The war in Europe was over. Hitler's Germany had surrendered unconditionally.

I was flying troops out to the Far East. I had been seconded to BOAC, but was still flying in my RAF uniform, and the civilian DC-3 I commanded carried the roundels of the RAF on its sides. My passengers were nearly all army officers *en route* to the savage war areas closing in a ring around Japan. Russia had now joined the forces ranged against the Japanese. A second atom bomb had been dropped, this time on Nagasaki. I had departed from Istres, near Marseilles, and was *en route* to Malta when the big news came over the radio.

"Skipper!" came a joyful shout from the flushed-faced radio officer.

"It's all over. The Japs have surrendered. We've won. The war is over. We've won!" I quickly broke the news to my passengers. Their reaction was jubilant. They were on their way to fight and perhaps to die against this very enemy. To them it was like a personal reprieve.

We stopped the plane that night at Malta according to a predetermined schedule. Already the crowded transit officers' mess at Luqa was in full cry. One whale of a party was developing. My crew came to me. Would I still be departing soon after dawn tomorrow as scheduled? Was there any point in it? The answer had to be "Yes". The war machine hadn't started to slow down and unilateral action would only lead to chaos; also some men further east would be awaiting my plane so that they could commence their long-awaited homeward flight.

Would I mind, my crew enquired, if they joined the party? After all, this was rather a special occasion. Normally crews on early call didn't hit the bottle too hard the night before, and we were not encouraged to indulge at all when in the sight of our passengers.

"Go ahead," I told them. It really required only one steady hand to manage a DC-3, and for my part I felt strangely out of tune with the merry-making taking place around me. I walked out into the night. It was one of those Mediterranean nights I knew so well. Every star seemed to twinkle with a personal brilliance like the carefully placed lights hung with loving care upon a family Christmas tree. The moon illuminated the pale yellow of the rocks and the shadows of the low stone walls stood dark against the horizon. As I walked slowly towards the perimeter track memories came flooding back. I half expected to see Warby's special Beaufighter parked insolently on the road leading to Ops Room. Or to see Hugh Pughe's pale-blue Lincoln with Sergeant Aquilina crouched over the wheel. In the pale moonlight nothing would have appeared as more appropriate.

We had won. But what kind of victory was it going to be? Warby had gone, and with him Jackie Sewell, Seth-Smith, Dick Reynell the great test-pilot, Sandy of the long train-rides, George Crawford, Ken Aldrich, the magnificently-built Heays, Hussey of the *Lively,* Steve and Howe of the FAA, dear old Brem, my boyhood friends Dick and Basil, my wife's only brother and so many others. Names and faces passed before me in procession. Fine men all—all gone. Gone for ever. Gone to earth.

Were there going to be enough good men left, or would the spivs and the growing army of Smart Alecks take over? Were there enough Dennis Reasons left? And if a few remained, would they now be dubbed the professional killers of wartime, would they even be asked to take part in the fight to win the peace? Were there too few of them? Were not all those in uniform too tired, too deathly weary to start a rebuilding operation for which they were not trained or mentally equipped. Was 1946 going to be 1939 all over again? Too few men against established forces?

A swaying airman with his tunic undone and his flushed face sweating profusely passed me by. "You did hear the news, sir?" he enquired. He was gushing with good cheer. "We won. We've beaten the bastards. It's all over. We've won." I nodded silently and he went his way bemused.

I retraced my steps, walked past the mess from which the sound of boisterous singing could be heard, walked slowly under the brilliant moon to my billet, yes "my" billet, on "my" airfield, on "my" island. My mind was so much on other days that I was half surprised to find sheets on the bed. Automatically I ran my hand down the walls to test their dampness.

Would I ever forget Malta and the days that I had passed there? Those days when I was literally "glad to be alive" at the start of each day; glad to be free because we hadn't been invaded. Glad to be British amidst such company. Glad to be breathing while others were dead.

Around me were ghosts and I knew that I could never again completely relax until those ghosts were exorcised. Perhaps in writing this book I will have exorcised some of them and removed for ever from the innermost corners of my mind the stamp of Malta GC. Who knows?

Epilogue

LOOKING back over the war years I am struck very forcibly by one fact.

My personal experience of war over the Atlantic, in Malta and at Dover show clearly that the Germans were not very efficient at using their equipment. This is at variance with the popular supposition that the German people on the whole are experts at war. They march well; they have endurance; they are easily led and have no conscience about "anything being fair in war". They "bully" well and they defend like the devil. But they fail to fight intelligently as individuals. They fail in fact to "think" war. They fight with their jack-boots and not with their heads. In the Mediterranean, at the time when I was there, the Germans possessed an outstanding aircraft. This was the Ju-88. This plane was almost as fast as our Hurricane fighters. It had excellent engines; it was well armoured and it could carry a big load a long way. It was well-equipped with offensive and defensive guns. At the same time they had air-bases in Sardinia, Sicily, Italy, Greece, Crete, Libya and Tripolitania and they could fly over brow-beaten Tunisia with impunity. They also had hundreds of first-rate Me-109 F fighters to give them cover.

Yet they allowed Allied convoys to reach Egypt from the south in large numbers. They allowed our Egyptian ports to accumulate huge stores. They allowed us the use of the Suez Canal. They even allowed some ships to reach Malta. At times they were actually on the defensive over a sea ringed by their air bases. If attacking pilots such as Warburton, Lowery, Lerwill, Powell-Sheldon, Ivor Broom, Gibbs, Gillman, "Dallas" Schmidt and "Dinghy" Young, etc, or their FAA equivalents had possessed such aircraft and had they been able to operate unmolested from such a variety of bases, I doubt whether our Desert Armies would have received half the plentiful supplies that they did.

The Germans bombed Malta *ad infinitum.* They attacked major convoys *en masse*—that was their forte—that was their limit. They were dutiful and brave, but for all their overwhelming strength and fine aircraft they were inefficient.

Again in Dover. In the first place they were hopelessly fooled by our mock invasion plans. They simply could not get it out of their heads that we were *not* going to invade across the straits of Dover—not going to invade at the obvious place.

Later they incredibly allowed our huge D-Day plus 1 convoys to pass well within the range of their excellent long-range guns without sinking a single ship. Apparently there was not a single officer with the necessary "sense of war" to realise the supreme value of these ships to our forces struggling on their beaches.

The German mind throughout seemed fixed upon the theory that surface ships should only be sunk by U-boat or by lone raiders such as the *Altmark,* the *Hipper,* the *Graf Spee,* etc. Thus when in 1941 they began to attack our Atlantic ships with great effect with long range Focke-Wulf Kondor planes under a rare gifted commander (I believe his name was Peterson), they never realised how successful this one squadron was. Instead of cashing in on its success, they moved the unit elsewhere and ceased production of that efficient killer aircraft. And they never made a decent four-engined aircraft for the rest of the war. This in spite of the fact that at one time this single squadron was sinking nearly as many of our Allied merchantmen *en route* to Britain from the factories of the New World as was the entire U-boat fleet. And not until the "MAC Ship" mini-carriers of two years later did we possess an answer to these lone marauders.

Since the war I have often heard it said that the Germans lost the war because of this or that mistake made by Hitler. "He should have invaded us in 1940" is the most common of these remarks. The implication is that the Germans could have won the war. I refute this. The German people, within my experience, were incapable of winning a war, because their overall strategy was wrong and because they do not possess the qualities that produce individual intelligent action. If they had decided to cross our Channel in 1940 I believe that the defence that triumphed in Malta in spite of our chronic lack of equipment would have been repeated on a vast scale. They would have been killed in the streets, killed in the fields and killed in their beds. It would have become the "national game" played with poison and hat-pin as well as the modern appurtenances of war. We even had the catchphrase ready: "You can always take one with you."

Churchill was the leader and down through the chain of command were men like General Brook, Admiral Vian and my own very great leader of men, Hugh Pughe Lloyd. Lower down the scale were the men like Group-Captain Cahill of Luqa and Captain Agnew of the *Aurora*. Below them came the Warburtons, Bibbys, the Husseys and Lowerys, and lower still came the Dennis Reasons, the Sgt Dales, the Corporals such as Few and Norman Shirley and the LAC Haddons. If one were killed another "natural" miraculously appeared. The supply seemed inexhaustible.

I say that the Germans would have been in dead trouble had they tried to cross our coasts.

I saw it all in minuscule in Malta.

I was there.

Postscript

SHORTLY after I completed the original draft of this book, even before it was published, my life was changed quite abruptly.

From the latter part of the war until 1964, I had enjoyed flying as a Captain with BOAC, British Overseas Airways Corporation, which later became British Airways. After short spells in charge of wartime Dakotas, operating from England to the Middle East and India, and a pleasant year flying Lockheed 14s from BOAC's base in Cairo, I was posted to Dorval Airport, Montreal, which was then the Corporation's transatlantic base. Here I was privileged to join the elite ex-Imperial Airways and other senior pilots who were opening up the post-war transatlantic air routes.

When the base was moved back to UK, (it was eventually established at London's Heathrow) I became active in the pilot's "Union": the British Air Line Pilots' Association (BALPA). I was twice elected as its Chairman, during which time I was nominated by the TUC to attend the initial Duke of Edinburgh's Commonwealth and Empire Industrial Study Conference at Oxford. Later I was seconded to the Turkish National Airline as its Operational and Technical Director.

During this time, I had become, in 1956, the Honorary Secretary of the International Federation of Air Line Pilots' Associations (IFALPA). It was while doing this job that I welcomed the invitation to test-fly and evaluate technically, for all airline pilots, the prototype Boeing 707 (the Dash-80).

When in 1960, BOAC itself began to operate Boeing 707s, I left Turkey to operate this great airliner on transatlantic routes. Later I was among those Captains who opened up the Corporation's round-the-world routes in the same aeroplanes. This was a very pleasant period; one which included spells of living in both Hong Kong and Honolulu.

It was while engaged on these services, and during the long lay-overs at such places as Beirut, Delhi, Singapore, Tokyo and San Francisco, that much of *In Full Flight* was written.

All this changed quite suddenly when, out of the blue, I received a 150-word cablegram from Montreal which offered me the appointment as Chief of Operations and Chief of Accident Investigation, of the International Civil Aviation Organisation (ICAO)—the Civil Aviation technical agency of the United Nations Organisation—at their HQ in that Canadian city.

I had enjoyed twenty-seven years as a pilot; pre-war; wartime and post-war, during which periods I had seen many dramatic changes in both military and civil aviation. However, I had already come to realise that I might one day have to seek a ground job, due in the main to increasingly defective hearing; a direct result of my wartime flying. Consequently, I wired my acceptance and within days I was representing my new employers at a major international meeting in Paris.

While with IACO, I was given the additional position of Chief of Airworthiness, put in charge of the SST Panel, the Committee on Aircraft Noise, the Sonic Boom Panel and had to stage-manage over a dozen major international meetings in Montreal.

However, during the nine to ten years which I spent in Montreal serving IACO, the assigned technical nature of that organisation became seriously undermined by the political edicts of the United Nations Organisation (UNO). For example, South Africa, a leading international civil aviation nation, was virtually expelled for entirely non-technical reasons.

As a result of this and other considerations, I finally resigned from IACO and set myself up briefly as an independent Aviation Consultant. Later still, I opted for a more interesting, if less lucrative, life devoted to golf, bridge (at which I am now a double National Master) and writing articles and further books.

In the aviation field, my books include the biographies of two famous wartime flyers.

The first was the life story of the greatest of all U-boat hunter/killers; namely Squadron Leader Terry Bulloch DSO and bar, DFC and bar. This is entitled *Coastal Ace*, published by William Kimber & Co in 1986.

This was followed by the story of Wing Commander Adrian

Warburton DSO and bar, DFC and two bars, the charismatic Malta ace pilot, whose amazing exploits from the island won him undying fame. This book, *Warburton's War*, was also a Kimber publication, in 1987. I had known both men during the war; Warburton in Malta and Bulloch while operating with Coastal Command. Both books were well reviewed and I am currently engaged upon similar projects, including the life story of Wing Commander "Bob" Braham, the RAF's most decorated fighter pilot with DSO and two bars, DFC and two bars, and another book on Malta.

Due to my wartime association with Malta, I am also a National Officer of the George Cross Island (Malta wartime veterans) Association. I now know more than ever that the memories of Malta can never be exorcised.

Tony Spooner
December 1990

Index